New Work
New Culture

Work we want and a culture that strengthens us

New Work
New Culture

Work we want and a culture that strengthens us

Frithjof Bergmann

zero books

Winchester, UK
Washington, USA

First published by Zero Books, 2019
Zero Books is an imprint of John Hunt Publishing Ltd., No. 3 East St., Alresford, Hampshire SO24 9EE, UK
office1@jhpbooks.net
www.johnhuntpublishing.com
www.zero-books.net

For distributor details and how to order please visit the 'Ordering' section on our website.

ISBN: 978 1 78904 064 7
978 1 78904 065 4 (ebook)
Library of Congress Control Number: 2018936101

A CIP catalogue record for this book is available from the British Library.

Design: Stuart Davies

UK: Printed and bound by CPI Group (UK) Ltd, Croydon, CR0 4YY
US: Printed and bound by Thomson-Shore, 7300 West Joy Road, Dexter, MI 48130

Contents

Preface

New Work had a genuine, full-fledged beginning. It did not start with a hesitant whisper high in the trees but instead with a bang. That bang was an unconventional, much publicized, very fought about proposal. It was during the recession of the very early eighties, which also was the time when computers suddenly appeared on both sides of the assembly lines. The place was Flint, the automobile town in the United States, the equivalent of what Wolfsburg signifies in Germany. There was no clear cut announcement but rumors circulated in rapidly upwards rising spirals: there would be lay offs in magnitudes greater than any that had ever occurred before. In response "we" (at this point this was a group of colorfully diverse friends – some came from the union, some from management, one was a priest, one another philosopher, one the assistant mayor of the town) established the first Center for New Work. I had written about work before, among other things a chapter in the book *On Being Free*, and I had also written, produced and broadcast a ten-part television series with the title: *Culture after the Elimination of Labor*. So I was not wholly unprepared, but the pace of the developments was far more rapid than I had expected. On the basis of what we knew about Flint – which was much since most of the members of the center had lived and worked in cars for most of their lives – and a bundle of then still very green ideas, we formulated a proposal.

That proposal, partly to our own surprise, set many minds in Flint, but also beyond that in Detroit, in Michigan and in the automobile industry, on fire.

There were articles in the newspapers, interviews on the radio and on television, and most everybody in the town was soon caught up in the debate.

In essence we insisted that there was an alternative to the

mass dismissal of workers. If that dismissal were to occur then "half of Flint would be unemployed, and the other half would be working fearful loads of overtime." Those were the words we used. The alternative was to not split Flint in two, down the middle, but to cut across, horizontally with a far superior division. "Even after the introduction of computers there will be enough work left for *everyone* to work 6 months of the year inside the plants." But most important would be the remaining 6 months, for in those the workers would not be waiting, or sleeping on their waterbeds. This is where the purpose of the newly founded first Center for New Work came in. That center would undertake *two tasks*: for one, we would do our very best to unearth the talents and buried skills, but also the values and desires of the workers – we would find out what work they "really, really" wanted to do – that was the phrase that, before we knew it, had been turned into our emblem. But, in the second place, we would also bend every effort so that in the other 6 months they would actually do that more meaningful and more fulfilling work, and beyond this even earn serious money with what that "pursuit" or "calling" had turned out to be.

In the intervening 25 years a good number of Centers for New Work, altogether maybe 30, have been established not just in the United States and Canada, but also in Europe, especially in Germany, and in Asia and Africa.

From the first day we took the view that the Job System was only one and a problematic and passing way to organize and structure work. We emphasized that for thousands of years, the vast majority of people did not work in jobs but on farms. The peculiar form of work that we call "jobs" is roughly only 200 years old, as old as the Industrial Revolution, and even when that system was first introduced many were skeptical and announced ominous predictions. By now the Job System suffers from a manifold and virulent pathology, and the time has therefore come to organize work anew, from the ground up:

the Job System is now dying and the next system, New Work, has to be created.

What is New Work? This book is a long and complex answer to this question. But, here, by way of introduction, is a very short reply. Central to New Work is a reversal. You can express it first in the language of means and ends. In much of the past the task to be performed was the goal, the end, the purpose. The human being was used by others, or also by himself, as the tool, the instrument, the mere means for the achieving of this end. We, human beings, subordinated ourselves. We placed ourselves into the service of work that needed to be done.

New Work is an effort that has now gone on for over 20 years to reverse this: we should not be serving work, but work should serve us. The work we do should not drain and exhaust us, it should give us more strength and more energy, it should develop us into fuller human beings.

These words seem too mild, too pale, too colorless. If one observes what working in a mine, or on an assembly line, or in a kitchen, or on a farm, or in a garage is like – then what has work in the past actually done? It has maimed people – every kind of work, the people that did it in its own characteristic way – the coal-miner his black lung, the farmer numb and stupefied from the sheer excess, the torture of too much work, the salesman stuck inside his fake joviality, the priest in his hypocrisy (imagine a wall covered with mugshots of how work has disfigured people). If one takes account of the enormous expanse of work, the great proportion of an entire life-time which work represents, then one could say that the relentless stress and pressure exerted a permanently constricting force on the majority of people, very like the wet bandages wrapped around the feet of Chinese women. When these strips of cloth dried they strangled the foot till it was dead like a specimen preserved in alcohol, and very small, the size of a baby's fist.

Let that be one of many symbols for what work has done

to the great mass of human beings. In the past work crippled people like the feet of Chinese women; it made them smaller, more desperate and far less alive than they might have been.

At the heart of New Work is the idea that this should be reversed. Not only halted, not just stopped, but turned around! New Work is not merely an effort to lift this burden, to lighten work or to create more leisure. The intention is very different from this. We have found in over 20 years of the most diversified experience that work that makes use of people's best talents, work that corresponds to their full and deep desires, that they believe in, that they experience as a pursuit or a calling, does not weary people, but does the exact opposite: it gives them more energy, it strengthens them, it lifts them up.

Instead of turning them into the crippled foot of a Chinese woman, it assists them on the upwards path toward becoming a fully developed, vigorous human being. The aim of New Work is not to free people from work, but to transform work until work will create free human beings. Freedom *through* work is the goal to which we aspire.

More vitality, more strength, more vigor is much desired in our present culture. We, therefore, run through the gamut of a great range of comparisons, some serious, some half in jest. We suggest that this kind of work strengthens people more than Ginseng, or vitamin E, or HGH (Human Growth Hormone), or any of the other dietary supplements you may have tried.

Doing work that does not make you ashamed but that excites and thrills you makes you more self-possessed than Dang Quo, or Tai Chi, or taking seminars in self-defense, or increased assertiveness. One of our much-repeated little sayings is that sex must be very good indeed, to stand the competition with this kind of work (ask those who have waited alone in bed for someone who was working with a passion and they will tell you).

We believe that each of these comparisons is literally true.

You can test, observe and see. However, in our culture a deep tradition inveighs against thinking of work as gorgeous or delicious. In fact a vast number of people experience their work as a mild disease. Not like a cancer or hepatitis, but like a cold. Notice that this analogy is very close: about a cold one says that it will pass in 2 days. In the case of work one says that it is already Wednesday, and that one will get through it until Friday.

Partly because of that tradition, but just as much because that mode of speech is so prevalent and so ingrained, we, who are associated with New Work, go out of our way to speak insistently about it.

The polarity of work

What we mean by this is on the one hand that very much of work is far from a mere *mild* disease. As we have just been saying, for many work is a crippling disease, and work of course also kills. I am not only thinking of the notorious accidents in coal mines or at sea. One also should remember that what soldiers and officers in all manner of armies do is work. They are hired and paid for it, and if one would count those who are killed in this line of work, then the number of deaths that work has caused would be staggering and huge.

These facts are much of the time not emphasized because we have been taught that work is always honorable, that sloth is clearly a great vice and that those who refuse some kind of work are reprehensible, for even the humblest and most menial work somehow magically becomes good and honorable if it is only done with sufficient discipline and care. What an utterly amazing transformation! Far superior to the wildest dreams of the alchemists who were only trying to turn lead into gold. And, naturally, for any kind of boss or master, the most welcome myth one could imagine. How could anyone who supervises serfs who carry ore, or weave, or pick cotton, ask for more?

However, it is the other pole, that for New Work is even

more important. We have already said that work that fascinates and rivets people, work in which they are totally involved and which they love draws more energies out of people than they imagined themselves to possess. That fact is so important for the whole enterprise of New Work that we habitually refer to some especially evocative examples. These are like symbols for us, or like light-towers that help us to steer our way when there is a danger of becoming lost.

The first of these is an occurrence that is frequently cited in textbooks on psychology: a woman steps out of a shop. She looks across the square to where she parked her car, an old-fashioned Volkswagen Beetle. To her utter horror she takes in with one glance that her 5-year-old son is lying underneath the car, and that the car somehow must have rolled forward, for the weight of the car is bearing down on the chest of her child and is pinning him to the pavement of the street. Without a moment's pause she runs over to her car, takes hold of one of its sides with both her hands and with one heave lifts it up. In this way she saved her son. But in the reports it is also emphasized that she did not injure her back, nor did she damage her body in other ways.

The essential point of this story is, I believe, quite plain. If standing in a parking lot anywhere, with her son safely at home, you were to say to her, "Why don't you walk over to this car and lift it up?" that would be laughable, grotesque. Even if as a joke she walked over and tried, she would not be able to budge it by an inch. It is therefore the *context* that is all-important. The context in this case is the entire situation that includes her and her son and the car. They are webbed together, a connection between them has suddenly come into existence, one could also say that the plight of her small son exerts an enormous force upon her. It is very like a *field* of forces in which she becomes *included*. That field draws forces out of her that she "normally" does not possess. Therefore, she is able to exert a strength that is quite out of the ordinary, and what she manages to do is hence thoroughly amazing.

Once all this has been explicitly and firmly stated, many of us, I believe, would go on to agree that, unusual as this case is, there nonetheless are countless others that in their basic structure are very similar or the same. Legendary examples can be found in almost every sport, for instance. Still, what is most important for New Work is that the same is true in the domain of work. We discover that something is more difficult than we at first thought. But we are involved! We care! The outcome is important! Not quite in the same dramatic way as the mother and her son, yet nonetheless we in these cases also find ourselves included in a nexus. We become part of a larger situation, and that situation draws energies out of us that we did not suspect ourselves as having.

When I personally am asked to define what I mean by work in one single sentence, I invariably decline. Still, often I do respond to that question by saying that I oppose the traditional, well-modulated, genteel view of work, and that I instead think of it as mainly close to one of two extremes. Work has the capacity to maim, and with frequency also to kill, but there is the exceptional kind of work that gives us more energy than we had before. Sometimes, I elaborate, and add that it is an integral part of these situations that we do not know in advance how much energy we seem to have. We are surprised, and often not only once but several times in a row. The demands increase and there is more energy than we assumed we had. Then the stakes go up again, but to our second amazement there is still more energy available this time round.

The fact that work has the rare capacity to make us *more* alive than we were before, and hence can raise us upwards from one level to the next, we, in New Work groups, often call the "pull" of work. It suggests that work indeed can be like a rope that pulls one upwards, very like in rescuing someone, or in mountain climbing.

That very physical increase in energy *through* work plays a key role when people pass into so-called "retirement." This is a well-researched and documented subject, and if one studies this material then the facts turn out to be startling. A very high percentage of people depend utterly on their work. Once their work is gone they are like a marionette whose strings have been cut and they collapse into a heap.

This also relates to experiences I have had many times with inner-city youths. There, too, the physical transformation of these youths, on working at what they wanted to do, changed their walk, their posture, the expressions on their faces, literally made them into altogether new and different persons. The pastors, with whose churches I was working, translated this into religious language: they spoke of work that the youths really and seriously wanted to do as performing on them a resurrection. That was strong language, but it was not inappropriate. It captured the life-giving, the life-enhancing capacity which this inordinate work often has.

One other example: this occurred along the banks of the Mississippi. In one spring the water level continued to rise beyond previous highwater marks, and still more rain and more water from the melting snow was forecast for a series of days. After all of the normal measures had been exhausted an appeal went out to all citizens to come and help build dykes. As in other such cases, the whole country was watching on TV. What impressed me enormously were the expressions on the faces of the people that were hefting the sandbags into place. I remembered that Dostoevsky, speaking of his time in the camps, wrote that one could drive a person into despair and nihilism by forcing him to move sand, first to one place and then back again to exactly where it had been before, and then once more again. Here on television was the exact opposite of that. Yes, it was moving sand, but these people were defending their own villages! They were in a struggle! They were fighting the

Mississippi! Their faces said it unmistakably: that they had done nothing this meaningful, this life-giving in many years. Even the memory of this would be a nourishment to them, as they would talk about it in their old age.

This example shows once more that the context, the purpose, the meaning is utterly decisive in determining the quality of work. The precise physical action *can* even be repetitive and grueling, as it was on the banks of the Mississippi *if* – and this if is all-important – there is meaning, there is a goal, a purpose to what one does!

It is a fact that we all know people who are well over 80 but who have utterly astounding vitality, energy and power. Martha Graham was among these, but so was Linus Pauling, and Toscanini and Einstein, most memorably in the celebrated photos in which he rides a child's bicycle and sticks out his tongue like a 6-year-old. Some part of that vitality is no doubt genetic, but a portion of it is certainly due to these people's work. They are living proof of the idea contained in the example of the mother and her son, and of the villagers fighting against the Mississippi. Their work gives them energy and raises them upwards with its uncanny draw. Their work has done that over the duration. There were pauses but then the upwards pull again came back with its full force. The result is the vigor of the people whose names I listed. But there is a hidden point: we know their names because they are all world famous. However, that is deceptive. There was a period in which I studied the effect that work has on the energy of older people. In that connection I must have met several hundred whose work affected them in a similar way. They were stunningly more alive than their cohorts, because the work they performed gave them one spoon of the elixir of life every time they did it.

We explored and tested and above all learned to make use of this one fascinating, lifting force in 20 years of New Work projects that ranged from some of the biggest and most renowned international companies down to many that dealt only with a handful of chronically unemployed or homeless people. This range has been important to us and we are proud of it, and in the body of this book you will be reading about highlights; more about Centers for New Work directly connected with mega-companies but also very different projects in which street-youths created roof-top gardens on top of the high-rise buildings in Vancouver, or of one in which youths in a maximum security prison assembled motor cycles, and of several with Indian tribes who live close to the Arctic circle, and created a business based on the invention of a unique, Lego-like building system, and of course of many more that worked more conventionally with state government departments, or with middle-aged managers, or seniors, or depressed people, or schools, or universities, or towns, or regions. The many-colored diversity of our efforts, constitutes in our eyes a kind of proof, a demonstration. Over the years we gradually became convinced that we must at least be near a promising and hopeful path and one main reason for this was specific: we witnessed in every one of our projects that we were not just offering ameliorations, that even in the case of the very down and low we were not just providing food, clothes and shelter. We were not just handing over alms, and creating what we ourselves, with some nastiness, called "comfort stations." No. Doing work that they valued, that excited them and made them proud raised people up, not just materially, but as human beings. It raised their spirits, it strengthened them, it made them more courageous, more alive and very much more self-possessed. We proved to ourselves that this ascent, this upwards climb could be undertaken – could be performed "under their own steam" – by great numbers of the low and down. But, also, and this was no less important to us: we saw that this also happened to many who lived in ease, prosperity and plenty. They, too, became stronger, more vigorous and more developed as human beings. It was this breadth, this advance toward a semblance of the comprehensive that gave us hope, that eventually led us toward formulating this as one part of our goal: to aim at the creation of a society and culture in which *everyone* would have the chance to work significant portions of their time at a task that excited them, in which they believed, that raised them up to being more alive.

Making this possible would accomplish much else in addition to this elevation of the spirit and the bodily vigor of people. Leading management personnel have been intrigued with New Work from the first day since they saw in it a twofold optimization. That enabling people to do work that they seriously desired would be good for the workers was self-evident and almost banal from their perspective. It was the other side, namely that it would simultaneously also be best for productivity and for profits that naturally captured more of their attention. But this double optimization was also of great importance from our own perspective, for it meant that if a raft of enterprises, or a town or region were to implement New Work on a larger scale their speed of development would be much greater than it had been before.

There was another, related dimension which in our view also had great weight: that one was made up out of the sum-total of actual work accomplished through the aggregate of "pursuits" and "callings" that a group might perform. If one asks people what they really, really want to do not very many want to write symphonies or poetry. After 2 weeks of conversations many say that they above all "want to make a difference," that they want to do "something meaningful" and that turns out often to be another phrase for something that will be of use to other people.

A functioning New Work economy thus would have two advantages: with so many people doing something that they seriously want to do, much more cheerfulness and pleasure would pervade the world of work, but there naturally would also be more creativity and inventiveness. We believe that the difference this could make is so pronounced that we sometimes use the expression "the Jet-Stream of New Work" for it. We also have a name for the other advantage. Half in jest we call it "the Niagra of New Work Energy." A society in which a sizable proportion of the population were available to perform "meaningful tasks" would have a resource of energy at its disposal that we like to compare to the energy that is possessed by the Niagara Falls.

Summary of the development of New Work

In spite of these hopeful and promising indications, we were convinced even before the Flint Project had begun that the pursuit or calling aspect of New Work by itself would not be enough. To provide the prosperity, but also the plenitude of work that seemed to us desirable – and we think of work as in principle *unlimited*, that is, infinite, as for that matter most housewives and most farmers do – we needed to develop an entire second half: a second, additional new type of work. The underlying thought was that the Job System, our current mode of organizing work, suffers at this juncture from such a debilitating and manifold pathology, that not just one, but two types of New Work would be needed to create a viable system of New Work for the twenty-first century.

This other mode of work is best explained through a brief reference to personal experience. After I had taught philosophy for a year at Princeton, I lived in the woods of New Hampshire. Following Henry David Thoreau, I was determined to eat only what I had first planted. To grow corn, cabbages, potatoes and 20 other vegetables was no problem. The problem was the fierce New Hampshire cold. I, on purpose, did not have a chain-saw, and, therefore I ended up cutting many chords of wood with a small bow-saw. In the April of the second winter I decided that this was not Freedom but Slavery. I left the woods, but out of that experience developed a monster project which I have been pursuing ever since.

I call it Hi-Tech-Self-Providing (HTSP). In essence it is the idea that one could use technology not to turn rivers into sewage or rain into acid, but for a wholly different purpose. One could develop an array of tools, devices, materials and machines that would enable a small group of people to *make* 60 percent or 80 percent of everything they need, so that they could live the exhilarating, independent life of which I had a taste – without the sweat of having to cut wood with a small bow-saw.

As an idea we introduced HTSP in all of the various projects we ever initiated, including even that in Flint, and as an *idea* it invariably generated enthusiasm and excitement. People understood that it was an indispensable training ground for the finding of work that one seriously wanted to do. To be involved from one's earliest childhood in the making of a large variety of different goods, and to develop the habit of choosing virtually every morning anew what specifically on that day one would want to *make,* would redevelop a capacity that we right now lack almost completely. What I mean, somewhat provocatively and oddly, is the capacity simply to ask ourselves which out of the 500 things that I conceivably could do today, will I decide to undertake. In our current lives we know already from the moment in which we open our eyes what we *must* do on that day. Many of us in fact, first thing in the morning, write down a list. In that way HTSP would *train* us to ask on a small scale every day, the Big Question that is at the center of a New Work life: what is it that I with real determination want my work, and my life to be?

Everyone working in the various projects also understood that *in the long run* the economic independence that HTSP enables one to have amounts to an indispensable prerequisite. The idea of doing what one "really, really" wants simply cannot be reached without that degree of material independence: without it the pressures of the real world – of the famous Brechtian "context" – will always extort a compromise.

I am saying that virtually everyone connected with New

Work always agreed with the idea of HTSP. The execution, the practice was another matter. The problem never was resistance, it always was availability: the vision of creating technologies that could eventually fulfill this purpose – that would allow a small group to manufacture most of what they themselves need in their own immediate environment – was inspiring. No one questioned this. The question was, where were the tools, the machines, the devices that would empower one to do this?

In retrospect one can say that in the first 20 years, progress on that frontier was frankly slow. The jump, the forward leap has taken place in the last 5 years. Naturally, inescapably, like everybody else, we started with gardening. I should emphasize, we did not do it *quite* like everybody else: we used the most advanced, the most sophisticated methods of permaculture, of container gardening, of growing even the most exotic foods, even tea and coffee, in greenhouses. Somewhat tongue-in-cheek we were "Hi-Tech" even when it came to lettuce and tomatoes. We also did very well with building: during our extended journey we stumbled across a large number of different building "systems," that in different ways favored people without skills and without experience, who nonetheless wanted to build for themselves. One of these was a special way of building domes. A picture of one of these is prominent on our website, for it became an emblem, one of the signatures of New Work. That happened partly because the appearance of it is stunning, but the method of making it also fits New Work. One simply takes a very tough, quarter-inch thick "skin" which is sewn to have the shape of the dome one wants and blows that skin up into a big bubble. Then one sprays either light cement or a clay mixture over the outside, and after that one merely waits. It takes 2 to 4 days until the dome has dried, and then one, very like a child, pulls the cork out of the bubble. The air leaves, the skin collapses, the dome remains standing and one pulls the skin out of the front door. It is the simplicity, the intelligence, the elimination of unneeded, stupefying work, and the humorous nuance, that makes this way of building typically New Work.

We initiated a raft of other efforts – some that used computers to accomplish tasks that are difficult for poor people, like the arranging of an appointment with a case-worker, or a physician – but the experience with HTSP as a whole remained daunting and elusive. We were not interested in puttering or playing. The crux for us was hard and economic, and the basic intention was audacious. Crucial from our point of view was the reduction of the *dependency on jobs*. We wanted to achieve a level that would make a significant difference on that score; that would enable someone to reduce the Job Work they were doing by a third or even a half, and to with ease and pleasure make up the balance with self-providing work. In the first 20 years we made inroads here and there, but on the whole we fell short of that.

That was the status until the last years of the nineties. After that juncture an ever-larger flow of ever more insistent invitations from Third World countries came to our door. First India, Russia and the Ukraine, soon after that Haiti but also several Pacific islands, then China and Japan, and in the last few years Morocco and other African nations, and of late and in a special way South Africa. The invitations said that one or another group had read (on the internet or somewhere else) or heard about our efforts and that they wanted one or several of us to come. The arrival was in each case a big surprise.

During the slow-going up-hill years we had accumulated a mass of ideas and information, that all amounted to different "possibilities." Wherever we went we explained that our idea was *not* to spend large sums of money so that global companies would arrive and create jobs. The number of jobs that can be created in this way is absurdly small and that strategy is also recklessly expensive. We proposed, instead, a panoply of small, mobile, inexpensive technologies with which people could make whatever they needed *for themselves*! In each case it was *decisive* that we did not offer "primitive" contraptions – the reaction to these is invariably that they are insulting – but that we on the contrary proposed machines that were "cutting edge," and for the most part more than that, brand new or still in development, and to the core "Hi-Tech." In every single instance, whether it was during a lunch with the Minister of Social and Economic Development, or with a smaller, local, struggling agency, the ignition was *instantaneous*.

We would put pictures on the table and explain that one of the German universities that partners with New Work is in Chemnitz, and that they currently are leading in the development of small, mobile factories; not really factories, but Hi-Tech-Shops that can be mounted in containers. One possibility might be a small, mobile factory that could travel from village to village and people could make their own electrical generators out of recycled plastic and aluminum – bottles and cans – while the "factory" stops with them, before it goes on to the next village. Another possibility might be a similar small, mobile factory with which one could manufacture tiles for roofs (the majority of roofs in India and Africa are made from corrugated metal. In the winter they are cold, in the summer they turn the house into an oven). A third possibility would be a small, mobile factory in which one could manufacture "serious" water filters – that is, filters that would turn poisonous water into drinking water. A fourth possibility might be a small, mobile factory with which one could make cement. And more of the like.

The reaction everywhere has been ebullient and somewhat overwhelming: why did you not come years ago? Is there any chance that you could stay? Do you have people who could come here in your stead and initiate a project along these lines? Tell us how we can get started, and please, if at all possible, today.

This is a point where I must intercede with a loud voice and waving arms: let there be no misunderstanding! The response I have just described is not by any means just to the technological trinkets that we parade across a lunch- (or also a conference-) room table! We never, ever present these as "solutions," as the "answers" that we clever white men have brought along in our fancy cases. Before we show any pictures, or introduce any talk of technical devices we invariably insist that they, the people with whom we are working, are in the driver's seat, that all of the decisions will have to be made by them, that we in fact will not do one single stroke of work, that the work, too, will have to come from them. "Nothing at all will happen, not one nail will be driven, not a single key will be turned in any lock, unless YOU are clear in your mind that this is what YOU really, and seriously want! In this there will be no wavering and no compromise: from the first day on, this will not be our project, but YOUR project. We only come with "possibilities." If there is any action whatsoever, then it is only because YOU *want* it to occur!"

We like to think and speak in terms of polarities, or juxtaposed extremes, and this, too, is only one polar extreme which has its corresponding and paired opposite. The other, second half of what has recently happened to New Work has to do not with the down and low but with the most gifted and most advanced. By some estimates close to a fourth of our younger current labor force is comprised of people whose insignia is the laptop and the mobile phone. A high proportion of these experience their work as far from a "mild disease" as can be imagined. When the bubble of the New Economy abruptly burst, many of these people lost their jobs overnight, but to the surprise of many, they were not downhearted or depressed. On the contrary many seemed relieved. Many had started their own companies in the proverbial "garages." The boom whirled them around and then trapped them in success and money oriented companies (like Microsoft) in which they had to work like galley-slaves. Hence, the relief.

Many of these people experience their work very like artists and intellectuals. Before the boom, their life was half-bohemian: when they were inspired they worked 4 nights without stopping in a row, and when their brains felt like porridge they stayed in bed for a week. The software they were writing, or whatever else, was their *work*, and like with artists, their work was close to the most important matter in their life.

Very understandably, great numbers of these people are hot with interest in New Work. Our root conception of what work should basically be is a strong common bond. But so, of course, is also the conception of Hi-Tech-Self-Providing. Many of them never cared much for the opulent and glitzy life. In their eyes it was more a carnival that seemed like a protracted joke. In addition, many of them now have undergone a financial plunge. That, too, makes the conception of a less expensive, less wasteful life attractive to them.

But there is one further major point: These are some of the most inventive and gifted people not just in the United States, but anywhere. Not a few feel that their best ideas were filched from them, and were then used for purposes of which they roundly disapprove. They are tired of this. One could also say, they are enraged. Nothing seems more natural than their desire to use their fabulous skills and talents for the development of new technologies that will enable people to live elegant lives, but at drastically reduced expense. For New Work this means that we have suddenly found many allies in this widely dispersed and marvelously impressive group.

Frankly, this book is an invitation. It describes efforts on which we have worked for over 30 years. However, we are absolutely clear that everything up to now has only been the beginning of a prelude to an overture. Our not silent, but on the contrary, insistent hope is that the steadily increasing number of different people in many countries will further develop this beginning.

Chapter One

The Post-Cold-War-Condition

Imagine a scene in a possible Hitchcock film. A train is going deeper into an arid mountain region, but the passengers are strangely becoming more and more apprehensive. A while ago it was only a sense of unease, then it became nervousness and now it is barely controlled panic. In quick succession a series of incidents suggested that the train seems to be running without an engineer, that there is no one at the controls in the locomotive, and the passengers also discovered that the emergency brakes don't function. The train is running downhill and by now is moving far too quickly for anyone to jump off. One further still more terrifying matter has become clear: namely, it seems that every last one of the doors and equally all the windows have been locked in a completely firm and indestructible way.

The image of this train is a metaphor for a belief and a set of emotions that very many experience in our culture. We feel incapacitated, stuck in a progression of events, trapped in the unfolding of an inevitable story. It is ominous and by degrees it becomes steadily more frightening. What is most characteristic and intensely awful is that we have not even a shred of an idea, not even the faintest ghost of a notion of how the progression could be stopped, or reversed, or even just redirected into an improved and more hopeful direction. Of course people run backward and forward through the wagons and gesticulate or shout, but everyone aboard knows with a frozen, ironclad conviction, that this is only a distracting and upsetting show. What is bound to happen, if not sooner then later, is by now inescapable and clear. The train will jump off the rails, will hit a wall, or will careen off a bridge and plunge down into a river.

The mass of often sharply divergent groups who nonetheless

all somehow find themselves on this train is genuinely astounding. The millions who construe the coming apocalyptic disaster in ecological terms have images for the calamities which we are approaching which are more vivid, more hypnotically compelling than those of any other. The train, as they envision it, runs downhill toward the depletion of resources such as coal or oil, but more lurid than that, some see us descending into a world of increasing salinity; of fertile lands turning into deserts and dust, of cities along coastlines collapsing into the rising sea, and of ever-larger regions of once verdant land covered and suffocating under layers of construction, tar and cement.

Other, by now equally massive and widely dispersed hosts of people see the most imminent, the most quickly approaching threat in the deepening and widening bifurcation between the rich and the poor. Many of them awoke only quite recently to the mind-shaking fact that the 80 percent of the earth which we so far self-deludingly called the "developing world" have actually fallen into a downward spiral. The sight of what is happening will soon eradicate the smug complacency of the fantasy that these countries are "catching up." As we come to face the form of life into which they are descending we may have to invent new categories and words for terms like anarchy or chaos which may become too placid, too smooth, too glib from long wear.

The many millions whose eyes are increasingly focused on the issue of poverty have of course long anticipated the nightmare of a last and final war in which the rich will be arraigned in battle against the poor. What is at this present moment slowly dawning in many different minds is the realization that what we now, at this stage, have decided to call "terrorism" may well be differently understood and differently named 10 years from now. It is possible that it will have become quite patent that what we now live through was actually one of the first stages of this war – different enough from what wars had been like before, making it necessary that years had to pass till we were ready to admit that this was the nature of the conflict in which we in fact were embroiled.

Still other throngs associate their sense of riding downhill in a welded-shut train with the decline, the fall, the steady drying out and crumbling of what formerly was our own upper crust culture. The point is not that we too suffer, and not that we should become exclusively absorbed in the horror spectacles of the Third Word. The point is to have at least some basic intuitive overall grasp of what is happening in the time in which we now live. In that spirit it is entirely necessary and right to insist that in addition to the environment and also the horrific deepening split, the life of the privileged, in any case of the vast majority of them, is also in a steep and fear-inspiring decline. These people react to the collapse of what was formerly the quality of their lives. This includes the provisions for their health-care and their retirements and really the whole of the social safety net. It also includes libraries and museums which from lack of funds reduce their opening hours, and orchestras and theaters that show the effects of budget cuts, and to the fact that one could write a requiem for virtually all universities except for some few in the United States. It could apply to the idiotification of television, or the pitiful erosion of what formerly once was journalism, or again to the descent of politics into prostitution. Or of course also to the vulgarization of our personal relationships and not least to the vastly spreading consequences of our ubiquitous lack of time. The results of haste and of the slow relentless crescendo of stress.

It is very important for the past history but also for the future prospects of New Work – in particular for the cardinal issue of "power" – that there are a good number of managers from the top echelons of the most renowned corporations who talk very much as if they too were trapped in this locked train. There is a difference, though. Among world-class managers the imagery is not that the train will plunge over a cliff, or that it will collide with a mountain wall. The prevalent fear is more that the terrain will become ever flatter but at the same time also harsher and more difficult, and that the climate will become more arid and ever less fertile. The train will slow down and eventually grind to a wheezing halt. Among the high-rolling elite the great and only partly hidden fear is of a chronic slowing of the economy, of a protracted irreversible decline, of a permanent, not cyclical, paralysis, of a standstill, and a final stop.

Certainly we have all heard by now that top managers feel pressured, driven, frightened, overworked and exhausted. In the last 30 years I have closely known, and often personally counseled, numerous executives who were proud of their corner offices and their thick carpets. Without exception their complaint was that they could *not* stop; that there was no such thing as rest and stability and permanence! Exactly the reverse: to desist, to cease was tantamount to slipping down and then hurtling into empty space. The true image is therefore not a cage, but a greased and slippery slide, steep enough so that one can stay in place only with the utmost exertion. The ghastliest part is that the slide is very short and right above an abyss. If one pauses one is first demoted and then, soon after, fired. The abyss below the slide is in other words deep, and just as in films it is full of snakes.

It is perhaps even more significant that the greased slide over the abyss describes by no means only the individual, personal lives of those who are (temporarily) at the top – and I, of course, mean not only managers, but also physicians, engineers, professors and attorneys. It describes very closely the situation of many of the most successful business people, financiers and entrepreneurs who conceptualize our society, our economic system and even our culture as a whole. In the last 30 years I have observed many times that not just executives in the auto-industry, but also many top managers in the computer industry and specifically in the legendary Silicon Valley, experience the entire economic structure in which we are now living with a sense of desperation that contrasts sharply with the surface optimism they are professionally obliged to wear as a mask.

But just as individuals cling with their hands and rudder with their feet merely so that they will not careen down into empty space, so our economy and society too must stay in white-hot overdrive merely to keep afloat. New products, new inventions, new technologies, new industries, new markets must be fed perpetually into the great chute. The question of how long will whatever is already in the big machine keep us going before we start to sink sits in most boardrooms in its own chair right next to the table. Constantly there is the sense that we need a new idea, another twist, maybe an entirely new stream of products, or as one says: the next "Big Thing!" Or else? Exactly, the "else" is the point. If nothing comes to our rescue, then decline and deterioration will begin and stagnation becomes omnipresent. It is crucially important to make this part of the picture: in our time, not only the miserable or wretched see us trapped on a downhill course. No, many of the pampered and privileged elite have exactly the same picture. This is a fact of momentous significance, for it indicates at the very start that not only the poor and inconsequential look for the possibility of a great change, but that many of those who are not far from the levers of power do the same.

Of course it would be easy to list and to describe still other large constituencies whose basic mindset is also that of being trapped in a cage-like train. Some see the coming collapse mainly inside the domain of health. Others formulate it as "The Coming of Anarchism" and point to fratricide in the Balkans, to tribalism in Africa, and to the dominant control that international crime – the mafia – has gained in a long list of countries. We could all add on to this list, but the point, the central and pivotal issue is a different question: whatever happened? What was the origin, or what were the separate and converging causes that reduced us to this condition of helplessness, of passivity, of dumbfounded desperation? Does not the sketched enumeration which we just reviewed, underscore how very extraordinary and weird this paralysis is. Does not the sheer number of those who feel altogether that they are caught in a giant machine contribute to the weirdness of it? If collectively our number is truly immense then why can't we muster enough energy to alter the direction of this descending course? Does not the enormity of the number who now live not just in a *silent*, but in a comatose opposition make this embarrassing and insulting to our remnants of common sense? To call it a majority would be a fatuous under-assessment. To come at all close to an accurate sense of the proportions one would have to turn the table and ask: not, who shares the conviction that we as a culture are on an ominous, ill-boding course but, *where are the exceptions*? Who still believes that we as a whole, the entire modern, industrial super-enterprise is on solid and promising tracks? The answer is of course, that this number is pathetically small. Which raises the insistence and the urgency of our question: why, given this fact, this tilted proportionality, why in spite of it does this grand and encompassing mass act as if it had been magically bewitched and was incarcerated in this spooky fairy-tale train? Especially, since in some nominal sense we still think of ourselves as in a democracy? Why do we feel so helpless, so incapacitated, so obviously trapped, so without recourse? What has reduced us to this condition? What was the sequence of events, what were the causes of this weird paralysis, this strange and specific impotence?

There are deep reasons, reasons with roots that go very far down. Brutally, the first very large part of this is that we exist in an economic system that careens in that direction with incredible power and force and we are helpless because there exist no alternatives to this economic behemoth. Try as we might to even vividly imagine an economic alternative that would be more powerful, or more productive than the system we currently have seems impossible. It lies beyond the boundaries of what we can imagine. Therefore we do not even have a notion of the direction, or of the ball-park in which an alternative could lie. We feel utterly helpless, quite dumbfounded and thoroughly nonplussed.

We all of course know that once upon a time an economic alternative did not just exist but that it in effect covered half of the globe. We of course also know the fate of that once mighty alternative: it vanished, it disintegrated, it collapsed.

The death of socialism

As with other deaths, more time may still have to elapse until the full reality of the dying of socialism will come home to us. Thirty years have not been enough to grasp it, in part because it was as strange and unheard of as any death that ever struck. For generations it had been *the* hope of humanity par excellence! Half of mankind had believed in it, and generations had struggled for its cause, had suffered and allowed themselves even to be tortured in prisons and in camps. Then overnight it was gone. It died so utterly and completely there was not even a corpse that remained which one could have mourned. Socialism had been a complete, detailed, coherent alternative! It was not only a column here and an arch over there; it was integrated and worked out and in some sense complete. It had evolved into a fully furnished counter-world in stark juxtaposition to the world that now is.

That anything so detailed and so vast, that had ruled half the world, could turn into mist virtually in one single night should have seemed like a mad, preposterous nightmare. By rights, half of the world should have sung dirges and worn black veils for years. Nothing like that came to pass. An uncountable number of people shrugged, brushed the dust off their lapels and went on as if nothing much had occurred. We never stopped. We never probed. We never thought persistently about the implications and consequences which the death of that colossus was likely to have. Even the most blatant and obvious of these we did not absorb. How could we not have anticipated right from the first day that our own system, suddenly without a counterweight, without the force which hitherto had kept it in check, would inescapably lurch toward the more extreme? Toward the unbalanced, the tilting, the brutal, the dangerous and the shrill? The effect in the regions of power was obviously enormous, but not only that. It also engendered huge changes in our political, intellectual and even our spiritual world. One talks of shift in the intellectual spectrum, of a movement by a few inches. This was deeply different. It was not a shift. A massive portion of our intellectual ground broke away, as in an earthquake. The fundamental polarity was gone; it had shrunk and shriveled and become infernally small. Where formerly there had been genuine issues and debates, there was now only haggling, quibbling and splitting of hair, an essentially futile rope-pulling by inches.

How truly amazing that we did not react, that the shock did not send us reeling? For as it in fact occurred, there was barely a muffled sob, in spite of the millions of authentic human corpses, and the countless lives that had burned in sacrificial hope with enough faith and energy to produce the light of a small star. That we simply turned and went on is an incredible performance, unequaled in history. Nero at least played the fiddle when Rome was burning. We carefully peeled a salami, and deliberately put thin slices of it on our next bread!

The other culture

Finding ourselves without any alternative is one main reason for our sense of paralysis, for the mentality of the locked train. We are dragged along by a giant machine that possesses such indescribable force that there is no question of changing its course. Our sense of impossibility, of being locked in stocks as in the Middle Ages is nonetheless strange and puzzling and maybe downright bizarre. For we do not live in one uniform, homogeneous, goose-stepping world. We are miles from that, and one could say, we do not have that excuse. In fact even though there very clearly is no economic, no systemic alternative, there oddly enough do exist two quite distinct and in most ways even opposed separate cultures. In a superficial way most everyone is naturally aware of this, and in a slipshod, cursory fashion most everyone could also describe the two. The finger-painted clichés attached to the official, conventional, "straight" and "square" culture are power-suits for both women and men and the accouterments that match them. Next would come that this official culture gives obeisance, preeminence and deference to the global corporations and that it therefore not only wants, but requires, as a necessity to have *growth.* Which means that it needs "free trade" and good investment and good business climates, which very often in turn amount to low wages and if possible no labor unions. That entails further a certain set of social policies, and of course a certain relationship to the military.

Of course we can go beyond that to the web of international power politics. No one would have difficulty mentioning representative, true-to-type examples of this culture. Bill Gates might be one, and George W Bush another. Bush is so perfectly typecast in this role that he performs a genuine service. With him for a mascot, it has become easier to grasp and to conceptualize the official culture. He is so graphic and picturesque: his limited speech and even the wooden cut of his face help one to imagine him sitting on the lap of one of the great ventriloquist corporations.

The other culture is often associated in the finger-painted cliché fashion with certain kinds of music and of course bands, with a wholly different approach to clothes and foods. Often it is sprinkled with ideas of New Age and also of Buddhism, almost certainly with a more casual attitude toward sex, and considerable resistance to hierarchy and elitism. Perhaps it's also related to the legendary and much misunderstood "sixties." The differences between the two cultures extend also to quite opposed opposite attitudes toward order, discipline, monotony and boredom but also to a great extent and more seriously to issues of war and peace.

Most everyone would probably agree that the second culture is enormously variegated and manifold. Which at once brings to light one of its most intriguing features. Though it is extraordinarily dispersed and diffuse, and cannot point to common insignia, structures or institutions, and even though there are countless separate formations congregating around distinct and separate issues, one usually *recognizes* it in the first instance. It does not matter whether one encounters it in the streets of Beijing, or in Tokyo, or in North or South Africa, or in Central Asia, or in the Ukraine. No matter where, it asserts its paradoxical quality, its instantly identifiable presence, even though it costumes itself in a carnival of different disguises and uses as many modes of speech. Often a single reaction; one glance, one smirk is quite enough, one knows on which side of the great divide between the two cultures one is now on. Needless to say, in terms of sheer numbers it is immense. There may not be a single country on the earth where one cannot find cafés, shops and boutiques which cater to the clientèle of this other culture. That, of course, is not the most helpful measurement. Yet the difficulty may be genuine. To attempt anything like an enumeration would not just become tedious, it would fail. The numbers that belong to it, the sheer size of it, have grown too large for this. Half in jest one could propose that it would be more appropriate, more practical and a more feasible procedure if one turned around and asked: who really is genuinely comfortable in the *official* culture? Who feels at home in it, who identifies with it, believes in it and experiences it with exuberance? As in the case of the train, the answer would be that those are precious few.

One indication of how very deep and wide the canyon is that separates these two cultures is the frequency with which communication between them breaks down. In fact, the division is deep to the point of speechlessness. Quite commonly there is frustration and then capitulation, and the similarity to a phrase much quoted by feminists is striking. "You simply don't get it" occurs as much between these two cultures as between men and women. The same crevasse also divides parents from children, and very often two bedrooms under the same roof exist nonetheless in these two widely separate cultures. That both sides "give up" is by no means a matter of language. Words become useless, one no longer knows what to say, because one has reached the bottom. There are plenty of disagreements about no end of surface matters and values but in the end one finally hits on the rock floor two different conceptions of how to live, of what life is for – and then there is no more to say.

On the surface the other culture is certainly disparate. Subcultures of it group themselves much of the time around one single issue and are not rarely even at each other's throats. Nonetheless, very large parts of this other second culture have roots that go very far down, that as a matter of fact are solidly embedded back in the soil of the Enlightenment. Which means that not only the official and public culture derives from those foundations, but that there actually were two sharply opposed sets of premises, two wholly distinct, juxtaposed sets of views from which the Enlightenment sprang.

There was of course the tradition on which all the familiar classical documents of democracy rest, and which we all know intimately from high-school and everyday life. That is rock-bottom world-view which holds that human beings are inevitably and inescapably controlled by their self-interest, by their egoism, by the direction of their own greatest advantage. All of those phrases have been smoothed from much excessive wear, and their original intent must be recaptured. If you recall the single most famous sentence of Hobbes that life in the original condition was "nasty, brutish and short" then this genteel middle-class language is obviously too mild. The fundamental idea was more nearly that man was rapacious and wild – very like one imagined animals at that time – and that above all he needed to be socialized, and de-clawed and tamed! That is how the most familiar Enlightenment philosophers justified morality, the social contract and the state (Kant, in ever so many respects at the opposite end of the spectrum from Hobbes nonetheless also insisted that the purpose of morality was to extinguish "the interests of the self"). Unchecked, untamed, left to our own impulses and devices we would not be safe on a bus. The person next to us suddenly might bite off one of our hands.

In this official, socializing, taming tradition the cardinal political idea of freedom is instantly hedged with caution and reservations. There must be freedom *with* responsibility, and of course numerous other restraints. In other words, freedom, but only as long as the leash is strong and in place.

Most of us are so entirely habituated to these ideas that they seem wholly inevitable and uncontroversially true. The very suggestion that there could be a set of foundational axioms that are diametrically opposed to these sounds strange and unreal. Still, the exact opposite picture of human nature is not in the least outlandish but very plain. It begins from the conviction that very many human beings are above all vulnerable and frail. They are easily discouraged, and much of the time downcast and very subdued. It is in fact all too easy to cow people and intimidate them. Great hosts of them are reserved and shy. The difficulty with legions of them is not that they are obstreperous and will not conform. Just the reverse. Surely, fascism should have persuaded us of that. So the opposition is by 180 degrees: reaching the point where people will stay quiet and hold still is not the difficult task. They muster very little resistance, and society can mold them like lukewarm wax. It is the other way round. To strengthen people, to bring them to the point where they will not lie down but at long last stand up and resist, indeed that is hard.

In the official stream of thought in which we were raised the great danger is too much will, too much wildness and too much rebelliousness. The task, therefore, is to trim, to cut back and to socialize. That patently on the face of it raises the question of just how emancipatory; how genuinely freeing anything enacted in that spirit could possibly be? Can anything based on the premises of the tradition in which we were raised become a serious "revolution" or will it be mainly, like so many other events that call themselves this, a changing of costumes; a sewing of new buttons on the same old uniforms? Certainly there can be a new administration, a new authority which ensures that there will be order and discipline. Instead of a king one can install a parliament or a congress, and of course the people will be allowed every few years to vote. Still, the purpose, the intent will be basically the same. *The* cardinal question will be merely under what circumstances one will be justified in killing, or in deposing a king. The new and of course differently dressed governing bodies will still see the controlling of people as the mandate of their roles. Fundamentally they will therefore use the whole panoply of social institutions and structures; from the courts, to morality, to the police, to the schools, to the army to guarantee that people will not break out of their cages, to keep it peaceful and quiet inside of the zoo.

The other tradition starts from the recognition that human beings are very incomplete and very dependent when they are born. This is *the* exact contradiction of the famous first sentence of Rousseau that "man is *born* free." On this view man needs to be nurtured, and strengthened. His individuality must be enhanced and encouraged and brought out to the surface. The last thing needed is to smooth that individuality over, to polish it till it has disappeared, to sing lullabies and offer pacifiers on trays. What is needed is not to sing people to sleep, but on the contrary to wake them up!

Nothing could be more fatuous than the presumption that the conventional and taming tradition is somehow more mainstream or better credentialed than the arousing and invigorating stream of culture. The pedigree of that tradition can easily hold its own for in its ancestry are any number of names of the first rank. One could list Goethe and Melville and Whitman among them, but also Hoelderlin, Rilke and Hesse, and again Lawrence and Gide, and of course also philosophers like Emerson and Thoreau, and certainly not least but in a special place Hegel and Nietzsche. If one wanted one sentence as an emblem, as a motto for this broad development then one might choose William Blake's "Energy is eternal delight," or Jack London's "I do not want to turn into dust, but into ashes instead."

There can be no question that the history of this other individual strengthening and enhancing point of view is mighty and has majesty. In large terms one could say that it had its beginnings primarily in literature, philosophy and art. However, by now it has had a pervasive and pungent effect on how a vast number, in fact an overwhelming majority, in our current culture think about morality and values and beyond that about how life should be lived.

It is revealing and significant that the kinship between this other basically life-invigorating movement and feminism is particularly close. Any number of vivid commonalities between these two leap to the eye. As fundamental as any other is the idea that the capacity to assert oneself must not be weakened but the opposite; it must be strengthened and even trained like athletes who develop muscles. That a spate of different seminars have been offered for many years in which this is taught and learned shows how intimate the relationship between feminism and the alternative foundations of the Enlightenment are. This is equally evidenced by the emphasis within feminism on the conception that many women are too hesitant when it comes to the fulfillment of their own desires. They subordinate themselves too easily and too much, and they even have trouble with the acceptance of their own success.

The culture that wants to arouse and wake-up has also built its tents in some of the territories of education. It has by no means won a decisive victory, but in discussions of how one should relate, especially to children, the many different strands of the affirming version of the project of modernity are playing an ever more important role. A rapidly increasing number of parents are coming to the conclusion that they want no part in the diminishing of their own children, in the weakening – and as one used to say – in the *breaking* of their will. A very similar kind of transformation has also occurred in many of the various approaches to counseling and to therapy. The overall general picture is surely that many have distanced themselves from rigid formulas and precisely defined often pseudo-medical techniques, and that at least in many cases one thinks much more in terms of a pervasive sense of depression. Ultimately this presents itself as a lowering of one's capacity to function and of one's level of energy. The most basic aim in many therapeutic situations is, therefore, the restoration of the client's well-being and sense of competence. This same gradual shift from the traditional and older ideas to the newer more life-affirming mindset is still more vividly noticeable in the manner in which one approaches the efforts to assist the seriously poor. Those who intimately and over a long period of time have dealt with that large and ever-growing segment of the population understand with ever greater clarity that the fearful sense of radical discouragement, of flat despair, of a solidified conviction of futility and of nihilism is the single greatest obstacle to any effort to alleviate and help. Predictably, this manifests itself in how one frames the entire enterprise of trying to be of some use to the impoverished. If a frozen, monstrous, indifference blocks access to them, then the first phase must be an attempt to thaw through the ice of that armor. That again falls typically into the province of the arousing and not the taming idea of culture.

Sadly, majestic though the other culture is in many ways, it never managed to translate itself into a set of social institutions. There is no such thing as a seriously developed political program. One looks in vain even for a firmly delineated, clearly defined conception of a goal. How would a society have to be structured and arranged to actually embody and support the basic impulse, which is to strengthen, and to enhance and to develop *individuals?* This surprising lack is in fact so flagrantly *not there* that we still, to this day, think that structures, rules and institutions must inevitably, and so to say by definition, curtail and limit individuality. In the USA one still waves the slogan that "less state means more freedom" quite particularly at conservative party meetings. We now live in a time where the excuse for still believing such absurdities has melted under our feet. These days one can visit numerous regions where the state indeed has died from anemia or from "withering away." One only has to pay a visit to the Balkans, or the Congo, or to Central Asia to learn the elementary lesson that the absence of the state easily means the absence of *all* freedom, and the beginning of mayhem. Therefore, that structures and institutions are able to enhance individuality and to support it, should go without saying. Astounding is the fact that there has been all along an alternative, life-enhancing platform.

From its first inception it had awesome powers in philosophy and art and it is undeniable that in its history the sixties played a role. Until then it had been somewhat secluded. It lived in theaters (think of Strindberg, of O'Neill or Buechner), in libraries, in universities, in studios, studies and museums, not in political assemblies, not in legislatures, or union halls, or anything that we call the market place. That was wholly and completely changed in that notorious decade. The other culture swooped down out of every window of every ivory tower and it was suddenly a mass-phenomenon. It had not just an affair with the media. No, it married them. It took possession of popular culture, turned itself into the cultural equivalent of fast food, but at the same time virtually usurped all the galleries of "high art." The aspirations in all of modern art became identical with the aspirations of the other culture. Whether it was a film or piece of sculpture, or a happening: crucial was that it was "alive"! Essential was that it had force, and energy and was authentic! Almost at any price, and also in the effect upon the audience: what one strove for even by hook and crook, was to disturb people in their slumber, to wake them up, if in no other way than through unabashed and vitriolic shock.

One could suggest that the ghastly birth-disfigurement of this mobilization became the pitiful, pathetic undoing of the sixties. Often not known about the sixties is that they had a magnificent and glorious start, at least in the USA. One should go back and pay attention to the language that people like Robert Moses and Stokley Carmichael used during the early freedom bus-rides into Mississippi. Even Martin Luther King was already slack and pallid in comparison. They did carry "fire to the mountain" and they were "evangelical" as many at that time already recognized. Of course not least because they had read Walt Whitman, Melville, Thoreau and Blake. The calamity occurred when the small and deeply idealistic civil rights movement became the mass movement against the war in Vietnam. Suddenly hoisted up on an enormous stage with TV lights bearing down from every side, the demand for a political program beyond the ending of the Vietnam war became loud. For that, one was lamentably, nakedly unprepared. And that is a crucial point: the other, life-enhancing great stream of developments had not addressed the political and social; the programmatic question. Suddenly the streets and squares were filled with people who wanted answers. Those who wanted to be told in which direction they should go, and what, with the towering energies that had now been loosened, they should *build*? They did not want to know what to "smash" or "shut down" or "take" – but what to *construct and shape and give new form?*

An awful silence fell. And the rest everybody knows and has heard too many times. Bitter sectarian squabbles erupted in every corner; splinter groups packed their bags and marched off in every conceivable direction. The worst part was two aberrations, both in retrospect not hard to understand. One was the descent into futile violence, (for example, the weathermen) the other the descent into mudslinging rhetoric and mud-bathing vulgarity. One did not know what else to do. There was no alternative! So one threw bricks at the police, or took off one's clothes and wallowed in the mud.

Predictably the pendulum swung back. The peace-movement produced a reaction whose name in the USA was Reagan. The sixties had come to a pathetic, shameful and revolting end. Ever since then a disillusionment with the whole domain of politics has gradually deepened. Indifference, apathy, cynicism and mere clowning waxed and grew like a growing region of quicksand in which an ever-larger number of people sank deeper inch by inch. Everyone agrees that this mood was intensified through the pressure on most people's jobs, which meant that they had to focus on their own survival. They were no longer able to afford the distraction and the luxury of participating in the larger, extra-domestic world. This also meant a greater concentration on materials goods, and hence the development of consumerism. There also is a near consensus that the spiraling down into the deepening numbness and the deepening coma was driven by the palpable decline into two entirely different worlds: that of the poor and the other of the rich.

There patently is truth in this narration. A perspective that creates an overlapping though in some ways different gestalt should be added. There is possibly a different and much more intriguing cause. The sixties were a very brief and smelly fire of mere straw in large part because they were the breakthrough, the coming out, the shattering its way out to the surface of a whole other culture that had long existed side by side with the official disciplining culture. The nemesis of that woeful little episode was that there was no form that could have given shape, flesh and substance to that spirit. Therefore that short burst befouled itself and turned into a besotted carnival even before it reached a toddler's age. The impulse that had been there from before the abortive French and American Revolutions of course lived on and survived that promising and nonetheless grotesque debacle. That impulse was a much more serious, a far more audacious idea of freedom than the mere substitution of a big committee for a king. The desire and longing vaguely anticipated in that idea gained in power, in strength, above all it gained enormously in the sheer number of those that it ignited and inspired. During the Vietnam period the other culture was a paltry and bedraggled group of students, forlorn intellectuals and artists. In the meantime the other culture has circled round the globe and you can find it in the remotest villages of China and Mexico. There are also the people who make and work with computers. You can tell them from their hairstyles and from their dress and from what they eat and from the coffee which they drink to which culture they belong.

The computer people are only one of many samples. The reason for singling them out is that they have been the locomotive that pulled the economy during the last 10 years, and locating them gives one an impression of the power that the strengthening culture conceivably could gain in the future. A very large segment of the young are also on that side of the deep crevasse. So also are a surprising number of managers and engineers, especially those who work in small and medium-sized businesses as opposed to the gigantic corporations. The political indifference has therefore possibly a very different reason. It may not be apathy or despair but a stance very far from that. It may be more a postponement, a lying in wait and conserving oneself for the proper time. The issues between our present parties – slightly cheaper drugs for the elderly, a still greater tax-advantage for the super rich – have no connections to the deep differences between the two cultures. They are squabbles between two relatives that both belong to the same camp: that of the "straight" and "up-tight" and ordering and disciplining culture. The difference is merely that one wants a 3-inch longer leash for the poor, and the other wants 5 extra miles for the rich. However, neither the Republican, the Democratic, the Social Democratic, the Christian Union, the Labor or the Tory parties have any notion of what sort of "program" would create stronger and more vigorous *individuals.* In fact, that exactly is the crucial point. This is where we face a towering cement wall. None of us seems to have even a ghost of a notion of what sort of "program," or what sort of institutions, or what society could achieve this goal. That is the impasse. The vast majority of people alive now on this globe could not care less about the quibbles between the branches of a dying culture from which they freed themselves perhaps already years ago. They do hold very still, and they seem strangely quiet but not from numbness and not from apathy. They hold still because they are waiting. One can even point a finger in the general direction of what they are waiting for. It would have to be a few first indications that the incomplete culture in which they now live cramped and uncomfortably could yet be realized; indications that this culture will not remain an impulse, or a torso, or a child with only half a chest and half a head for ever. Something would have to suggest to them that there might be an agenda, that there might be stepping stones, that there could be an ascending staircase up to the culture which they *want!* If signs of that appeared on the horizon, then they would move!

The Job-Business-Nexus

In optimistic moments the existence of the other culture and quite particularly its phenomenal size do give us hope. We are growing by leaps and bounds and the conventional, subduing, taming, socializing culture is shrinking and drying up. In 5 years the world could be wholly and completely different from how it is now. Except! Except! Yes, except for monster-factors whose grip holds us like a vice, and who seem utterly determined to railroad all of us into a yawning grand canyon abyss. The colossal dynamic in which we are trapped is primarily the result of the absence of a viable alternative, whether that is the departed socialism, or another culture that *could* perhaps develop into an alternative. Yet so far there is no alternative that has power, an agenda or even an image of its goal.

We are trapped by a mechanism that commands immense and inestimable forces and all talk of hope and coming changes is wet and wasted drive till that mechanism is lucidly and clearly understood, and more than that: until it is dismantled and disarmed.

Four cogwheels drive each other like gears in a transmission, and each of these four has to be separated out and looked at coldly once it's on the table. The first of these is: the fact that jobs became our omni-value. There were some Indian tribes (which the white man exterminated) for whom the buffalo was by no means only meat. Yes, they ate the prey they hunted, but from the skin they also made their tents and cloths and even moccasins, and from the sinews they made the strings for their bows. There was no part of the buffalo they did not use, and the buffalo met the sum-total of their needs. That is what I mean by "omni-value." For us, in our time jobs are what the buffalo was for those Indians. Jobs of course supply us with our income, but they do ever so much more than this. Our jobs are the source of our social standing, and give us access to other people. "The phone stopped ringing" is one of the most frequently heard complaints among the unemployed. They also hold up our self-respect. In the moment in which we become unemployed the sense of our own dignity caves in like a house of cards. Many of the unemployed with whom I worked hid that fact even from their wives and their own children. They took their lunchbox in the morning and came back with it in the evening – from the public library. Without a job one is "dependent," therefore not a full person. One is superfluous, a nuisance, a burden. One is not properly entitled even to one's food. This is decisively different from numerous, possibly most other cultures, and it is not fixed. It is a rapidly advancing process. Every year we load some of what used to furnish our lives onto a cart and burn it on the great stake of our jobs. In the village in the Alps in which I grew up Christmas was celebrated for 6 weeks, and that meant caroling and candles and feasts and many get-togethers. These were by no means only church functions, and whenever anybody died the whole village went to the funeral, and afterwards did not sober up for at least 2 days. By now it is much grimmer and closer to our skin. We have no time for friends, not much time for our children, and have to make "appointments" when we want to sleep with our partner. All this is gone, but there is no empty space. The work we do, like water, fills every nook and cranny.

The second gear in this mighty mechanism is: automation. For years the most munificently salaried experts on the "Future of Work" wholly underestimated the sea-changing effects that automation can easily achieve. No end of supposedly learned articles were written in the early eighties proving that the introduction of computers would only polish the *quality* of work to some degree, but the all-important *quantity* would stay intact. No one believes this any longer, but most people still resist the suggestion that we are still in the preparatory stages. That what we have seen so far is like the noise from an orchestra when the musicians tune their instruments. The concert has not yet begun. The conductor has not yet rapped his baton against his stand (something analogous to that might soon happen in the internet). Then the music will begin.

It is best to illustrate this with a few examples. There exist already one or two ultra-modern factories close to the border in Mexico that offer to their clients to manufacture anything whatever on demand. One week they make refrigerators, the next week television sets, the week after that DVDs and a few days later X-boxes for Microsoft. It is most useful to think about these factories in symbolic terms, and to regard them as a metaphor for just *how* flexible, and *how* agile factories can become.

Only a few years ago a curious belief was frequently discussed. Now it has distinctly faded and soon people will look at it in the wax museum of amazing credulities. I mean the desperate conviction that the growth of the service sector will compensate with new jobs all of the losses in the manufacturing domain. It is now common knowledge that exactly the reverse has started to occur. Service jobs are much more easily automated than those focused on "making things." The automation of banks and insurance companies, and of course of service stations and of the purchasing of railroad and of airplane tickets, will soon be followed by great waves of dismissals in the private and the public bureaucracies. No doubt that will be one of the most widely welcomed advances in this field. The tedious filling out of forms for applications, licenses, permits and visas, as well as for loans and credit cards will soon be put to rest and the grave will be covered with software. The clownish, comic irony in this is of course hard to miss. First we endowed jobs with every value we could find. We not only dressed them so that they would be sexy and seductive, we made them indispensable. Life became impossible without them. We made very sure there was no substitute, no replacement, no *ersatz*. We pinned every medal and encomium on them and then placed them on a high and throne-like chair. Having done that we turned around and invented 550 ways to abolish them, indeed to bury and to burn them and to drown them in the sea. So, with the assistance of no end of different machines, jobs became wildly rare and impossible to find. Anyone could have predicted that there would be a mad and insane rush, that people would kick and bite and twist each other's nose and ears. That was to be expected, but we still added one small twist. It dealt with those who lost out, who were pushed aside in the great scramble. One would have thought that not receiving one of these all-valuable cornucopia baskets was punishment enough. Yet that was not the case. Rumors were circulated about those who could not grab a job: stories to the effect that they rotted gangrene-like from sheer inertia, and that their limbs turned into an evil smelling slime.

So far we have a mad, paradoxical collision. First we hoisted jobs up high and decked them out with every value, and then we turned and made them parsimoniously rare. That might have been enough, but a third giant element was brought into the situation. This was not intended. Nor was it anticipated. It was a by-product of other developments that came as a surprise. We moved forward and perfected several technologies. These were not arcane or controversial like the genetic manipulation of foods or like making engines out of individual molecules. If anything they were on the banal side. Mainly they all had to do with transportation and with covering great distances in a minimum of time. More specifically, crucial were the development of large transcontinental planes, of very quick and inexpensive cargo ships, of trucks and trains and of course of one of the most elementary capacities of computers; their ability to send and receive email. Naturally, there also were a multitude of other causal factors. Still these technologies did much to produce the third ingredient: globalization. The astounding surprise effect was a change in the entire order of our basic magnitudes: with one leap virtually everything left the era of the local, and the regional, and even the national behind, and in an amazingly short time we had entered the new era of the *global*.

One of the oddities of this sudden transformation is that businessmen quite generally talk about it from only one and the most narrow-minded possible perspective. To their minds, the word global suggests primarily a global *market,* and on top of that their imagination is limited to the single product which they happen to produce. The auto-industry thus sees the whole of China as one windfall giant market in which many millions of Chevrolets can be sold. The ability to think this way is almost acrobatic: it is a feat in the mastery of the one-sided and the asymmetrical. Almost like the famous ability to clap with just one hand. How is it possible not to see the other side of this coin? Namely, that the Chinese will not only buy, but also manufacture, and possibly cheaper and with better quality – like the Japanese of course have done for years. Perhaps it is still more astounding that the very same automobile industry managers who speak with glee of China chew their lips in rage at the mention of Japan. Importantly though, the topic of trade should not monopolize the conversation. Unfortunately, that is the established pattern when the pros and cons of the leap into the global are discussed. Neglected is the side that has to do with work. Imagine the combination of three actions: first, jobs are raised on high, second through automation they are decimated and reduced, and third, one brings not products but as many *people* as one can. What if there existed a marvelously curative medication (say, for Aids), but unfortunately the supply of it was inadequate in the extreme. Think of a mass of people already restive, standing in the heat and waiting. And then with trains, ships, buses, carts and cars one brings thousands and further thousands of additional patients to that same place.

Take careful note! Insane as this would be, this is not an accurate portrait of what actually happened. The truth is worse, and it is worse by an entire level of the dastardly and the horrific. Until far more recently than one is apt to realize the overwhelming majority of people on the entire globe lived in villages and made their living by farming their own or someone else's land. Even in the United States and Europe the percentage of people living on the land was in the neighborhood of 80 percent as recently as 150 years ago. Everybody knows that farmers receive mighty subsidies in these countries, but that farmers "are in trouble" even though they are given this support. Therefore whole villages, even in Europe and the United States, are abandoned and turn into ghost-towns. It should be mentioned that the subsidies over the last 80 years were designed to help corporate, mono-crop farms; not the multi-crop, family farms of old.

This is mild and gentle compared to virtually the entire rest of the whole earth. In every country of Africa, Asia and South America huge migrations are in progress. The former peasants leave the villages for many reasons, but in part brutally, because they must. Largely for two reasons: one, because large agri-corporations bought their land, and because food stuffs the world over have become too cheap. On a small lot one cannot raise either enough corn or rice even to subsist. So the true picture is that these people do not just come in buses, ships and trains. They are *forced* to come! The form of life in which they lived longer than anyone is able to remember has quite suddenly been pulled away under their feet, and so they walk like refugees – millions and millions of them – in the direction of the cities.

This then is the third component that must be joined to the other two: jobs became the buffalo of our culture, we utterly relied on them, then they were killed off in droves by automation, and in addition a mass of people that is without exaggeration in the hundreds of millions (just one example: Zimbabwe has "officially" 70 percent unemployment at this moment) now wander over land in search of jobs.

We have now seen how the pressure bears down from three sides: jobs became all-important, then automation eliminated reams of them, and the migrations from the villages and farms immensely escalated the need for them. The number of people involved in these migrations is so very large that the figures that measure unemployment in our genteel world are laughable and puny by comparison. If one does not include the virtual elimination of most traditional farming in one's picture, one never sees the true magnitude of the job scarcity we face. The fourth still needed cornerstone that joins the issue and with one flash illuminates a great deal about our situation is: the job monopoly.

The job monopoly

The result is very crass and plain: think of it simply as a stupendous, overpowering *increase* in power. Whose power? The power of large business of course. Business builds new plants and thereby makes new jobs, or business also closes plants and then sends the people home. All three of the giant forces we have just described are relatively new. All three have grown like a fire-storm since 1989. Twenty years ago work did not fill as much space in our lives and did not have the status it has now; automation was a kitten compared to the voracious tiger it is now, and millions who now live in slums at that point were still on their farms. So the pressures are not the same. They are vastly greater, and the power of business has grown commensurately.

"We, the people" to use that great and ringing phrase have descended down into the position of petitioners, of beggars, or of supplicants. That is the essence of the Post-Cold-War-Condition. One often hears that towns, or regions, or even countries make an effort to "seduce" business companies to please settle down inside their territory. That image is not accurate: to lean back in nothing but black underwear on a red couch requires considerable confidence. One has to feel desirable and attractive. For the most part that is not how cities or countries feel when they deal with corporations. They are much humbler. They offer bribes and blandishments, great sums in subsidies and tax abatements, but beyond that they very often downright plead.

In relation to the business sector we the people are not like a seductive woman. Far from it. We are more like the famous sculpture of Rodin's: the Citizens of Calais. We come barefoot and in sackcloth. We wait in the lobbies, and the keys to our cities hang around our necks. That posture and that encounter is the foundational building block, the arch-typical module out of which the economy and political life was built in the era after the Cold War.

It may be pathetic and infuriating, and is yet nonetheless true that a single crude and ham-fisted wrestler has been given that much power over an ever shrinking group. Hold that primitive toggle mechanism up, for example, against the success of Reagan's campaign, or for that matter up against the careers of Clinton, or Blair, or Schroeder, or Bush, or once more up against what has happened to the labor unions, or more broadly to Liberalism in the United States, or specifically to the Democratic Party. Is it not easy to see how dominantly powerful this Job-Nexus-Mechanism has been? It is centrally important to see clearly how this grip has managed to *immobilize* us. How we were paralyzed by it. How it held our minds – and above all our political imagination – like in medieval stocks. It hardly could have been still simpler, still more banal: jobs are our omni-value and the twin forces of automation and the unification of the entire globe ensured that they were permanently and increasingly in desperately short supply. To that harrowing famine we had only one response. That was to raise, to elevate and to coddle business; to become ever more subservient, and subjugated to it. We believed that there was nothing else to do. We thought that we were in a train that was locked and welded shut.

The demise of the left

It is not only the true and central core of socialism that was killed off. Not only the fortress or the castle of it fell, but the entire countryside; all of the land around it was also depleted. Since

1989 also the attenuations of it, the milder, diluted, watered down versions, many of which had flourished on this side of the iron curtain, became tepid and lame. Even the shadings of it that were barely left, those that were certainly not red but only the palest shade of pink, the "respectable" social democratic, liberal, genteel, bourgeois labor parties – even they grew weak and weary and lost their purpose and their identity.

Why did this occur? One major factor was that they were *tainted!* Tainted by association. They had a resemblance, a kinship to a system that had pitifully fallen. Therefore, they smacked of failure and defeat. Which made it far easier to denigrate and dismiss them than it had been before. One other major factor was that they had been *deracinated;* they had been cut off from their roots. We had not troubled ourselves to determine the deep and serious causes from which socialism died. We blabbered about inefficiencies and corruption and party-bosses, and the result was awful and could have been predicted. With socialism dead and no corpse anywhere to be seen, people rifled through the mementos and trinkets they could find. What formerly had been a coherent forward thrust, (misguided, yes, but still coherent) was now gone, and out of the remnants of found furniture one now heaped up pitiful defensive barricades. This became the hallmark of the left in politics, but the ineffectual defensive rear-guard actions became characteristic even of the labor unions whose keyword became *limits*: *limits* on the speed of the assembly line, *limits* on the number of hours, *limits* on the degree to which we will be exploited. The same spirit wafted across much of the rest of what previously had been the left culture. Regardless of which group, or enclave, or camp one visited, it was the *defense* of jobs, or wages, or the *barrier* against drilling oil in a region, or against a technology, or (biological) research of a certain kind, or the protection of this species, or of that rainforest; those were the slogans and the battle-cries. This was, sadly enough, reactive and defensive and therefore forever close to a mood of retreat.

One could say in summary: the history of the left since 1989 is the story of a longish line of rear-guard actions.

In the larger picture a third and different factor far overshadows the two I have just mentioned. That, unsurprisingly, is of course the Business-Job-Nexus. In a nutshell: the power of the business sector increased upwards in an exponential fashion and the left was hopelessly outmatched. The politics of the left basically turned into efforts to control the waxing power of business, and for that very reason they failed. The Job-Business-Nexus constituted such an incredible boost in power that business could no longer be controlled. In earlier more favorable times, the more liberal, left-leaning parties were like a bundle of strung together ropes. In the Post Cold-War-Era different strings and threads and lesser wires were separated from this one giant rope and were applied in softened and attenuated ways in no end of different situations. Every one of these attempts was in truth some mild or also not so mild constraint on the arbitrariness of the forces of business. And in that exactly lay the rub. For at every turn one could raise against them the fear, the spectrum that they represented an employment axe. Whatever they might have been, whether they were an effort to raise minimum wages, or to increase health benefits, or to tighten the rules that allowed a company to fire people, or any of a great variety of taxes, or naturally the effort to organize the workers in a plant in the first place – in regard to one and all of these one could invariably and forever raise the cry: this will bring about a decline in jobs! This will give the company the excuse to pull up its stakes and move elsewhere! This will hem in the expansion of one or another of these corporations and fewer job-calls will be the result. Often enough, to give a different example, groups did come together and even grew to a considerable strength in the name of their support of peace. There were signs on the doors, and white pigeons even circled round the roofs. Then by chance, in a wholly unrelated way, the local military base, or the munitions factory down the road spread the word that they might leave, and that with them the jobs on which the town depends will of course be gone. It is deeply significant that before long many of the peaceniks would drift away and would now paint signs different from those they carried through the streets before. Now they want the base or the factory to stay, and there is of course only one way to accomplish this: the town must make itself still more attractive. It must woo the business interests in still more alluring, more seductive ways. With what? With tax abatements? With larger subsidies? With labor contracts still more favorable to the company side?

Once we understand the dynamic and the logic of the Business-Job-Nexus we also get a far sharper understanding of the progressive deterioration of our own culture. What is happening is far from a mere "crumbling," far from pieces dropping off from weariness, or old age. It is more a demolition, a deliberate and willed destruction in which we play an active part. The need for the creation of more jobs clamors on every side, and that demand is ultimate and not negotiable. At the same time we know only one response: to elevate, to boost, to enlarge the benefits that flow to business. So we take from the social and cultural institution and give *en masse* to business. The business sector receives more space while the social and cultural institutions huddle in ever smaller corners under the impact of their budget cuts. The largesse handed to the pharmaceutical corporations and the big insurance companies as part of the funding for the new home security department is only one of the latest and most shameless of these massive transfer payments.

We are not only taking away from "culture" in the narrow, ethereal and effete bourgeois sense. The economy is like an enormous Goldberg contraption that we expect to manufacture; to produce jobs. Since jobs are constantly eliminated (through automation if nothing else), new jobs must continuously pour out of the great chute of this machine. Yet the engine is voracious. To keep its steam up at the highest pressure we grab whatever is to hand and toss it into the furnace fire. And that's the point: metaphorically speaking, we burn old family pictures, precious furniture and even our violins. Not metaphorical, but in crass literal fact. The demands of our jobs have so encroached on the rest of our lives that we have sacrificed much of the relationships to our children, large parts of our family lives and even the frequency of sex. It's become common that we must leaf about in our small black book to find an open spot where we can meet with our mate. This frantic "burning of our violins" has by now reached the point where an ever greater number of harried people sum up their great complaint into the one much-repeated sentence that they "no longer have a life!"

The pressure caused by the twin giant factors of the spread of automation and of globalization lowers not only the level on which the "working class" lives. No, the force of that pressure has also reshaped the professional life of physicians. Hospitals and much of the rest of medicine were turned into for profit enterprises. Many other professions have followed suit. In fact that is very much what the increasing dominance of business means: realms that formerly were not wholly subject to calculations of money were conquered and became part of the business empire. Similarly, that same pressure also exerted its downward force on the territory of the service sector. Social workers, to pick one example, suffer from a perfectly old-fashioned "speed-up" – more cases, in less time. They are also subjected to a great increase in regimentation. The upshot? The distinctive value which this work formerly possessed, which was inseparable from personal attention, and personal involvement has largely been eviscerated: the pressure has desiccated what they do, has rendered it bureaucratic and close to meaningless.

Once again, one can understand the history of the recent setbacks of the ecological movement as a consequence of the same dynamic. The connection between the multiplicity of ecological apprehensions and the Business-Job-Nexus becomes apparent as soon as one strings words like "blackmail," "extortion," "ultimatum" and "jawbone" together. That in our world is one of the most patent, flagrant patterns. Irrespective of what the particular cause may be, whether it is the quality of air, or of water, or the preservation of the beauties of a valley, or of a stretch of beach: sooner or later all of these campaigns collide with the interests of a part of the business system and then the either/or comes sharp and quick: "Fine, insist on your water or your air. If you do we will simply relocate our operations where labor is cheaper, like to the Ukraine or Brazil." As the demand for jobs becomes ever more intense the force of that threat naturally grows. That is one reason (to my mind only one of many) for the long line of defeats and withdrawals which the ecological movement in the last few years has suffered.

Clearly, this is the monotonous repetition of one and the same pattern. In fact this pattern has been repeated so consistently that the basic quality of politics has changed as the years passed. Politicians of course make promises; that is in the nature of their trade: they will improve the lot of the great majority that has lost ground, they will reverse the well-known trends toward ever greater inequality, toward more work for less pay, toward... and invariably these promises raise hopes and a following comes together in support. Yet again and again this has turned out to be mere show, merely a spectacle, a theater and no more. Once the conflict is joined, once the battle takes on form, after the stage of mere posturing and rhetoric is over, once more the well-worn sequence of events unfolds. It becomes clear that the hoped for promised changes for keeping it would imperil the further growth of jobs. At that juncture two things happen at the same time. For one, the politicians become toned down, they back-paddle, their stance becomes far more conciliatory, softer, gentler. At the same time, we ourselves become uncertain. We waver, much of the time we turn and disavow and reverse course.

This means that no genuine conflict is permitted to arise. There are no longer genuine negotiations, or a serious meeting in the middle, a compromise, in which the different parties are honestly represented. None of that. Instead, for a short time the growing apprehensions are allayed, a little calm and comfort spreads, vague signs of hope; a little cheerfulness.

To go back to our picture of the train: by now we have painfully learned that no matter what our politicians say, there is no question of their changing the course of the train. Indeed we have now reached a later, more advanced, still more upsetting stage. By now the politicians no longer speak about the train, or about where it is going, or what anyone could do to stop it or to slow it down. They no longer address the encroaching situation. They do not mention with a single word the fundamental fact; namely that formerly there were alternatives, but that these have disappeared. They are as helpless as the rest of us. Therefore, we have begun to see them differently. We have assigned to them a different role, they no longer perform their previous function. They have been demoted, degraded into porters. They knock on the compartments and offer pillows, some red, some black, some green. A little comfort so that we can catnap for a spell, a bit of sweet-talk for this or that especially offended group, some soothing words so that all on the train will stay reasonably quiet. That is all that is left. No more.

In many Punch and Judy shows that I saw as a child, the large and very toothy crocodile would forever lurk behind Punch's back. All the children saw the huge crocodile clear as day, only Punch for some strange reason was totally unaware of it. No matter how loud the children screamed, no matter how repeatedly they explained that its mouth was terribly wide open, and only 4 more feet away, Punch looked merely baffled, and was constantly distracted by no end of happenstance events. That our politicians are like Punch and we like the children does not need spelling out. It is the outcome that contains the lesson: the children always stayed to the very end of the performance. Yet many of us left this puppet-theater long ago; it was tiresome and we grew bored (for one indication of *how* bored, glance quickly at the percentage of participation in elections in the USA).

The mayhem spreads

The film *The City of God* depicts the life of young street children in one of the favelas of Brazil. In one scene the 14-year-old leader of a gang tells an 8-year-old who wants to join that he must prove "of what stuff he is made" before he will be received. The test assigned to the boy is that he must shoot at close range one of the two other also waiting children. After hesitating for some moments, the shot rings out.

How does the Job-Business-Nexus function in the Third World? What effects has the enormous increase in the power of the business sector had in these two-thirds of the globe? The comparison is not just grim. It is revealingly instructive. It is impossible to really understand the nature of the forces that in these decades change and re-shape the world if one observes things only from the protected vantage point of our world. A great deal that we see here only through a fog, as shadows, as suggestions, becomes unmistakable and stark in any one of these so very different countries. It is of course vastly, incomparably, monstrously worse! The reasons for this hit us in the face. For one, because unemployment is five or eight or ten times higher than with us. If we wear sackcloth and wear the keys to our cities around our necks because we are desperate for jobs, what do you suppose the people of Africa or of India or of any other 50 random countries are prepared to do? Come naked and walk on their knees? They of course compete against us, and one should add this to the moments in which the new and greater power of the business sector becomes manifest. With very little talent for theater one can easily fantasize a scene in which two representatives, one from a pleasant spot somewhere in Ohio, and the other from a slum in which 8-year-old boys kill to get into a gang, plead their case in front of an only half-listening businessman. What infrastructure do you have to offer? How skilled and trained are the people who sleep on newspapers in the street? How many years of schooling do most of them have? How familiar are they with the latest version of "Word" or of "Windows." And last but by no means least: "(You there, you from Ghana) how much can you pay us if we do decide to come?"

And yet, and yet – and this is truly important – all of the governments of every one of these countries nonetheless do precisely this. They have masses of people that are unemployed and live in slums and they beg and plead with businesses to please come and settle in their territory, just as we do this between Michigan, Indiana and Ohio, or for that matter Michigan and Germany. At this point I know a good many people in the governments of some of the Third World countries, and I know that many of them are corrupt. Nonetheless I cannot imagine that there is a single one who does not in his heart of hearts know that this peculiar contest is utter madness and a full-fledged monstrosity. The point is of course, that they in spite of all that *do it*, and of course for the very, very best, and the most overpowering of reasons. *Because there is no alternative.* Because there is nothing else to do. Because development means creating jobs, and assuredly and without any doubt: jobs do come from business and from nowhere else. Speaking of riding in a thoroughly locked train – I suspect these government people know exactly what I mean. Take South Africa as one example. For years the South African people carried on a revolution that most of the world watched with breathless excitement. It was an extraordinarily left revolution, even though many people in the States prefer not to know how close the ties between Mandela and communism in those years were. It was also fully and completely a black revolution. And, above all it was victorious. And in spite of all that, what is the path that the black government since 1994 has followed? Everybody knows: after some initial resistance it is to the letter the path that will invite and please and hopefully attract and bind Big Business.

It is a bitter crashing irony that precisely the condition of the black population has in many respects *worsened* since the victory of the revolution and the election of a largely black government. Unemployment has risen sharply and together with it, naturally violence and crime. The utilities have become more expensive and the social services have declined. It is not at all unusual for a *black* taxi-driver to say that he preferred the time of apartheid. In this respect South Africa is entirely in step with the great majority of Third World countries. It may sound shocking to our ears, but many people who live in the territory of the former Soviet Union refer to the time of Breshnyev as "the good old days." Why? "Because then there were sausages in the butcher windows, and everybody worked."

The fearful descent that has occurred in two-thirds of the world in roughly the last 15 years teaches us a crucial lesson. Of course the policies adopted by these countries are at fault. In every one of these countries they have aggravated the division between the rich and the poor. Since the poor were numerous and quite poor before this decline started, their condition is now calamitous. And once more there lies an ironic twist in this. Many blame the World Bank and the International Monetary Fund (IMF) for aspects of this deterioration. Doubtless the IMF has acted peremptorily in numerous situations, and has browbeaten governments into economic policies that are to Washington's liking. Equally, the World Bank has acted like an unscrupulous loan-shark. If sleazy pawnbrokers in the poor inner-city districts of America had practiced what the World Bank has many times, they would have gone to jail. Even granted all that, one should not imagine that the World Bank or the IMF are *responsible* for the disaster which has now arrived. It is useless to blame them, except of course for some of the timing and the sheer dogmatism with which "privatization" was foisted onto several countries – perhaps most especially the former Soviet Union. No, actually, the real responsibility and the real blame lie elsewhere. Namely, in the absence of any conceivable alternative. With or without the IMF and the World Bank all of these countries were trapped in the Job-Business-Nexus. With or without the added prodding from the IMF and the World Bank they were all desperately trying to find the fertilizer that would grow bumper crops of jobs. That was the big coercive reason for the policies that they adopted. That is why they cow-towed to Big Business which very often was expensive and used up the funds that could have helped the poor.

I have insisted in a permutation of several ways that the most massive and overshadowing characteristic of our system is the fact that it drags us down into the bifurcation and the polarization between the ever fewer that are growing ever richer and the ever more that are becoming ever more destitute and poor. The sum-total of those already stuck in slums and particularly the number of those now migrating into slums from virtually every rural area in the Third World has become unfathomable. Probably only a very small minority has an at all accurate conception of what the numerical count of slum-dwellers would cumulatively be. One mind-boggling number might in any case be no more than yet one more empty cipher that floats past us in the night. Conceivably, the simple fact that every Third World city – whether it is Kiev, or Moscow, or Calcutta, or Bombay, or Johannesburg, or Cairo – is both a city and a slum, and that the slum-part growing around each of them covers many miles. Miles on which people live like refugees, huddled together, crammed, with only pieces of plastic sheets for roofs, and often only the barest minimum of water, and toilets that I will not describe. Perhaps that sentence comes a little closer to shaking us by the shoulder, and waking us to this massive and foundational fact about our age. Possibly no sentence, or even poem written by anyone could come close to doing such a thing. There may be no substitute for spending a longer period of time, not just 3 days with a tourist guide, in a slum, and to live there in every respect exactly like the slum-dwellers do.

There, nonetheless, may be one purpose that quoting one select statistic could well serve. Some experts have estimated that roughly 2,000,000,000 people live now in urban settings, and that approximately two-thirds of these 2,000,000,000 are seriously poor. Guestimates of this sort are of course notoriously and fabulously problematic, but this does not thwart the one thing I have in mind: regardless of whether this number is farther or closer to the truth, virtually no one in the face of it believes that the one tunnel strategy that we have been pursuing could eradicate this condition. No matter how obeisant our bows before the Lords of Business become, no matter what heaped up sacrifices we burn on the altars of their boardrooms, no growth of businesses or jobs will be elicited that could ever match the order of that magnitude. If some inkling of the size of what we have been trying to suggest has come across, then we can imagine the next few steps in the development of what we so far label "terrorism." The question that must be posed focuses on the relationship between these two: given that terrorism is now a fact, that its existence is a given, how will these two world-encircling phenomena interact? More spelled out: how will terrorism effect the further development of poverty and the slums, and vice versa. In what ways will the festering and spreading slums influence the next phases in the evolution of terrorism? Almost anyone who knows life in the Third World slums from direct experience cannot help but be amazed at how placid, how patient and truly long-suffering this great mass of human kind has so far been. For those who know this first-hand, it is hard not to see in terrorism, a perhaps overdue first outcry of reaction, a long-delayed, maddened, furious flailing that obeys no rules, and most certainly not the "rules of war." Poverty will continue to deepen and to engulf more. Not because of sheer fated, preordained ultimate necessity, but because that is the all else overwhelming drive of the Job-Business-Nexus.

The widening of terrorism is at rock bottom a matter of contagion, of proximate location, of geography. As the frequency and the ubiquity of terrorist attacks increases and intensifies, any number of them will obviously be launched in the vicinity of slums. Inescapably this will bring in its train measures of protection and defense. Also measures of repression will be taken against all those in the neighborhood; guilty and innocent alike. Since September of 2001 we have seen this pattern enacted all too many times. Sooner or later this of course multiplies the number of potential terrorists. The ghastly history of the combat between Israel and Palestine is like a didactic text-book illustration of this upwards spiraling logic which before long we will be observing in hosts of other places. Part of this is plain, understandable tit-for-tat reaction. The awesome, deeply depressed, near catatonic passivity of the typical slum-dwellers is not bottomless. Enough violence and steadfast repression eventually pushes them far enough down to produce a reaction. That reaction has by now been modeled, demonstrated and rehearsed. It has been analyzed and explained countless times in the newspapers and on TV. Everyone at this point knows in detail what to do, and with sufficient provocation will of course eventually do it.

Another element is as old as the psychology of sin. If I am being treated as if I had already committed the transgression while I am actually still innocent, then I am a doltish fool if I don't plow ahead. I am already paying, so I might as well sin for what its worth – or in other words: why not become a terrorist if they have begun to treat us as if that is what we are? If terrorism will indeed spread in this way, if gradually more and more war-like acts will originate in areas that are slums (and to a large extent that of course is the case already) then, naturally, Al Qaeda and all other circumscribed, specific conspiratorial groups will fade and blend into the background. In the United States this will erode a very basic and foundational perception. For a long line of reasons, the dominant emotional posture is still that "clean," surgical strikes will be all that is necessary; that essentially this entire conflict will be kept at a distance from us, and will thus be like other recent wars have been for the United States. We will look back upon this mad conceit a few years from now as a high-water mark, as one telling measure of just how calamitously and madly deluded we were. This will change very gradually as through a slow persistent grinding. More than likely there will be many acts of terrorism in many different places, and gradually they will become so ubiquitous and so persistent that we will realize that we have no effective defense against them. Slowly our life will become more like life is in Israel already. No one will feel quite safe when they shop. Parents will have anguish in their eyes when they send their children off to school. One will start to walk across a square – and not make it to the other side.

In slow degrees we will discover that Iraq was but a minor skirmish, and reluctantly we will piece by piece admit who our enemy in this struggle actually is, and how huge the numbers that have come to "hate us" really are. Piece by small piece our picture of the whole gestalt will undergo a transformation, until we face the fact that we are in the early phases of the long overdue great war, the first genuine world war, the war of the utterly desperate four-fifths of humanity who are down and out against the uselessly and absurdly rich.

To fill in this picture with a few further touches, most of us have seen films and read books in which the territory into which the locked train is moving is described in detail. If we continue in the direction in which we are now going then the canyon that separates the poor from the rich will have become much deeper and much wider. Possibly in 10 or 15 years most of the rich might live in "protected communities" – in some states and countries, these, of course exist already. They will be a lot like fortresses. High concrete walls with spirals of electrically charged barbed wire on top of them; surveillance cameras turning in their sockets in unsuspected places; children who are driven to school in armored cars, and wave at their parents through glass that is bulletproof. The everyday life of the rich, of necessity, will be disciplined and guarded – in many ways a military life. Life in barracks but with Jacuzzis.

The other side is also predictable. For it, too, models exist already. Poverty will be still deeper, and the number of the poor will be vastly greater than it is even now. If the downwards pressure on all social services and safety nets continues then the slums, or camps, or barrios, or shantytowns of the poor will of course be enormous. They will sprawl across miles and miles. Very few people will still live in the rural country and the rich will have segregated themselves from the areas of the poor. How everyday life in shantytowns rolls on, many of us have already seen. So it is easy to imagine different snapshots. Some areas might be very like leper-colonies in the Middle Ages, others might look like the camps of guerrilla fighters, not so very different from what we recall from Vietnam, or witness now in Iraq, in East Timor, in Afghanistan and Palestine.

The division that we so far only morally lament, the bifurcated culture that we so far regard only as a moral scandal will have become something else: small, fortified enclaves surrounded by a hostile roiling sea of last-resort, last-ditch, fighters unto death. Life will have become a hysterical struggle for survival – also for the rich – and both the poor and the rich will be lost in a landscape of great slaughterhouses.

Yes, the train is headed for Jerusalem. Not what Jerusalem once was, but what Jerusalem in the last 20 years has gradually become. In retrospect we will understand that Jerusalem did play a prophetic role: that life as it is there now – with bombs exploding in discos and in cafeterias – was the forewarning of the life that was to come. The locked train in which we imagine ourselves to be riding may not crash into a mountain wall, or careen down into a river: the train may stop and the conductors will be shouting: "Last Stop! This train ends here! Jerusalem!" The question is: must this happen? Are we bound to continue in the direction in which we have been going? Or, is there an alternative, is there another way?

We started from the idea that a lot of people experience the condition of our culture on the analogy of a locked train. That there is only one path, one trajectory, one end. I would like now to suggest a different picture. In this picture, we in effect have been moving through a broad and long fork, huge like the Mississippi delta. There is not one moment of decision, one quick final either/or. Instead, our culture is making its way in the tension between two poles, two alternatives. It has been doing this for some time, and this will continue for several more years. Between the two paths exists a field of forces. We cross through currents that pull us first in one then in the opposite direction. The outcome, along which of these two paths our culture will eventually develop, is still wide open. Both are possible. Much depends on the decisions and the actions we will take.

We know that spreading forever bigger and redder carpets for the moguls of Big Business will not work. We have now known this for some time. That exactly is the heart of the Post-Cold-War-Condition: Of course we know, certainly by now, that the entire frantic effort to coddle and assuage them is to no avail, that it is a useless, self-destructive strategy. Why do we nonetheless continue and persist? Ultimately for only one, but that an utterly final and door-closing reason: there is no alternative! We do not have the ghost of a shadow of a notion of what else to do! We are hypnotized and believe ourselves to be in a locked and welded-shut train. In one sentence: this is the purpose of NEW WORK. To show that there is an else, that there is an alternative, and to make that other way as visible as a great streak of light.

Chapter Two

The Job System

In the last 20 years people sometimes responded to me with outraged and incredulous irritation when I would explain that we have so far lived only through the mildest precursory beginnings of the automation of jobs; that the real hurricane was so far still miles out in the sea, and that in the very near future the scarcity of jobs would be vastly, incomparably more severe than anything we had experienced so far. Quite often people would behave as if they had been offended. That idea was simply preposterous, wholly outlandish. Surely there had been ups and downs many times before now, but the conception that we could seriously and permanently run into an ever more severe and ever more painful shortage seemed just plainly grotesque. Many times I pointed out that the mood in which they were speaking appeared to come from the conviction "that there of course had always been jobs. Back as far as anyone could remember. So, why on earth, should have all things in our time occur a sudden and mysterious drying up of this immense and gigantic river that had been flowing for eons through uncharted vastness of past time?"

"We" – I mean "we" who have just read the Preface can give any number of other reasons of why they sound as they do. Yes, the idea that there could be alternatives to the Job System seems not to have ever occurred to them, but there are also the harrowing experiences of the last 20 years. We are at the end of our rope. We have brutalized most every fabric of our environment, we have looted much of the furniture of our culture and burned it like violins, and nonetheless the horrific bifurcation between the powerful Big Brother Few and the drowning mass of the poor has only grown worse. And now we should face the fact that automation, which is one of the main causes of these calamities, has only barely begun? No wonder they react with indignation and rebellious rage.

Usually I apologize somewhat for the shock, but then go on to explain that I in all seriousness want to propose that the entire Job System has only existed for about 200 years. For many this is a second, additional shock which throws the minds of most who have come into confusion. That, I then continue, is indispensable and exactly the point. We must start from a fresh point, and pursue tenaciously a strange and somewhat frightening path. To announce now what the end-result, or the goal will be like, is utterly out of the question. The only assurance that can be given is that we can begin the right first steps on the way to New Work. To put it less abruptly, certainly people did not have jobs when they still lived in caves and cleaned the skins of bison with scrapers of stone. In fact if you step back and look at the main outlines in the big mural of time you can see very quickly that the vast majority of people moved into jobs, into that quite specific way of working, around the time of the Industrial Revolution. Prior to that the majority of people worked on the land. In one way or another they were farmers or craftsmen for the farmers. So the peculiar structure that I will be calling the Job System is historically speaking extraordinarily young. Two hundred years in the evolution of human kind is no more than the last 5 minutes on the gigantic clock. So one could say that jobs are a late-comer in the meandering history of the whole of work. They as an institution are very young. On the face of it there is thus nothing so weird and contrary to common sense about the possibility of their disappearance. They arose under the pressure of a highly specific array of circumstances, and now that those circumstances have waned, they too might disappear in the sand. There would be nothing in the least unusual about an institution that has a life-span of approximately that long.

I happen *not* to have a romantic view of farming (in essence simply because three times in my life, I have done it with my own hands). Nonetheless, there is no question that farmers work very differently from people who work in jobs. In a cartoonish way, one could say that they work for themselves: they are not hired and fired, they do not punch a clock, and they do not dress up for the life-determining interview. In many countries, especially African and Asian, the transition from farming to jobs is still in full swing right now. Indeed, we all know that many millions of peasants have been leaving their villages in the last 10 years and that they have wandered into the cities in search of jobs.

From the very start the Job System was not welcomed with jubilations and cheers. Far from it! When it first took root and began to spread, nightmarish, monstrous things arose. They were so new and so unheard of that they took on a symbolic value, which reverberates down even into our own days: sweatshops, child-labor, the English coal-mines, Manchester, the Weavers in Silesia, the festering slums in most cities. To a degree all of this was new since, for good or ill, people previously had lived far more in villages than now. It is not totally irrelevant that the expression "the good old times" initially referred to these pre-industrial, rural, bucolic village times. Nothing is more absurd, more a carnivalization of history, than the fantastic notion that it was mainly Marx and socialism that reacted with uproar and rage against this new system and this new life. It was more like a trembling, an ague, a fever that shook the entire social organism from its hair to its toes. If one wanted to mention only two of the most obvious names, one could refer to Thomas Jefferson, as one towering figure, who never tired of warning against the new job-oriented life in the cities, which was in his estimation worse in every respect than the more vigorous, more independent, healthier and far more virtuous agrarian life. Or, in outlook and origin as different from Jefferson as can be imagined, one could read again the novels of Charles Dickens, and maybe not only *Oliver Twist*, but also the much-sentimentalized *A Christmas*

Carol. For that story was not by any means only about the ghosts of previous plum puddings, but very much also about the Job System. What was he describing? The feel, the ambience, the "spirit" that would be the travesty still remaining of Christmas, if you are working in a job, and for a boss who like Scrooge counts out the pieces of coal that you can put into the fireplace while you freeze and work for him late into the Christmas-night.

Many thus regarded the Job System as dubious, questionable and flawed even when it was young, and for a sizable group these words are too mild; in their eyes it was a calamitous invasion, an illness from the start. One could easily suggest that, illness or not, the system as a whole suffered from defects even when it first sprouted out of the ground, and that with wear and tear and stress and age these defects have become worse; that this system is now very much in the phase of its terminal decline and hence suffers from a grievous and multifarious pathology.

The pathology of the Job System

The idea that the only defect, the one great disease of the Job System is unemployment seems an utterly wrong-headed and fantastic notion. Note, merely in passing, that this assumes of course, in self-serving fashion, that for those who have employment life is sweet and rosy, and that there is only one small fly in this ointment: the fact that some are excluded. Even the glance we have cast at the origin of this system should expose the grotesque and comic over-simplicity of this *idée fixe*. For it is like an *idée fixe* in the big arena of mainstream politics. There, employment and unemployment do function like a single, sufficient temperature gage: low unemployment is like a normal temperature, whatever the complaints, it can't be too serious; high unemployment is like 105 degrees, at once the economic doctors are summoned in haste. Surely this is far too simple. The interrelated complexity of the shortcomings of this system must be considered, also and no less, the enormous changes that occurred over time. In the initial phases the Job System broke like a pack of wild boars into the rather orderly and placid village life. People were displaced, torn from their roots and excesses of all kinds hailed down upon them: abuse, illness, exhaustion and a mind and body torturing poverty. Eventually, some containment of these excesses, some measure of comfort and calm and security were achieved, in large part due to the organization and often the courageous struggle of the Labor unions. The result was many-sided, conflicted and paradoxical: a hefty portion of the old brutality and rawness remained, but it was combined with an obdurate and dogmatic adherence to often arbitrary rules, and worst of all – the times changed in galloping and turbulent and upending ways. The Job System, however, made the most needful adjustments only reluctantly. That became one of its gravest, most debilitating flaws: it became obsolete, anachronistic, a relic of a by-gone age.

The "pathology of the Job System" as it now presents itself to a sociological physician comprises a fearfully extensive list of different symptoms and diseases. The most unmistakable and apparent is the great division, the monster canyon that separates the poor from the rich. It is a three- or four-fold error simply to identify this with unemployment. For one, there is a great deal of poverty outside and beyond unemployment. It has become proverbial that large numbers of people in the USA who have jobs do nonetheless not earn enough to pull themselves out of the quicksand of poverty. Also, the manner in which unemployment statistics in the USA are compiled is a stand-up comedian's slap-stick joke: to be counted as unemployed one must *prove* that one has applied for several jobs in the last few weeks. In other words, those who have given up are not counted. If one makes the comparison to a flood, one can see the absurdity clearly: imagine that during a flood only those who still come up to the surface at regular intervals and scream for help are counted as victims! Those already drowned are not admitted into the statistics. Indeed, the US Labor department has a separate category for such people: their official label is "the discouraged." Beyond this, there are the three-quarters of the world's population that live in what we still call the Third World. That the unemployment statistics there are even more dubious goes without saying. Still, that is not the more serious point: a vast number of people, possibly the majority of the Third World population, is in the middle of a sweeping "mass migration" that is moving from the villages into the cities; the name for their suffering is not unemployment, but poverty. And that is also the right category for the one side of the great division. The Job System of course also created unemployment, but the more accurate, more inclusive name for the disease that it is now causing is the word *poverty*.

However, it is still half-blind and one-eyed to perceive only this *half* of the disease. The phenomenon is more systemic: it has two mutually interacting sides (that is one reason for the term Job *System*). Long ago (1982) in one of the first New Work projects in the automobile town of Flint, Michigan, we reiterated tirelessly on radio and television that computer-aided manufacturing would eventually result in a *split*. Again and again we used the image of Flint as a *divided* city. We said that on one side there would be rising unemployment, but that on the *other* side there would be steadily increasing pressures and demands. We insisted that the requirements that work would have to meet would climb upwards in a spiral, until unemployment on the one hand, and relentless poverty on the other would face each other and as a result *both* halves of Flint would be in anger and rage.

In her prescient book *The Overworked American*, Juliet Schor swam against the mainstream, in which pundits and academics drifted, and demonstrated in exemplary detail that contrary to all manner of expectations, the time-span American workers spent in their jobs was not falling, but was instead *rising*! In the meantime that has not only been acknowledged, it has become proverbial, the butt of a rain of jokes. It also has become the bane, the harrowing affliction from which lawyers and doctors and managers and really all on the fast track, and quite especially those on the fast track with computers, suffer – very literally, day *and* night! They are overworked! They put in 10 to 14 to (in extreme cases) 16 hour days, and much of their lives are like walking barefoot on burning coals.

This polarization is not finished. It is a process of a progressive and deepening bisection. It is an ongoing dynamic, the evolution of a set of bundled trends, it is one of the key and cardinal effects of the Job System. For an understanding of the perspective of New Work it is quite especially important to emphasize that this bifurcation is not a one-sided but a two-sided, a symmetrical phenomenon (one could add that in Germany in particular this duality has been overlooked). A concatenation of by now quite familiar factors on the one side increases and deepens the great mass of those who live in poverty. These same factors at the same time also raise the growing pressure, the stress, the perpetually rising speed-up in which especially the successful and those on the fast track are now trapped. This duality is of special significance for New Work for one straightforward reason: as long as one imagines that the waxing unemployment, or poverty is the solitary alarming side one can cling to the delusion that still greater pressure, still more growth can somehow or other solve the problem. Facing the duality or the symmetry of the widening split tears apart the cobweb of that delusion. Pushing the revolutions of the economic engine still higher up will certainly not help those who already suffer from an *excess* of pressure and speed. The solution, whatever its exact nature, must therefore be far more drastic and innovative than the mere pressing down on the economic accelerator which neo-liberalism prescribes.

However, this is only one of several disproportions, or more precisely mis-allocations, which constitute the diseases of the

Job System. Structurally similar to this first one, is a related, neighboring malfunction. It, too, has two interrelated and interactive elements: on the one side there are great numbers of jobs which serve no convincing purpose, jobs that naturally and easily could be eliminated, but that are not. The cartoonishly exaggerated, poster-boy and -girl example of this is the fast food industry. Very recently Eric Schlosser published a scathing book on this subject (*Fast Food Nation*) in which he exposed not only the filth, literally the excrement often mixed with the meat, but traced the ramifications of that industry, its far-reaching implications for our economy as a whole, and in that context also the consequences for the lives of the predominantly young who work in the franchises of it.

If one adds to his book the perspective of the Job System, then two additional features stand out. One is that the technology it would take to automate the hamburger business is child's-play. In the last 20 years I have been close to the automobile industry. I am convinced that robots, which have the capacity to assemble a carburetor or a distributor, could with ease put the slice of ground meat between the halves of a bun. The other fact is that this automation nonetheless is *not* performed, and that in itself has a many-stranded relationship to the Job System. One of the clearest of these relates to the employment situation in many of the hard-hit villages and small towns of America: that so many of the young people of the town, who otherwise would be unemployed, have at least this kind of work (never mind the wages and the working conditions) is marvelous PR, is powerful advertising which in its effect is inseparable from the famously special flavor of the McDonald's fries.

Viewed more from the perspective of the economy as a whole one naturally could ask: how much genuine "added value" – the very grail of the economists – is created by this industry? And in particular, how much more of that added value is created because the work is done largely by the youth of our nation, rather than by machines? That question points toward the fact that among the closely clustered diseases of the Job System, the one that needs to be emphasized most is the sheer inefficiency, the gross lack of productivity of the Job System, the immense heap of *waste* for which it bears responsibility. This needs to be stressed because normally that kind of critique of the Job System is never broached. Which in turn has a reason: for normally we do not think of the Job System as having alternatives, so the question of its efficiency *as a whole* does not present itself. This is novel in the posture and perspective of New Work. That there are alternatives to the entirety of the Job System is for New Work a pivotal and cardinal fact: indeed it is one of the very few components of its essential credo. The sheer wastefulness, the in fact calamitous and absurd dysfunctionality of the Job System as a whole is therefore a significant and fertile subject for New Work.

For the moment this is only one first indication of the magnitude of this waste. What if the close to half a million fast food workers had the chance to perform incomparably more creative and productive work? What could they invent, or manufacture, or compose, or explore, if the system were different? By how much would that conceivably raise the so important Gross National Product? And would it not in addition be a cheering relief, if the one and best-known contribution of America to the culture of the world were something other than a hamburger with ketchup on the side?

In slightly more summary terms: I am suggesting that the Job System requires a great billowing mass of "fillers," of jobs that are not work in any serious sense, but keep people busy, or occupied, or employed. To a degree the whole fast food industry can be regarded as such a "filler," because we so obviously *could* automate 80 percent of the jobs which that industry provides. Of course this is only one (somewhat tongue-in-cheek) example. Once that perspective or that question is raised, similar and often blatant examples rush in through all the windows and doors. Just because it goes so well with the idea of "fillers," the category of "featherbedding" should be listed next. This is one of the baits with which unions are sometimes hooked, but the concept is so marvelously graphic and illuminating: soft, downy featherbeds lie in machine shops, in factory halls and on building sites. Take it as a kind of paradigm of how problematic the Job System in some ways is, and how old and crotchety it has become. Great struggles have been carried on, so that people need *not* work, so that some can sit in a corner through the bigger part of a whole shift, or so that importantly the "line" (that is, the assembly line) moves only at a genteel and measured pace, or of course, so that a person with one job description cannot be asked to help with a task that lies outside his official limit. A rambling, huge machine has been gradually jerrybuilt to protect people from their work. Is there not something suspect and paradoxical in this? Could it not, all by itself, suggest that the time for a new start has come? And perhaps not just the time for a new start, but the time for a new *system* of work that will allow people to do work they *want* to do, and sometimes even to do work which they love as they love a child?

We encounter here the same duality or symmetry as before. While a great mass suffer from a lack of work, others suffer by now intensely from the too much, from the excess. Similarly here: massive quantities of fake work are squandered upon some areas that have no need of work, that could well do without it, while again, in other domains in which work is desperately needed, a fearful dearth, a miserable, lamentable shortage prevails. The common text-book examples for these are education, nursing, the care of the elderly, the education of children and so on. While the Job System on the one hand creates mounds of empty shells, it on the other hand leaves great regions of needed and important work undone. This imbalance is precisely what a properly functioning system is presumed to avoid. Still, one could push this envelope further. Labor-shortages in the categories I have just listed are well known. There is no need to stop with these. One could paint a bigger picture and point out that there is an unlimited demand and need for more imaginative, more creative work, work that expands science, engineering, the arts and the humanities, and what of those? Are they not fillers, elements that perform no function, that are of no real use, that are being dragged along in every instance, an indication of poor organization, and poor management? Is, therefore, the Job System not seriously wanting on their account? And does the fact that the huge number who now go through pretend motions, who sham work, but who indeed could perform imaginative and inventive and creative work, not add greatly to this accusation? Is not this misallocation of people a dreadful, most especially a fearfully wasteful and inefficient characteristic of our current job-arrangement?

There is a third, again structurally similar maldistribution to which we have become so thoroughly habituated that some effort is required to recognize that it is as skewed as the two we have just considered. I am thinking of the deficiency, the virtual absence of work in people's youth and old age, and in a monster contrast to this, the relentless, ceaseless excess of work in most people's stretched middle period. Why is it that the Job System banishes people from its domain once they have reached a certain age, and that it then sends them out onto the ice, only not as the Eskimos do, at a point very near death, but that the Job System imposes this act of ostracism and of exclusion at a time when many of these people have still 20 or 30 years to live? This will probably become known as one of the great cruelties of our culture. Not many years from now people will be shocked to learn that this was done almost as much as the tales of Russian labor camps shake us now. It seems likely that this different perception of the meaning of "retirement" will become dominant once the number of the "forcibly retired" has become so very great that they will be able to throw off the bedspreads that so far muffle the cries of their humiliation and rage.

A similar outcry might also at a not distant time rise up about the corresponding deprivation imposed precisely and ironically on our well-educated, and well-cared for youth. That the children whose parents can afford to send them to school, and way beyond that, that young people who are trained to become physicians, lawyers and teachers are often barricaded off from genuine engagements with work, sometimes until they are fully certified doctors, or professors, or attorneys will not be branded to be one of the great cruelties of our culture. It is far more likely that it will before long be pilloried as one of the great "stupidities" into which the Job System tricked us. The preposterous idea of young people being prevented from "working" for as much as the first third of their whole lives. To many it will seem utterly incredible in very few years that young people precisely in their period of supposed *growth* allowed themselves to be caged into such an anemic, dependent and sterilized life – a life of pure learning sans work. I expect that this bifurcation of theory from practice, of mind from body, really in serious lack of knowledge from the real world will be undone not by a rebellion, but more by storms, maybe by hurricanes, of unstoppable laughter, simply because it is so ludicrously self-immolating.

If one combines these three maldistributions, and takes stock of these several ways in which the Job System is tilted like a ship that is about to sink, then certainly some first doubt about the permanence of the Job System, about our normal conviction that it is of course here to stay, should begin to arise. Yet the list of the maladies of this system is still far from complete. There are grimmer, still more dismaying, still more debilitating diseases to come. A yet more ghoulish deformity is a general, pervasive, seemingly even humdrum characteristic that we have come to accept as normal and merely a fact of life. It is actually so grievous that one could wonder whether the Job System is indeed really a Work System, or maybe, considered more closely, really serves very different social and political functions.

What prompts this question is an almost banal, uncontroversial fact: namely that with relatively rare exceptions the vast majority of people employed inside the Job System spend their time on tasks that are far below the level of their capacities and their talents. Truly huge numbers, millions and millions of people, work every day in the settled conviction that the talents which they possess, most especially the deep-seated, so far still hidden abilities inside them, are not called upon, are not utilized by their job. They spend the entire immense duration of their work-time like a flame turned down as far as it will go, sputtering, on the verge of going out. One's first inevitable instant associations with this are of course the worn clichés: the factory-worker, the rote repetition of the endlessly same identical primitive task, or also the office person, shuffling meaningless sheets of paper in a traumatized, stupefied, half-conscious state. This demoralizing condition is by no means limited to these stereotypes. Far from it. Working so far below the level of one's potentialities that a single finger is really all that one would need is also rampant in the professions, and of course in the higher levels of politics and emphatically of management.

I will illustrate with one quick example. A group of physicians from Seattle contacted me about 8 years ago. They felt that they had gone into medicine with high ideals and resolutions, but that their actual practice had gradually deteriorated. One touch I recall with great vividness: most of their well-paying patients, so they said, were often hardly ill at all, not seriously; seeing a doctor for them was very much like buying a new hat. From the physician's side, this was not always easy. To announce bluntly to the elegantly dressed lady that not much was amiss would have been close to insulting. Also, perhaps she indeed had a slight cold. Again, to prescribe after 30 seconds flat the one inevitable remedy was once more very much not wanted. Time needed to be taken, and attention needed to be paid. So, the physician was forced to spend 12 or 14 minutes on questions that were almost small talk and also on a few manipulations. Only then could the doctor say out loud what he had actually known instantly, after the first glance.

The group of physicians that contacted me found these small bits of "theater" upsetting. They symbolized the quintessence of their professional lives. We talked about how medicine for them could again become what they originally wanted and expected. They wanted to heal, to be useful, in earnest, and not merely write exorbitant bills. Eventually, they made arrangements to spend part of every year in a Third World country, where the need for them was unmistakable, and return only for the balance of the year to the northwest.

Analogous stories can of course be told about lawyers. The monotony, the boredom of the formalities; the routine of writing yet one more will, after having done this hundreds of times, the tedium of negotiating the details of yet another minor civil complaint! Teachers fare if anything worse. What they end up doing in their job has lost all relationship to their capacities or their talents. The restrictive and supervisory rules of our school system discourage and depress them until they are ground down to the point where, like insects, they emit only a buzz that hypnotizes all within earshot into deeper and deeper sleep.

Clearly, the reasons for people's descending down into jobs that lie far below their talents are like confetti or chopped straw. Many are of course financial. Others have more to do with the fear that incompetent superiors feel for the talented beneath them. I have worked as a consultant to the computer divisions of numbers of organizations, and in those this conflict is often particularly pronounced. Many who work in these divisions are gifted, and their angriest complaint is often that they are pressured into doing shoddy work. With a little time the piece of code that they are writing would give them genuine pleasure, it would have the elegance, which they know they can achieve.

Yet the extra time is refused.

An additional panoramic perspective may be important. Possibly it is in the nature of all tightly structured *large* systems that they *necessarily* perform a *negative* selection. This might well be the result of a stringent logic. A large system depends on order, on the reliance that a mass of wildly tangled rules are faithfully obeyed. The high-spirited and the imaginative, that is, the talented, always tend to dance out of the ordained lines. That is their very nature. Conflicts are hence inevitable. In the sprawling bureaucracy of General Motors no end of life histories hung like scarecrows from the cafeteria ceilings: a marvelously gifted, rambunctious junior manager or engineer stepped "out of line" just once. Once was enough! Instantly he was transferred to the GM equivalent of Siberia, which would be a hopelessly outmoded plant far away from Detroit. It is relevant that scores of such stories also circulated in many of the communist parties when they still held power. The despair of many, who originally joined out of idealism and a great appetite for hope, was the fact that imagination, or intelligence, or talent were *objections* and that those afflicted with these *defects* were systematically weeded out.

I am suggesting that this lies in the very nature of quasi-military organizations: with enough emphasis on correctness, on etiquette, on rules and hierarchy and order, this downward pressure becomes inevitable. Hence that dynamic operates also in the behemoth system of the totality of all jobs. In the higher regions there is scarcity, a shortage of personnel, most notoriously at the moment in areas that require a talent for computers, or for mathematics, or for science. Correspondingly there is a glut, a density, a leaden-weighted excess down at the clay-feet.

There is one singular and probing reason very different from these that taps directly into the underlying root of the matter. We have to recall the origin of the Job System. It came into being in the early factories, mines and mills. There, a very precisely specified, sharply delimited task had to be performed, usually in an exact rhythm, over and over again. What was required of the hired person was wholly and exactly that she or he would execute this one task. Whether this person had talents for a myriad other matters, whether she could have performed tasks far more complex or far more nuanced was completely irrelevant. She or he was hired for this one thing, and it alone counted and was at stake. The deeper and far more instrumental reason for the fact that the vast majority of jobs do not utilize people's real talents is therefore the very structure and design of the Job System. If most fundamentally, I hire you to perform this very precise task for me, then this give and take is alone in the center. If I hire you to shovel sand, then the fact that you can also sing or recite poetry is of no concern to me.

This deep-seated feature of the Job System can of course not be remedied with a few cosmetic gestures. If one in seriousness wants a work arrangement in which the work that people do will have a genuine correspondence to their natural aptitudes and to the talents they cultivated, then the foundational structures will have to be re-arranged. Which is of course exactly the agenda which New Work pursues.

The now confronted raw fact that the majority of those in jobs perform work that is far below the level of their gifts has one enormously debilitating effect. Doubtless there are other contributing causes like the fact that work in the Job System is for the most part supervised, that it moreover did not originate with the person who is doing the work, but that it on the contrary was commanded, so that submission and servility are inescapably part of the attitude. Still, these are only additional tributaries that flow into this one effect. It is the laxity, the passivity and insolence, and above all the descent into an ever and ever deeper morass of self-loathing, that accompanies the recognition that one is not even half trying which is the main cause of the central meaning that work has for most people in jobs. Therefore: what is this meaning?

Simply, that they experience their work like a *mild* disease. Not as an immediate crisis. Not like cancer, or hepatitis but like a mild cold. When one has a cold one typically says, "It is already Wednesday, only two more days. I can make it till Friday, and after that I will be all right!" The similarity to how many experience their work is amazingly, no, disgracefully close. One's job is not like cancer. It is like a cold. One can endure it. One is not a baby. One has learned that life is not always pleasant, and one can outlast it. There is nothing to do, but to keep quiet until one gets to the other side. One's job, one's work is at bottom only a test of one's patience. Crucial in this is the passivity, the holding still. One does not want to be seen or heard. Most telling is the readiness to suspend, to put the entire job-time into a pair of brackets; to not really live this stretch but to count the months and years as they pass. To a degree one is like a part on an assembly line: one has withdrawn. One is frozen and does not move. One barely notices that things around one do change, that one is occasionally picked up and placed onto another belt. In some ways one really is like a small child that pulls the featherbed over its face and believes that it cannot be seen, that it has ceased to exist. The fact that this is the meaning of work for so many is crucial because even though the experience is "mild" ("mild," by the way, like the Chinese water torture) it ultimately bears responsibility for the appalling fact that vast numbers of people are crippled by their work – crippled like formerly the feet of Chinese women: the steady "mild" pressure which the wet bandages exerted is very like the pressure from the "mild" disease of one's work. The long-range effect is as deforming as it is because of the huge space which work occupies in our lives. And that space continues to wax, for as other forms of life – notably, the family but also friendships, the neighborhood, community in general and even religion –

wither in the barren climate of our culture, work expands into the vacant spaces. That much of the mass of humanity finds it so very difficult to become human, that great numbers are as misshapen, as shrunk as those who ride the subway next to us often are, that great parts of the so-called "masses" truly are in a miserable, depressing mental and physical state – one could call this the great disappointment, the most heartbreaking failure of the long string of frustrated efforts which began with the French and the American not-revolutions. The high, the dancing, the exuberant hopes which intoxicated much of that time are in horrible contrast to the faces, to the dull glances, to the lack of life and spirit that the advent of so-called democracy has in fact produced. Oddly, it is in the face of commuters, of people traveling to and from work that this historic disappointment becomes graphic and vivid and unmistakably concrete. It was this sight, the display of these amputations that shaped the original impulse from which New Work arose.

Work experienced as a mild disease is just one summary. It is not of the pathology from which the Job System suffers, but rather of how that system has lowered and transformed, and degraded what work once was and what it of course again can become. There is one more way of bringing this home that is perhaps still more compelling and leaves an even more indelible mark; that is a look at the misery the Job System wreaks in the "developing world," that is, in the descending, the collapsing "Third World." That it causes poverty and unemployment we know, but it also causes something different though related and that is right now the point. One can observe it on every sidewalk, every train-station, certainly near every hotel whether one is in Bombay, or Moscow, or Buenos Aires, or Mexico City – or for that matter Detroit. You see people crouching, squatting, standing, above all *waiting*. They stand in an intersection and offer oranges to every car that stops, or they post themselves at a door and wait for it to open or they squat in front of two little pyramids of tomatoes and one of mangoes and spend all day hawking those fruits which very likely will rot before they are bought. They are "working," some supposedly "for themselves" (that is, as entrepreneurs, as independent business men) others of course do it because it is their job. Ask the taxi drivers who stand in a long line of wrecks how long they wait, and how many rides they get in a day; ask the people who stand in groups and clusters and wait to carry a suitcase, how many minutes during any one day they actually carry a piece of luggage? And do not forget that many not long ago still worked their farms, one can tell this from their bodies and their hands. How does the "work" they do now compare to what they have done in the past, and even more importantly to what they *could* do – if the Job System were not what it is? Do take this as a symbol, as a metaphor, as a graphic representation of the degradation of work which the Job System has wreaked. Seeing these great numbers of people that do feel "employed," though they in fact do almost nothing but wait with an astounding, incomprehensible patience one could wonder whether the Job System in the end really is a system of *work,* or whether it subtly serves a bundle of entirely different functions. For these hundreds of millions are not slaves. Slaves were kept because there was work, and more to the point slaves were dangerous and rebelled. It seems as if one has fed these masses one small idea-pill every day: the idea, the fantasy that they are "employed" and that idea has made them as docile and easily controlled as sheep. That of course is only how they still *seem*! The fact that there is more and more so-called terror means that the Job System is losing its capacity to pacify, that in this regard, too, it no longer functions as it once did.

The advantage of observing this aspect of the Job System in the Third World is the advantage of magnification. The differences are of course painful and great, but one can all the same see far more sharply from this comparison how work has been sterilized and diluted and ruined also in the world in which we exist. This pathology of course is not intended to be complete. Yet there is one further malfeasance which played an enormously important role in the last 15 years, and which we for that reason discussed in considerable detail. It is perhaps more debilitating, more destructive than those we considered so far, but one nonetheless cannot see it unless one looks from a quite different angle. In one very short sentence: the Job System afflicted us with the *delusion* that work is limited, that there exists a fixed total quantity of it, that it is analogous to other natural resources such as coal or oil, so that it makes sense to speak of our "running out of work" in the same way in which we indeed might run out of resources drawn from the earth. Obviously, this is not a view held by peasants. For that matter, there is the saying that a woman's work never ends. Still, it is impossible to exaggerate the dogmatic fortitude with which the Job System imprinted us with this conviction, just as the pervasiveness, the wide diffusion of this belief is truly astounding. Merely the number of books that have been written which allude to the "End of Work" (Rifkin) is so large that their number should be measured in meters of shelf-space. However, the number of books is the least of it. One could say that the entire political drama in the last 15 years revolved more around the pros and cons, the ominous forebodings that this running out might occur, and the heated, or cajoling exhortations of what needs to be done to prevent this, than around anything else. Even though we traced the effects of this *delusion* from flat plains up to vertiginous heights I want to add one small vignette to capture how the claws of this belief have dug themselves into ordinary everyday life.

Among the many different groups with which I have worked in the last 20 years were a great number of widely dispersed chronically unemployed people. Among the many things they had in common was the near unshakable conviction that their unemployment was their own fault. In the same way, they had the conviction that there was nothing whatsoever that ultimately could be done about the scarcity of the work situation. All anyone *could* do, whether it was Nixon, or Reagan, or Bush, or Clinton, or now Bush again was "stimulate the economy," that is, cajole with arousing words, and wave the smelling salts of lowered taxes. Beyond that, in their minds, there was nothing that anyone could do. Beyond that there were walls of ice and rock and the laws of physics; beyond this was the relentless and stern face of nature – and none of the politicians could be blamed for that!

These are of course only one small severely disadvantaged group. The real point is that this belief is held, dogmatically, and without question, by everyone, that it is universal. We believe it as firmly as we believe that the earth is round, which is why this belief held us captive in what I symbolized as a locked train.

We now come to a point that is ironic and bitter and foul. Yes, since 1989 we have lived with the ever-increasing power of the Job-Business-Nexus. The success or failure of the business sector determined and controlled the flow of jobs, and since jobs are for us the encompassing omni-good we became petitioners like the Citizens of Calais with the keys to our cities hanging around our necks. We ourselves raised the moguls of business upon higher and still higher platforms of wealth and power and status. Whenever they threatened us with a shortage of jobs we eagerly looted and pillaged our natural world, but also the entire gamut of our cultural traditions and institutions, and by no means least, also the ethos and style of our personal lives. Still, our obliging alacrity was of no avail. The threatened shortages became more severe and more debilitating in every country of the world, seriously so in Europe and the USA but spiraling downwards to mayhem and murder in the other four-fifths we inhabit. Now we must face not just one but *two* combined and overlapping dastard perspectives. We have made an enumeration of some of the ill-effects, the dysfunctions and flaws of the Job System. Therefore, we must now ask a question that waited in silence for the last

15 years: whatever possessed us to make such unconditional sacrifices for a social contrivance that was so miserably and ghoulishly and absurdly *flawed*? Was there any equity, any smidgen of sanity in this disproportion? An arrangement so plump, so distended with glaring disadvantages, why ever did we use the bodies of our own children to preserve it?

The second perspective pulls back the curtain from a very different mistake. How long will it take to recover from the disgrace? We rushed to make all these sacrifices, flapping our wings like chickens that drown, because we were deadly convinced that any minute now we would be useless and idle like empty bottles in a grass field. We believed in the apocalypse of the end of all work. Was that not preposterous, deeply, incredibly comic, hilarious and abysmally sad all at the same time. Why? Because it is surely easy to see, on the face of it, that the idea that work is like a natural resource, or like a river that could dry up, is flagrantly false. Work is clearly not limited. Anything but!

Work is infinite

Start from the obvious, from the most near to hand and quite specific. Self-evidently, there are more books to be written, there is no limit to new ideas that can be spun. There is no end of room for more poetry, more music, more dance, but also for new inventions, new theories, whole new sciences that are so far still asleep under a stone. If this gives the impression that the open fields of work are all high and lofty and up in the mountains then think of the innumerable things that can be done down in the plains. To take one example, close to the heart of New Work, one could plant roof-gardens on every building in most cities. The view from every high window would be of countless gardens. One could plant gorgeous flowers along both sides of every turnpike, as is done in parts of Mexico. It need not be flowers, why not grow cabbages along the highways in all the places where we now have useless grass? Why not experiment much more with growing crops on the bottoms of innumerable lakes and *free* the land of the need to forever bear new crops. Grow enough on lake-bottoms so much land could go back to wilderness.

Advance again up a third venue: consider people in terms of work. How much *more* effort, *more* devotion, *more* care could be given to every living child? If you want one further picture for the infinity of work, consider this: why must 30 children usually suffer under one single teacher? Thirty is the worst imaginable number. Far too many for direct communication, for intimacy, and far too few for theater, for grandeur, for the unashamedly dramatic. So why not reverse this? Why not do for the minds of most children what we are already doing, but so far mainly for one specialty, one piece of acrobatics. If Steffi Graf, the professional tennis player, can have six coaches, one for each elbow, one for each hand and one for each of her legs, why not reverse the proportions in schools? Why not have ten teachers for each child? Calculate how much work, how much labor that would "create?"

This was half in jest. The notion of ten teachers for every student was of course not meant literally. It was a metaphor for the magnitude, for the drama and for the size of the upending changes that our schools at this point need. More in dead (rather, in *live*) earnest, one more measure of how much undone work there exists, of the vast efforts that could be intelligently organized and expended is the world of potentialities that lies fallow and uncultivated, and rotting in the overwhelming majority of human beings. Sitting for 2 hours in any train, never mind in which city or on which continent should be enough. If you look around and pay attention to the faces, the expressions, the eyes you can gage how many thousands of miles we are from realizing the twentieth part of the talents and capacities which most people possess. If one made even just a half-hearted effort, did anything the least bit serious in that direction, then mountainous energies would have to be marshaled, and probably would not suffice. For New Work this is not just one more idly enumerated example. Through the entire stretch of the last 25 years, we addressed in virtually every project whether there are practical and realistic ways to make progress in that direction, and what arrangements would be required to achieve this advance.

The interminably debated so-called "scarcity of work," the shortage and lack of is therefore a cultural creation. It is an artifact. It is the product of an economic institution, namely of the Job System. It is therefore an egregious mistake to think of this shortfall as a natural catastrophe. The relentless use of images like that of the drying river which formerly like the great Nile fertilized everything, while it has now ceased to flow, so that famine will spread across the land, are profoundly misleading. They convey the impression of one more fated, mind-boggling disaster that has come down on us like a cloud of locusts. The basic conception that underlies this is doltish and silly, and it is of course what the Business Elite and the politicians want everyone to believe, for unemployment then is not really their fault. They do everything that anyone could possibly expect from them. If, in spite of tax-cuts and stimulus packages the economy does not "produce" enough jobs, then this is like a bad wheat harvest – awful, but not the hard-working farmers' fault.

All of that is wool pulled over credulous eyes. The dearth of jobs is the result of a social, human arrangement that we artificially and perhaps not very intelligently contrived. There is nothing final, or inescapable about them. It is not the result of laws that are as intransigent as the laws of physics. And it is nothing like an affliction that is being visited upon us like leprosy or the plague. It is the result of a sequence of arrangements that we humans put into the world, and these arrangements can be examined and understood. Most importantly, if these arrangements – and

I do mean the sum-total of them, that is, the entire Job System – eventuate in results that are miserable and debilitating then we can *change* them. We cannot only make minor cosmetic nips and tucks. No, we can create a New Work system from the ground up! At the bottom it is the artificially created scarcity of work that is ultimately responsible for both the manifold pathology of the Job System and the gallery of nightmare apprehensions through which we passed earlier in the Preface. Clearly and most crucially it was this shortage which led directly to the raising of the Executive Caste onto higher and still higher platforms, until the might of its members was close to absolute. Again, it was this same shortfall that created the enormous and still growing split between those who sit on ever higher pyramids of wealth, and those who sink ever deeper into the quicksand of poverty. No one can fail to see that this bifurcation is the inevitable and immediate effect of the insufficiency of work. In one sentence: because to be unemployed is to be poor. And it was yet again this same dearth that led to the pilfering of the beginnings of a culture that we had started to make. What has brought us to the point where step by step the socially erected protections against sickness, unemployment and old age were leveled to the ground? What caused us to shift a seemingly unending flow of funds away from children and schools, and away from everything that has to do with emotion and feeling and art? Where did we pump all this money if not right into the stomachs of the Business Elite? And yet, paradoxically, in spite of all that, large parts of that very Business Elite are also afraid, and under the surface their fear has the same cause. Their worry is of course not that there will be no further inventions and no further ideas. Their underlying panic is that these new inventions and new explorations will not create enough jobs, and that as a result the entire economy will gradually slow down. Slow even until their own job and their own standing and their own security will turn into a mist.

If one can comprehend all of this in one single glance then

maybe one should at least consider for one moment that it might not be proper and right to remain ever so mild and genteel and to discuss with great politeness and calm the pros and cons of the Job System. Possibly the air of academic detachment has resemblance to the detachment of pilots who fire missiles from altitudes that are high enough to ensure that they remain quite impersonal and unmoved. If one tries to sum up in one's mind the ghastly destruction and the utterly incalculable quantity of suffering that the Job System has caused – do recall some of the images that portray what the descent into poverty in much of the world has in fact done – then real rage might be a very justified response. Maybe it should be rage like in the Old Testament and in Greek plays; where in rage one tore the flowing coat one was wearing, and rent it apart from one's neck to one's feet. Still, after the rage the one most cardinal point should be implanted with firmness and depth in your mind: namely, *that there are alternatives to the Job System!*

The Job System is not the only way in which work can be organized. There are more inviting, more intelligent, far more productive Work Systems on either side of the track on which we have been. Nothing is more bizarre than to have an overview of what damage that arrangement has wrought, and to still persist in the ossified idea that the Job System is eternal, and was bequeathed unto us by nature or God. Once we can see into what landscapes that social creation transports us we cannot pretend as we have so far that there is nothing that we can do, that there is no exit, that we are condemned and bewitched to sit in paralyzed desperation, that it is impossible for us to leave the locked train.

Jobs are scarce

Work has no limits. It is infinite. Nonetheless, jobs are scarce. Why is this the case? What are the reasons that make it so? Not by any means simply because jobs are of course paid. There is no question that the structure of payments can and of course should be changed. And that not only because some important and valuable work fetches wages that are much too low, but also because those in the upper echelons of business are ludicrously and grotesquely overpaid. Certainly that whole spectrum could be shifted and moved. That, like so much else would only be a change inside the Job System and nearly all of the evils we listed would at most be somewhat attenuated. In the main they would go on and persist. In fact if one decided to pay the now low-wage people more, then this would make matters worse! Jobs would become still more expensive and hence still more scarce. The real reasons for the great scarcity, for the fact that jobs are difficult to create and expensive and therefore in limited supply, lie oh so much deeper down, but are nonetheless patent and not hard to grasp. What transforms work into a job is in essence that I work *for somebody else*. That immediately means that I must accomplish something that is of value to this other person. It must be something that he needs; something that improves his situation, that increases his power or his wealth. Otherwise it would be absurd for him to hire me, and moreover he could not pay me if this was not the case; that is, certainly not in the long run.

That may sound banal to a point that is near sleep, but it actually constitutes an enormously stringent limitation and establishes with one blow that jobs are bound to be scarce, and what is more, it immediately throws a shaft of light on the further fact that the development of technology has increased the pressure on the shortage of jobs in an exponentially rising curve. If the crux of the matter is that my working for somebody else *must* in the end be a paying proposition for him, that my working for him must "create value" for him, then the forces that create the crunch are at once on the table and exposed. In different terms. He or she must inexorably *need* me. If a set of machines can make the same product or provide the same service cheaper, then he can and obviously will do without me. Then I would cost him more money than he has to spend, and I do not contribute a value, but instead a loss. This comes into still sharper focus if one underscores that this applies all the way from top management right across to domestic help. The far-flung and extended array of labor-saving appliances that are now not only available but indeed cheap – from the washing machine to frozen food – creates a situation where for most people a domestic servant is no longer needed. A significant aspect is that the servant is not just superfluous, but would in fact be an inconvenience, indeed even a nuisance. One loses the advantages of privacy, of being undisturbed and truly master in one's own space, and the very few chores one might not have to do, do not begin to compensate for this loss.

The measure of how very limited and restricted Job Work thus is – in contrast to the expanding and infinite universe of work as such – can also be understood as the set of criteria which Job Work is coerced to meet. These are a manifold of intersecting and stringent requirements that might be eight or ten in their full number. Someone must *want* to make or provide something in the first place, and he must require my help, in a way that is cheaper and more efficient than the help he can get from machines, and my help must still meet additional conditions that must finally assure him that he is in possession of more value or cash through my assistance. Only if this complex configuration (which of course omits a host of additional regulations and rules) comes to coalesce does the precarious reality which we call "a job" come to exist.

One could say that each of these criteria is like a cut, and that work itself is therefore like a very alive, large roving animal. Meanwhile jobs, after an elaborate sequence of cuts are in the most startling contrast to this very like a bowl in which some few very select rectangular cubes of meat are neatly arranged. The increasing gap between the number of jobs that are desperately needed and the number of jobs to be had has thus very deep and compelling reasons. The basic criteria we have described permeate the structure of the Job System on every level and inside that architecture is not very much give. This explains why the reaction to this debilitating and extremely painful shortage has been strangely monotonous and nearly everywhere identically the same. Ultimately, there really has been only one almost mindlessly reflexive response. One steps on the accelerator and gives the economic engine more gas! One increases the pressure and hoists the level of production, or the sheer speed, or the amount of advertising, or the amount of invested capital to ever higher and more dubious levels. Both in the United States and in the "developed" countries of Europe this instinctive reaction has been repeated rhythmically a great number of times. One could say that it has driven us in a vicious and futile cycle. The entire gamut of social problems, from poverty to unemployment to violence to old age, and health issues seemed dangerous and severe. So one forced the economy into higher rotations. Bringing the result that all of these problems became even worse, which then in turn leads to still greater efforts at acceleration, with the predictable outcome that the spinning wheels had dug themselves even further into the sand. The rock-bottom reason for this monotony is also the first foundation of New Work: one could turn one's head 360 degrees without seeing an alternative anywhere on the horizon. Every government advanced the same programs and policies, always accompanied by the brass-music of fatuous promises. The result was that there was nothing new about the so-called "*new* middle," that New Labor was no longer *labor*, that Schroeder and Blair seemed to blow into the very same horn, that Clinton was forever charged with being a Republican in sheep's clothes, and that the choice between Bush and Gore was indeed very like making a vegetarian choose between pork and beef.

This monotony, this excruciating sameness is by no means

restricted to America and Europe. Very to the contrary, that same inescapable, pre-programmed reaction has also been slavishly performed in the whole of the *not*-developing world. And as in other matters, here too: observing the Third World is very instructive. They obey the same pattern that we follow as well, but their situation is in so many ways more extreme. The gap between rich and poor is incomparably wider, and in addition many of them have a revolutionary tradition. In fact some governments came to power through the victory of a revolution. South Africa is one patent example. That their governments in spite of these massively potent facts follow the same policy of presenting humbly and on their knees invitation cards to every mega-corporation in sight is one more indication, one more measure of how utterly bereft of all alternatives we have become. They of course know that these "knee-falls" will aggravate the split between the rich and the poor still more, and they of course also know that doing this kicks with boots the face of their former revolutionary religion – but they nonetheless do it. Why in heaven's name do they follow this path? Doubtless for only one reason: *because there is no alternative*! Very like all of the rest of us they are trapped inside the Job System, and therefore they categorically believe that development can only occur in one way. Namely, through the creation of jobs. Every child of course knows that jobs are like buns that are one and all baked in the big oven of business. With hands uplifted they pray that the geese that lay the golden job-eggs should land on their patch of land. It is, therefore, doltish to assume that their obedience to these business-obsequious policies is mainly prompted by the threats and pressures and blackmail maneuvers of the IMF and the World Bank. Not that these two robber-baron castles are sweet and innocent. No. On this score they are less effective than we might think. Indeed, they are close to dispensable and superfluous for none of these countries would dance very much out of line. None of them would pursue a different course, even without the supervision from these masters. What else could they do? There is only one way. The locked train careens downhill on a single track, and in the case of these countries, these two-thirds of the world, the train runs moreover between two high cement walls.

It seems incredible that it was not patently obvious all along that people will of course *not* voluntarily sacrifice hours and pay precisely at the juncture at which these are becoming horribly scarce. Just as it should have seemed self-evident to any clear-thinking child that people will not opt in hordes for social work in precisely the time in which those who already do social work wish to heaven that they could do something else. That is a bald fact, which is easy to understand. Because the very same adulation of the business model that has been part and parcel of the general elevation of the Business Elite has naturally also produced the *lowering, the demotion* of social work. Just as hospitals, and schools, and also roads, and police forces, and parts of the military were "privatized" – which really means "businessized," – that is, just as these were transformed into competitive, for profit, squeeze as much juice out of the cheese as you can enterprises, so of course also the agencies and institutions that addressed social problems. They too were steadily burdened with greater loads, while their pay was reduced. So why anyone ever supposed that the alluring and promising *future* of social work would cure the manifold malaise from which the Job System suffers – how anyone could *think* that is a dumbfounding question.

One large and sweeping thought has to be added to place the entire set of these ameliorating proposals into the perspective which they deserve: they utterly lack all sense of proportion! They are in a blind naivete about the enormous size of the forces that have been unleashed. Even if some workers would accept the option of working only part-time, and even if changes in policy and the mood of the country were to attract larger groups into social work, these adjustments would never compensate for the decimation of jobs that the combined forces of automation and globalization have brought about. And it is not a question of falling somewhat short. The disproportion is downright comic. It is laughable and pathetic as if someone fussily carried cups full of water to the edge of a raging forest fire.

At the very heart of this is one single intellectual step and it is not really large. As long as one allows oneself to believe that the Job System is ultimately a fixed, natural and unavoidable given, one indeed has no options. There is only one course of action in the face of the wildly growing disparity between jobs and possible workers, and that is bluntly to create more jobs. In order to understand, one needs to settle inside of one's mind that the hunters and gatherers had of course a completely different structure of work from the organization of work that came hand in hand with agriculture. Then again, the change from this to the work pattern of the craftmen's guilds of the Middle Ages, and that this was again true for the transition from the Middle Ages to modern times; then one can begin to see that our current Job System was a wholly strange and new invention when it was ushered in through the Industrial Revolution. In the very moment in which one's intelligence has firmly grasped this one can get up and walk out of the locked and downwards rattling train. One is then free of the frantic, constantly driven creation of ever more jobs. One can then see the invention and the devising of and construction of an altogether New System of Work. A system that must be as startling and brand new and novel compared to the Job System as the Job System in its time was in contrast to the agricultural Work System that had gone before.

It is not a hyperbole to say that the taking of this intellectual step will take only a flash, that leaving one world behind and entering another will take no more than a split second. This is not a poetic exaggeration, but a mundane factual description. As long as we were stuck inside the Job System we faced a "wall-

ignorance," which is to say, that we faced a wall that had no cracks in it. We were dumbfounded; nonplussed. All we could do was somehow increase the number of jobs. We had tried that in every conceivable way, and they had turned out to be expensive. In spite of the red and green and black pillows of our political parties, and worse, one and all of them had abysmally failed. The ghoulish, surreal calamity has become ever more virulent, ever more painful, and ever more paralyzing in the last 20 years. However, as soon as we understand that altogether New Work Systems can be created, that claustrophobia drops away. We wake from it, as we wake from a hypnotic trance. It does seem a bit magical or miraculous, but that is because we are talking about a mental, an intellectual change. And sometimes, very occasionally, that is what the mind is like. All the same, this act of the mind *is* the decisive act of liberation. What opened the train was not an act of violence, and not a crowbar, but a thought!

What does the idea of a different Work System in the end mean? Where is the line between the making of emendations and modifications of one system, as opposed to the construction of a new and different system?

An answer can be drawn from the conception of what a set of axioms are: the core, or one could also say, the definitional essence of the Job System is the nucleus of "working for somebody else." That coiled up in this are a spate of conditions which in very short order generate the mind-boggling shortage of jobs we already explained. Much of the quality of Job Work, as opposed to the quantity follows as well; that one is normally supervised in Job Work, that one is subject to irksome rules – in short a great many aspects that in the end contribute to the experience of work as a "mild disease."

First steps toward New Work

The definitional essence of New Work is that one does not

work for another but *for oneself*! This *working for oneself* is the basic building block, the molecule out of which New Work as a system has been piece by small piece gradually constructed. In fact, right from the start of the very first New Work project in Flint, Mich, USA, the intention was not to repair or expand the Job System. The intention was not to divide "jobs" into a different set of pieces and to distribute them in an innovative and more equitable fashion. The proposal that factory workers should do work that they "really, really" *wanted* to do in place of the factory work that was being automated away was quite deliberately an attempt to push a first small wedge of a different *kind* of work into place. In the almost 34 years since then we tried to advance these same central ideas in the by now very extended string of colorfully different projects. The common element in all of these projects is that they are not efforts to stretch or to re-format jobs, but that they tried to give shape or organizational support to the infinite mass of inchoate work, which lay fallow beyond the narrow confines of the lined-up cages; the zoo of jobs. Naturally, we groped and experimented and of course also lost our way. However some things were clear under the clutter right from the start. The labor of creating these new structures would require a great deal of patience and time, but the aim was to make them grow stronger and more resilient so that they eventually would be vigorous enough to compensate with forms of New Work the ever further diminishing number of jobs.

Our goal was the overcoming and the transcendence of that organization of work which in our eyes seemed like one of the least intelligent and least productive Work Systems so far contrived. From the plateau which we now after almost 35 years have reached one can discern that the plenitude of these different beginnings slowly coalesced into two subdivisions. One of the forms of working *for oneself* involved progressively more the use of certain advanced technologies which allowed small groups – not isolated, secluded, monk-like individuals –

but groups of between 50 and 100 to *manufacture* for themselves a very large portion (roughly 80 percent) of the total number of products (in the neighborhood of 64) which one requires *not* for "subsistence," but for a meaningful, pleasurable and fulfilling life. (Paradigmatic of these are *not* the raising of one's own tomatoes, or the making of one's own jam, but – surprise – the manufacturing of one's own espresso machine, and of one's own microwave-oven and of one's own mobile phone). This is the form of New Work that we most usually call "Hi-Tech-Self-Producing."

The second group of forms of New Work evolved out of the original offer that we first advanced in the context of the New Work project in Flint, Michigan, *the* automobile town in the USA. In the first formulations we presented it as a sharply defined *alternative* to the mass-layoffs that had become common in the recession and automation period of the early eighties. Our proposal was that instead of dismissing workers the company (GM) and the union (UAW) could introduce a "6 months – 6 months" schedule. The basic idea was that even after the introduction of computers enough Job Work would remain for *all* workers to spend 6 months of every year in the plants, while the first Center for New Work, which we had just founded, would undertake two tasks. We would assist workers in the difficult discovery of what work they "really, really" *wanted* to do, and we would also leave no stone unturned to ensure that they would be decently and even handsomely paid for work that they seriously and deeply *wanted* to do instead of the factory work which they experienced as a "mild disease".

The phrase "work that we really, really want" was picked up, much reiterated in the media and soon became one of the hallmarks or mantras of New Work. The forms of work associated with that expression also developed in fits and starts, like those associated with Hi-Tech-Self-Production, and eventually a second and very strong sense of "self-production" emerged as the core around which these building blocks formed a mosaic. One dimension was the idea that human beings *require* a far longer and far more assisted period of development than other creatures. One only has to compare a new born baby with a new born foal that can run across a meadow – awkwardly, to be sure – on the very day on which it was born, to feel the thrust of that observation. Gradually a second dimension was added to this first one. Namely, that work which one truly *wants* to perform is very possibly the single most accessible "staircase" for the upwards climb, for the mountain-path ascent that the development of every individual represents. That work which one seriously *wants* to do can be more realistically and practically *useful* than any number of much marketed practices and therapies. We insist that the Job System is only ONE system of work, that there are OTHER comprehensive superior organizations of work. This is the idea that wakes one up and allows one to walk out of the locked train. Once one has understood it, one can observe the progressive abolition of Job Work with indifference and ease. One can comment that Job Work is in any case thoroughly problematic, and that all things considered, leaving that System behind is very good riddance. For work itself to become scarce is in principle impossible, and the appropriate response is therefore the development of a NEW system of Work. Implied in this is that there might be any number of different and still to be invented Systems of Work, and that one quite possibly could even create a new academic field that studies the logic of these systems in the same fashion in which we have already done with political systems, systems of production or could in the future also study different systems of *pay*. Paying people for work that they do for somebody else is naturally only one possibility. It happens to be the arrangement that was built into the Job System and of course for good reasons. Here, too, basic alternatives too long overlooked do exist. One example of these is the mode of payment for work practiced by foundations. From the very largest foundations, such as the Ford or the Kellogg foundations, down to the smallest private family foundation arrangements, all of these basically make payments for work. They pay groups or individuals, sometimes for producing a report and sometimes for writing a novel. However, the fundamental approach is almost the opposite from that of jobs. For foundations encourage one to write a proposal. The proposal locates the initiative in the person or group who is wanting to perform the work, while in the case of a job the initiative lies in the person or organization that hires, and the work is therefore done at their behest.

Sharply distinct from this is the fact that during the last 35 years we have begun to develop one particular possible New System of Work. In this specific new system the idea of human development has played an utterly pivotal role. On one extreme we announced with all the force we could that work in the past has had an enormously deleterious effect on the unfolding of human beings. However, we tried to insist with the same force that work also *can* be the most potent instrument for the strengthening and the enhancement of human beings. In New Work the fuller development of human beings, far beyond the levels achieved hitherto, is not associated with anything like the achievement of a new species, of something like a next step in a very problematic conception of evolution. Our aim takes its cue from analogies like that to the trained left hand of a violinist, or the astounding virtuosity of a singer, or a writer, or a mathematician. The gap between what we consider a "normal" hand and the agility of a violinist's fingers is huge. Our hope is that doing work they seriously want to do will raise people one step at a time from the crippled state in which many are now to a condition analogous to a violinist's left hand. The great difference is that we are talking about the whole person; body, soul and mind and not only some fingers, and that we are not talking about a privileged few but about human kind. As Whitman put it in a single great line: "I sing the Modern Man."

Chapter Three

Work That We Really, Really Want

The last chapter was very like painting a portrait with a broom. My hope was to convey in very broad strokes the very big picture of the intellectual and conceptual armature that under-girds New Work. It is amazing, but in the dark of night one cannot drive a car. One must have headlights, or one can only crawl at a turtle's pace. That is one of the functions New Work wants to perform. It wants to shine a light forward so that after this long period of paralysis and disorientation we can again move.

It was important to glance backward at the vivid, brightly colored and ever so high expectations which the French Revolution utterly disappointed, and to assert that these hopes had not died and decomposed, but were only covered with several layers of dust. To blow off that dust and of course also remold these ideals in any number of ways – and above all to launch an effort that will finally reach and attain them – are part of the hope and of the vision of New Work. Both, the disappointment and the hope are compressed into the one.

The Poverty of Desire

The one question that almost invariably is asked first in any discussion of the Flint Project – with such a famished curiosity that the asking interrupts everything else – is always, and somewhat strangely always posed in terms of the "workers." The phrasing is often like this: "How could we possibly suppose that after twenty years on the line, a worker, stupefied from the monotony of it, would still know what he or she seriously and deeply wants to do? Are we not hopelessly romantic and naïve?"

To that question we have a ready and long-prepared answer, long-prepared not only because that question we have heard a great number of times, but long-prepared also because it has roots that go all the way down into the thought of the great German philosopher Hegel. The rote answer that we by now have given a large number of times says: "There is no need to focus on workers." The fact is not at all that in their particular case 20 years of work on the line has slowly buried under layers of ashes their knowledge of what they "really, really" want. On the contrary, not to know what one "really, really" wants is a far more general plight. Indeed, it is part of the human condition, part of our general fate, or if you like, part of the curse under which we exist. If one turns and asks people what it is that they "really, really want" then the vast majority catch their breath, look embarrassed and shrug. Not only workers, but most of us also cannot answer that question. Indeed this is so much the case that we in the New Work groups have become accustomed to having a name for this widespread human deficiency. We call it: "the Poverty of Desire."

There is a relatively mundane, not at all unusual occurrence, which illustrates that the Poverty of Desire really is pervasive and sweeping. It also illustrates that it is not a subtle or vaporous phenomenon, but that it actually is obtrusive and blunt, a little like the darkness inside a cave. It is a story about someone who is in therapy. Focus merely on one scene, on one brief exchange in a single session. It is perhaps 2 years since the client first began to see the therapist, but the last time he arrived, he burst excitedly through the front door and could hardly contain himself till he had sat down and said:

On Wednesday, I believe it was four o'clock in the afternoon, I for the very first time did not do what my parents in their subtle ways programmed me to do, nor did I do it because I was inwardly afraid of what my teachers, or my colleagues, or my wife would say. It was like after a downpour on a humid summer day. Everything seemed clean and cool and very fresh and new. Layers of accumulated muck about what one should or had to do were washed away. Like someone after a cold swim, I simply and directly acted. I believe it was the very first time in my life that I did what I myself and not anyone else seriously and from the gut wanted with all my heart to do.

This vignette is like a summary. Conceivably it really might require several years of intense therapy before one forlorn first act is truly done by "us." Done simply and straightforwardly and directly because that is what we want. Habitually we act from considerations, from cautions, from regards that have been drummed into us. What we apart from all this actually desire, that hardly comes into view.

I alluded to the philosopher Hegel because we are now face to face with a conception of human nature that is head-on opposed to the one with which most of us have grown up. In a vast variety of different contexts, from child-rearing right up to morality and religion we are customarily told that human nature is obstreperous and unruly, that much of the time it is dangerous and wild, that by nature we are indeed downright rapacious, so that if that nature were not somehow governed and tamed – and "tamed" here is the key word – then the person next to us on the bus might suddenly bite off one of our two hands. What we now meet in that story is the exact reverse of that. The idea that we are by nature frail, easily intimidated, easily subdued and cowed, easily manipulated and easily lead; that very little is needed for many of us to be crushed, that much of the time a vast number of us live our lives not far from surrender, from capitulation, from giving up. Therefore, the needful and urgent task is the task of giving us strength, of encouraging us to become more of our actual selves, of coming closer to the condition where what we want has any degree of influence over what we for the most part do. The needful result where our actions are not performed in one or another modality of cynicism or detachment, so that quick as the wind we already disown them though they are still half-done, but that we instead can stand by what we have done and claim it as our own.

The phenomenon I am trying to describe does not always present itself in quite as bald and explicit terms. Naturally, it often remains more disguised, but it is nonetheless very common and widespread. There are many words with which this condition is named, but the expression "Poverty of Desire" seems to me most unembellished and literally accurate. In any case, many of the New Work groups seem to have adopted it, and it is now the parlance they use. I first used this term in a longish paper about street youths and homeless people ("Proposal for the Poor," Toronto, 1984). In that paper I suggested that efforts to engage such young people in projects were bound to fail if the fact that such youths had sustained a specific injury by society was not faced. We call it apathy, indifference, ennui, cynicism, discouragement, hopelessness, despair, despondency and depression. More precisely it is a particular organ, namely their capacity to *want*, to have desires, that has been injured, or worse: that organ has been destroyed, has been amputated. They radically lack the capacity to formulate a want, to fix it in their minds and then to marshal a sequence of actions toward the fulfillment of that goal.

I went on to propose an approach that in the meantime has become extremely typical for New Work. Namely, I suggested that this would have to be the first problem addressed. In one way or another, even if it should require great inventiveness and tough endurance, the attempt to discover something that they really, really *want* would have to be made. Not a whim, not an impulse, not a momentary desperate attraction, but something that even after much examination would still stand up to their scrutiny, their doubts, and especially their vacillation. Arduous as the required effort may turn out to be, my argument was that unless some such solid ground could somehow be discovered and established, all subsequent efforts would be a thorough waste, would be like water poured down a sinkhole.

Many people so far have not done one thing that they really, really, deeply and with abandon wanted to do. From upper management personnel who become listless and virtually ill in their late forties because in their long and crowded and complex and tiring days there does not seem to be one single exceptional golden thing that they actually *want* to do, to the members of Native American Indian tribes, who have descended into a state of catatonic, deep paralysis simply from lack of anything whatever in their world that anyone could still meaningfully do.

In all of these different groups are many who suffer from this Poverty of Desire. You can make a very small experiment for yourself. Ask at an appropriate moment in almost any random room, how many people recall doing something that they deeply and seriously wanted to do. You will probably find that a good proportion will admit that so far they have never yet done anything of which they knew with utter assurance that they deeply and seriously wanted to do. This evokes a surprising picture: seriously wanting anything is not like the plenitude of sand on the beach. It is rare, exceptional, precious. Go further, and ask any of the myriad who lack this capacity, what they would give in trade, if they could only *want*! Many I have known would not just empty all their pockets, they would be prepared to turn their skin inside out, if that would only help. That this desire, this yearning is so very widespread and so very strong in many different groups is a key fact in regard to New Work. The Poverty of Desire is clearly the exact converse of "really, really" wanting something, and since so very many do suffer from the Poverty of Desire, the same great number responds with a wide-awake interest to what New Work most centrally offers.

The conception of the Poverty of Desire has a powerful effect on the tone, or the spirit, one could also say the mood in which the New Work conversations that deal with finding what one really, really wants (RRW) is carried on. The tone is miles removed from the arrogant wisdom which tells you from above, what it is you are searching for. With our approach we are humble and equally come from the position that many of us are ignorant of what we seriously and deeply want to do. Yet there is hope in our mutuality. In many hundreds of conversations I have experienced this: less as a professor and more in the Centers for New Work. The difference between feeling that you alone are cursed, that everyone else around you seems guided and assured and to be walking with the blithest confidence, while you are singled out – and in sharp contrast to that, to start from the open and proclaimed admission that *none* of us know, that we are all in self-ignorance, is huge in its effect. To sit in the first interview across from someone who easily and quickly says that not knowing what you seriously want is as common as wool is on sheep is reassuring. If a little more of what I have just said is then explained to the "visitor" (never: "the client"), then some of the humid and oppressive quality of such first conversations begins to evaporate. More specifically: the invariable expectation that something spooky, slightly mystical, only a shade away from the occult must now occur, is undercut.

This relates directly to one of the many crass misunderstandings which attached themselves to New Work. Our starting point is that desires are weak! That we suffer from the Poverty of Desire means both that we enter a fog, or a darkness, or a cave of confusing shadows when we ask ourselves what we want, and also that the desires many people have do not seem to possess very great strength. One asks a graduate student: "Do you really want to write your doctoral dissertation on this?" Saying this with no more than a frown and one eyebrow raised, maybe sufficient. The student pulls himself back and replies: "You don't think much of my choice." One off-handed remark, and the course of a whole life can be changed. We easily surrender our desires, we leave any number of them in the lurch; the power with which they influence us does not seem very compelling. Compared to any number of imposing external forces, our own private desires often pull us not with formidable ropes, but with thin and breakable twill. In our view this Poverty of Desire represents a genuine danger. Many people are like bits of wood tossed every which way in a strong surf. In their case the outside forces almost always have the last word. The result can be dreadful. From the perspective of one who turns 60, not a life at all, but a mess of escapes in forever new directions of least resistance.

To be very clear: the idea is the Poverty of Desire does not only strongly influence the tone and demeanor of many New Work conversations. It does far more: often it sets the direction of what an engagement with New Work will mean. The story, or also drama, of such an engagement takes its starting point, its beginning, even its *raison d'etre* from these complaints, and the outcome, the possible goal or success is defined as the overcoming of it. The emphasis on this deficiency, on the fact that we in earnest and literal truth do not know our own desires has thus the most immediate relationship to our practice. Why go through all the different stages of presenting possibilities and of assisting people to become more discriminating about the nature of their desires, in fact why have Centers for New Work in the first place, if it were not for this difficulty.

The work really, really wanted by the down and out

During the years in which the Flint project was most active (from 1981–86) we initiated a great variety of other New Work initiatives. Some of these dealt with the automobile industry in other locations (for example, Chrysler, in Kenosha, Wisconsin), but the majority engaged entirely different industries (among others, small computer and software firms particularly in Silicon Valley, since some of these had been started by former students of mine from Stanford and Berkeley) but even more intensely groups that had no direct connection to any industry at all. The wide range in which these many projects occurred was in part deliberate, since we were trying to discover how very different populations responded to the proposals that we were developing.

Some of these projects took place in schools, some in divisions of state governments, some involved consultancies to towns – through the mayor's office – or even to small regions. A cluster was focused on what are called "at risk" youth, which usually means youth that are with one foot in the world of drugs and crime. Quite a number addressed groups that are called "seniors." With them I always emphasize that "ripeness" is a better concept, and that ripe fruits, like seniors, are usually juicy and sweet, instead of green and hard like youths. Many of these seniors admitted early in a round of conversations that so far in their entire life they had not once done something that they deeply wanted to do. In response to them we often said, that in that case there was no time to waste, and that we had better look quick and hard for a first beginning. Some of the most intensely pursued projects sought to assist groups of women who were on "welfare," others took place in prisons, or with long-term homeless people, or with groups that were chronically unemployed. Not least, there were also New Work undertakings that worked with various Native Indian tribes.

To describe all of these in turn would be tedious and without point. I will highlight a few major features and events and begin with one endeavor that was located in Vancouver, Canada. This occurred when I was still very much a novice, an apprentice, learning, in the early period not long after Flint.

Gardens on the roofs

People had heard that our approach involved finding out what people "really, really" want to do. That is what they expected from us, and that is why I was invited. The assignment was to engage inner-city street youth, and the opening situation was that the usual methods had been to no avail. The invitation came partly because the relevant agencies, and also the available cohort of social workers, had tried every approach imaginable, but without results. I have a little adage which applied to this situation: "the situation was so desperate, that people were forced to come to a philosopher for help." I recall vividly that in the first encounter I explicitly said to these young people that I had not come to discuss jobs! After half an hour's discussion on the pathology of the Job System as that pathology applied to them, in which I went out of my way to explain to them that there were no jobs for people with their records and their habits (a fact about which many social workers lie), a good deal of the ice had melted and we began to ask what they would want to do. In this instance several months of intense effort on other people's and on my part were spent before what this group really, really, wanted started to emerge. I had the most wonderful help (from Betty Tully and later from Anna Kambel) and tirelessly new suggestions, new possibilities were brought into the quarters where they lived and were then discussed. Many of these young people were committed ecologists, which at that time was common among street youths, and after 50 other ideas had been assessed and found wanting, the one that survived all tests was the idea of growing food and flowers and other plants on the rooftops of Vancouver in unusually efficient containers, which they would learn to build. Indeed, the image of these rooftops with corn, beans and broccoli and also flowers growing on them, and with some vines hanging down on the sides of the building, soon achieved the status of an emblem: it became one of a number of much-cited symbols for New Work. There were many pictures in the local papers, and the youngsters certainly basked in every bit of the publicity they could garner. Still, the one conclusion I would emphasize above all others is this: if one is working with a truly difficult and resistant group, one that has been through several stays in different jails and transition "homes" then there is no substitute; if one hopes to make any difference at all one absolutely must discover something that they want! To cajole them into any of a hundred different activities, even if it is done with humor and imagination, will be a waste of time. It will be like water poured down a sinkhole if they do not have the clear sense that this is different, because this is something that *they* want. Another project, to adduce a further instance, took place in a maximum security prison school for young males. The director of the school contacted me for what seemed to me an entirely plausible set of reasons. Apparently, he had tried the entire quiver of disciplinarian and controlling means. He did not feel that he had flatly failed. It was more complicated. Violence, fights, small uprisings erupted at every turn. What concerned him in particular was that the "boys" (as he called them) started to fight with each other. On top of that there seemed to be no pattern, no predictable factions, no coherent groups that engaged in fights with each other. To him it seemed random, spontaneous ignition that hung densely in the air. So, he had decided to give the exact opposite from what he had applied a try. There was quite overtly an element of the experimental in his attitude. He was intensely curious, and could hardly wait. He wanted to know what would happen if one tossed into the mix one element that these inmates really, really wanted. The cells for solitary, the food, everything else would remain unchanged, but they should have one common task, as entirely different as could be imagined. Though many miles from the project on the rooftops of Vancouver (and not just miles in distance, but miles in culture) the structural, underlying pattern that evolved was astonishingly similar. I came many times with pictures and posters, models, catalogs and magazines and there were many times when I felt certain that nothing whatever would materialize, that my wits were leaving me in a painful lurch. Nothing I suggested came even close to generating a consensus. Then, as always in such stories, close to the point where I was ready to throw in the towel, a shaft of light broke through the clouds. I had come across a small struggling company that was selling kits out of which one could make motorcycles that had chrome in many places. It turned out that they were close to going under, and they, therefore, gave us a reduced price. In any case, the idea of assembling motorcycles and of selling them for profit, or of storing them until they were released, was an instant hit by acclamation.

Their enthusiasm was not a short-lived fire of straw. Many of them worked on their cycles in every spare moment they could find. It is easy to imagine the details, how dramatically the atmosphere in that prison changed. Indeed, that eventually led to the judgment that this was one project that under no circumstances would be replicated. Why not? Simply because compared to the extremely unsafe streets of Detroit even the normal jails were not always perceived as frightening, as an effective "deterrent" penalty. Three meals a day, and a place to sleep, were, despite the behavior of the guards, not totally without attraction. Our effort with the cycles, but also our other similar attempts to introduce the idea of genuine work – instead of making license plates – into other prisons, work that the inmates seriously wanted to do, ran predictably into the objection that this would be the last straw, this would put prisons on the other side of this teetering balance. With good work added, there soon would be lines in front of the entrance gates, lines of people who would want permission to please be admitted so they could be living behind bars. The very ingredient which might have "reformed" these youth (that is, inspiring them to do something other than destroy), sadly was denied them. Interestingly, Scandinavia has penal systems which strive to find what inspires their inmates and then they work to give them training in those areas. As they complete modules, they earn more and more privileges as well as more responsibility. Interestingly and perhaps consequently, they also have the lowest recidivism rate in the world.

While the cessation of the program was maddening, it was also a welcome further confirmation, for a single "Yes or No" ran for me like a red thread through the first 8 or 10 years of New Work: did I assess correctly the drawing or the upwards-pulling power of work that people really wanted, or was I mistaken on that pivotal, Archimedean axle point?

From observing them there was no question that the magnetic upwards-pulling power of that work was, if anything, even stronger than I had hoped. During this same period I also worked in the inner city (specifically, the East Side) of Detroit, but also in a number of other rural communities and cities. One invitation came from a very vigorously organized extensive group of churches, the Detroit East Side Coalition of Churches. A protracted theological debate had preceded my being asked to come: was the purview of the churches only the spiritual well-being of the parishioners, or did the mandate of the churches also include their bodies? Those who insisted that without bodies there would be no souls prevailed and a long process was initiated. My involvement lasted for about 3 years.

One highlight was definitely the focus on urban gardening. In the background was the project in which the street youth of Vancouver had grown vegetables and flowers on the rooftops of Vancouver. Urban gardening was now much more in the air, and New Work was by no means the only initiative which fostered it. Still, in the years since then, gardening in the city of Detroit has spread in quite amazing ways. In certain parts the immediate impression of the city is quite changed: instead of empty lots on which weeds grow forever tall, one now sees many fenced-in and well-kept garden plots. That we were working on a daily basis with a group of about 20 churches was important. In many other places, and in Flint, too, we had used the word "calling" as one of several names for work that people seriously wanted to do. Yet in the mouths of ministers that word took on a still richer and more compelling tone. It avowed purpose to assist folks into a calling, and took on a firm religious meaning. In other places we had been struggling to convince people that all work was not debilitating, that there was work that increased one's energy and gave one "more life." That was of course verbatim the language to which these ministers were long accustomed. I remember sermons in which the language went yet one step further.

This area of Detroit was one of the most drug-infested. In many of the empty lots and on street corners were clusters of people who were no longer standing, but whose addiction had exhausted them to a point where they were squatting or lying on newspaper, giving the impression of being closer to death than life. In that context, several ministers I worked with spoke of work in which one believed as a "resurrection!" It is a carefully researched and well-documented fact that gardening is therapeutic. All this congealed into a single and to us quite awesome fact, namely that some people who looked very ill indeed, and worked in the gardens through the admonition of their ministers, and understood the work they did as their calling, approached it indeed with extraordinarily high expectations. And there was no question, the health, the bearing, the spirit of many improved in quite astounding ways through their doing work in which they believed.

While not everything about the project in Detroit was this inspiring, there was much else to admire. In addition to initiating some gardens we also placed some computers into churches. People could come and get help from someone who was computer literate in getting medical information, setting up appointments with case-workers and importantly, in buying goods far cheaper than one normally could in the inner city. Still, the syndrome here was very like that in a host of other places. People certainly responded to the proposal to unearth something that they seriously wanted to do. And that was not minor by any means. Even to classify it under the heading of "motivation" seems a mistake. The ministers of Detroit were on that count close to right: it was not what one ordinarily means by "motivating someone," it was more like the difference between death and life. Nonetheless, the economic impact of what we were doing was clearly far from adequate or sufficient. In each of the spate of many different projects we explained the idea of High-Tech Self-Providing, and people certainly grasped it and wanted to take off their jackets and go to work. At that point we still lacked the technologies (and of course also the money and the know-how) that would have brought that aspect of our projects up to the level that the people we worked with and we ourselves expected. In a nutshell: we were ahead of our times. Years of technological development still needed to occur.

I decided to describe these attempts as examples, because in all of them the relationship to the central idea of discovering what people seriously want is direct and uncomplicated. In each of these patience and information was required but most importantly they should illustrate that there is nothing in the least arcane or esoteric in how we actually discover what people in one or another group seriously want. There is no gazing at tea-leaves, or swinging of crystals from a thread. More than anything else it is "trial and error" – however, pursued with relentless insistence.

Stumps of frozen flesh

My next story will be very different from the one's I have shared so far. Central in this episode is a contrast, the juxtaposition of the normal, standard government supported approaches to the whole range of these situations set into opposition to the very different approach developed by New Work. The next project became for me the most vivid demonstration of why the traditional – old culture – approaches are bound to fail. Indirectly, it thereby affirmed to us that we were perhaps on the right track. In that way it turned out to be crucially important for the further development of New Work.

I received the compelling demonstration of this lesson from two Native American tribes, from the Gitskans and the

Wettsuetsens in the high north of Canada. I will start with a single condensed story of my first encounters with them. Early in an October I arrived in a very small plane at the very small airport of Hazelton, BC. The snow was already deep and for several hours we drove with a pickup truck through unbelievably gorgeous mountains. When we arrived, what looked to me like a large part of one of the tribes sat in a circle in a very low-ceilinged room, which lay behind a restaurant that was itself located in a trailer. When I entered, a shuffling went around the circle but no one spoke a single word. I sat down in the silence and waited. After several minutes the elder of the tribe, a woman of legendary power and intelligence, at last spoke. Enunciating every word quite slowly and distinctly, she said: "Everything that we have done in the last twenty years has been a mistake!"

Nothing followed that first statement. All the same, after another silence, conversation slowly started to seep up between the seated people and not long afterwards we all went to sleep, without anyone having said a word about the opening remark which Val Napoleon, that was her name, had made. On the next ice-cold morning Val waited for me in her truck and we drove again for hours while passing hardly any houses and certainly no villages. At last she abruptly pulled up to a steep hillside and quite unexpectedly stopped the truck on the edge of a sizable village square. There was a school and several houses.

Not together, but at distances from each other stood the men of the tribe. In silence. Immobile. Wrapped in blankets. She again said nothing, but after a while I found the courage to ask what these men were doing. She answered, "They are waiting for the mail." After another pause I asked, "About what time does the mailman usually arrive?" She replied, "Around noon." "Around noon?" I asked, with puzzlement in my voice, "What time is it now?" Valerie said, "Ten past eight." I ventured to follow this up and said, "And how often do most of these men get a letter?" "Mostly, it is once a month, and not a letter but the check they get from the government," was her answer.

Two days later she finally broke her silence, and explained: the great mistake, which spanned 20 years, came to a head in the men who stood waiting in the snow. They stood there because there was nothing else for them to do. The work in the forest and the work in the sawmill had stopped long ago, and even the fishing and the hunting had come to a complete end. So, the Canadian government, which treats the Indians very differently from the US government, provided for the totality of their needs. Not just food and clothing and housing, but also counselors and social workers and nurses and trained therapists for every imaginable and conceivable requirement. For alcoholism. For domestic violence. For child abuse. For the old and dying. For chronic depression. For rehab when one returned from prison and so on. There seemed to be as many social workers as members of the tribe. She said there was nothing whatever for the men to do, so they no longer moved. They became so utterly dependent on being provided for that it was an effort to still feed themselves. Sometimes they no longer managed that!

The image of the men of the tribe standing wrapped in their blankets in the cold stayed with me through the years since then. They were waiting because there was nothing for them to do. All of their work, down to the last shreds had been taken from them. They could only wait. Also the other way around: they also stood and waited, they no longer moved, they stood stock-still in the cold and winter silence because the government provided for every last one of their needs! That double aspect was Val's point: the fact that the dependency did as much harm as the lack of work.

In the days after that I also learned about their culture and the details of their condition. They showed me the giant saw mill which had become so fully automated that I literally only saw one single person working. He sat in front of a console in a hermetically small cabin made entirely of glass. The buttons he pressed controlled inordinately large machines that picked up a big bundle of virgin trees all with one grip, as we would pick up wooden matches with one hand. The tribe's people explained that this had been one of the last stages; the last remaining jobs were automated out from under them.

Naturally, I asked them what ventures they had tried. One of their last had been making coffins out of wood, but the cost of the transportation from so far up north was much too high, and also they no longer had access to real board-feet of wood. Weyerhaeuser, the international lumber corporation, told them that they were allowed to take only the waste-wood, that is, remnants and trees too small for making useful lumber.

Much time during my next several visits was spent on generating an idea for another business that they would be able to build up inside the narrow confines of their situation. After a very large number had been explored and discarded one idea seemed to withstand every one of the objections that anyone could think of raising. It was again a point where I felt that it was utterly impossible to come up with still one more "possibility" when I suggested that they could mount a small manufacturing operation. I had encountered a building system which functioned very like the world-famous Lego game, with the difference that the building pieces were about 2 feet by 10 inches and were made entirely out of treated chip-board. The brand-name was Ability Blocks (about 2 years ago, a group of homeless people in my hometown of Ann Arbor, Mich put up two duplexes for themselves. They built their own housing and for that undertaking used these very blocks).

There were rounds and rounds of discussions. A business plan had to be developed, but finally the members collectively decided that this proposal also passed a different test: they liked it, the idea at the heart of it thrilled them, they believed in it. This at last was something that they really, really wanted to undertake.

The two tribes obtained a grant and for a time a few of them made money manufacturing those blocks. That was a very mixed result, and the picture was the same also in the other tribes with which I worked, in North and South Dakota. None of the enterprises we initiated came close to giving employment to the entire tribe. This was therefore another lesson I absorbed: it was quite out of the question to create enough jobs for these tribes, isolated as they were up in those mountains.

Oddly, the situation was in some ways similar to that of the homeless people in the city of New York. There we had decided, even in the densely populated city, that some modern form of self-providing was the only way out of a permanently marginal existence. Here the inescapable conclusion was the same. Clearly they could earn some money, just like farmers in agrarian times had earned cash with a cash-crop, but it fell far short of being enough money to purchase everything they needed.

The pattern that emerged had much in common with the development in Flint. It need not be said that "self-reliance" and "self-providing" were terms to which Native Americans responded. They organized Pow-Wows and danced in celebration of starting on this path. And they were determined and inventive and much was undertaken. Still, just as in Flint, large chunks of technology that have been developed in the meantime at that point did not yet exist, and the idea of HTSP therefore remained a mere beginning, a hopeful but unfinished start.

For me, in my own personal development, far and away the most powerful image was that of the men of the tribe, wrapped in blankets, standing still in the cold wind and the snow. That image bore some resemblance to what I had seen in the East, to how I had experienced the stage of socialism when it was less than 10 years away from its death, and indirectly it also became for me a metaphor, an emblem for the demise of what in the USA is called liberalism. Of course, everything left and liberal has now become extraordinarily diluted. It has been mixed with much water, and has thus turned very thin. Nonetheless, if one remembers its roots, its original flavor and greater strength then the resemblance to what was done to these Indians is patent. There were counselors for everything, also protections against most conceivable adversities, and the whole was based on an elevated version of hand-outs, crudely said, of alms. Admittedly, this was far and away more extreme than what one normally associates with the left or with liberalism as this is understood in the USA. Still, the direction was the same, and the picture of the men in these tribes (not, the women, they had work!) that I confronted refuted therefore in my mind all of the different variations, or shadings, or colorations that fundamentally embraced the same strategy. One main result was that New Work made a redoubled effort to sever the connections to these roots. Our resolve became firmer and more plain: to plant something different into a different plot of ground.

By further extension, the truths embodied in this image also became one foundation stone for the skepticism and the opposition I developed to schemes like the Minimum Guaranteed Income, or Buergergeld, or for that matter Buerger-arbeit, or any scheme that hopes to patch up the holes in the Job System with more social work on behalf of the disadvantaged, with more "comfort stations." All of these share the two sides of the Canadian Government's treatment of their "First Nation" (that is the Canadian term): the dependence and the lack of work, these two together produce a paralysis; they have the effect of turning people into ghastly stumps of frozen flesh. From then on, anything that seemed to lie in this direction was for me precluded.

If the problems of dependence and lack of work are not faced sharply and in a bright illuminating light then the whole intention and idea of HTSP is completely missed. The idea and practice of HTSP is positively shaped by the attractiveness of self-reliance, by a high regard and an admiration for them. In contrast are the horrors resulting from dependence and lack of work, as shown in the Canadian experience. Something needed to be put into the world that would not produce these stumps of frozen flesh. HTSP was from the beginning the dream of a different use of technology, that would give one independence with not too great a quantity of sweat. Those were the original impulses, but it now also became something else: one-half of a larger system that with fanfare and emphasis wanted from the start to meet the problem of poverty, the problem of destitution in a wholly and radically different way from the one that has been so far tried. Through that opposition the task of New Work, what it tries to accomplish on this score, can now be succinctly stated. In effect our question is: how can work be organized so that the result will be as far from this death, from these frozen stumps, as can be attained? Given the multiple functions of work, how could the structure, the organization of work be optimized, so that work will render people most alive? The image of the frozen men standing in a circle was not just a confirmation, it was also a directive, a signal, a pointing hand – there, in that direction you must go: to be blunt: as far away from this as we can get.

Aside from that memorable image there also was their different reaction to our one and only inescapable hallmark question. What is it that you seriously and deeply and with your soul want to do? When asked such a question a melancholy that I had not noticed even in Flint clouded their eyes. They believed that once upon a time, when their culture was still alive, they knew the answer to such questions. That they now did not know what was in their minds was one further indication of their being uprooted and of their no longer knowing who or what they were.

In retrospect this seems to have turned into a common theme. Past local traditions, to aspects of Hinduism and even to Ghandi were made. It was similar among the urban slum-dwellers in

Mexico and even in Russia and the Ukraine. To some of these people the question signified above all an invitation to pause, to stop in one's tracks and to reflect. Since they associated the West with perpetual motion, with a continuously excessive, driven speed, this rest meant to them something not Western. They associated it with the destroyed, the now lost.

The one most pronounced reaction in Flint was that this question had never been asked. In these settings the reaction was different. These people lived amid the rubble of their blasted, pounded down to the ground culture, and the question to them hinted that there could be a return. They caught sight of a path that would conceivably lead back to the culture they had lost.

Sighs of envy

In roughly that same period I also worked in numerous other cities besides Detroit and Vancouver. For extended stretches, for example, in New York where I was first affiliated with the then legendary "Manhattan Bowery Corporation" which in the meantime has been renamed "Project Renewal." My attempts to work with the down and out gradually took me also ever more into Third World countries. As time passed we added in slow steps more of the technologies that made the body of HTSP richer and more viable. In every one of these situations we naturally always emphasized that we only presented "possibilities" to the people with whom we were trying to work, that crucial was what they wanted, or chose, or desired. In New York I worked mainly with women most of whom had been on welfare for a long string of years. The Manhattan Bowery Corporation was in the early preparatory stages of a large building project and asked me to find out what sort of architecture and housing these women seriously and in earnest wanted. This was a context where the contrast between the usual "request for your input" (on one sheet of paper, by making crosses in these boxes) and what we were about, was not hard to establish. We talked for weeks, but I remember one outburst, one exclamation in particular that happened long after the utter importance of doors that one could lock had been nailed seven times onto the table. It seemed to me that people used to beds probably cannot imagine the truly fierce, the maybe by some standards hysterical importance that after years of sleeping on benches becomes attached to the simple fact that no one, no one at all, can peremptorily shake one by the shoulder and demand that one get up and move. We passed through a long sequence of many talks in which a long list of other concerns was discussed. Among these was having security and privacy, privacy so much that it was like being placed out of reach, becoming untouchable, so much so that we sometimes wondered whether we would be building a homeless shelter or a secret underground fortress. After all this there occurred the one unforgettable moment. As with the Indians, it involved again the matriarch of the group with which I was working. A woman at least 7 feet tall, at any rate in my recollection. Gaunt, lean, towering above the rest, melancholic of expression, extraordinarily like Don Quixote. It had been a petty, drawn out, interminable, pointless evening, and everyone's nerves were very much on edge. She rose. There was silence. She looked down upon us from her imperious height and explained that all of this was ultimately not important, not significant. There was only one thing that counted. Just one thing, she said: "Whatever we build, however it exactly looks, however many of this or that it will include. What matters, what counts will be that 'they' shall sigh with envy at whatever we have built."

This sentence, that is often quoted in seminars and workshops, has become yet one more signpost by which we orient ourselves. In this it is the frozen stumps of flesh in the snow, but also like the 90-year-olds that still perform somersaults between trapezes. Like the other expressions or images that are for us like points of light in the fog, this sentence, too, is alluded to and played within a host of different contexts. When someone says in the middle of a planning session: "Careful, this is not going to produce 'sighs of envy,'" the point may be very direct and plain.

Anyone who has spent much time at all with what I call the down and out knows of course that their sensitivity to condescension, to a patronizing gesture or remark has become very short-fused and explosive. By now it should be commonly known and it also has no importantly special relevance to New Work. It is simply a fact that many of these people look back upon a seemingly endless history of slights and rebuffs and failures, but also upon a history of having forever been treated like junk-yards or dumps. They have been at the receiving end of cast-off clothes, of rickety furniture, of half-spoiled food for so long that they often have an allergic, virulent hatred for anything second-rate, not to speak of the trash that is their furniture every day (I remember numbers of homeless people who indignantly refused the gift of a pair of worn-looking shoes, even if they were in better repair than the shoes they had on their feet).

With that meaning understood, the "sighing with envy" becomes one summation of one of the core beliefs or also of one of the core strategies of New Work. That hand-outs are a disaster, that they humiliate and diminish and in the end paralyze was part of the point of the story of the Canadian Indian tribes. For a very large part of that huge population jobs, too, are not the solution. Jobs for them much of the time simply do not exist. The gap between need and supply here is enormous and continuously growing, and to show and establish this in many different ways was one of the results of our detailed analysis of the Job System. Yet there is an additional main component, large enough to be almost a whole second half that we have so far left out.

What is that still missing second half? To see it one has to recognize that the lack, the non-existence of jobs is for a large proportion of the seriously destitute only the external part of the problem. The internal, more personal side is the fact that the sequence of traumas and rejections that their lives have been, together with the fashion in which they have been shaped by the culture in which they have amazingly contrived to survive, has turned them into creatures which in no way whatever fit the Job System. From their sleeping habits, to their ways of becoming distracted, right down to how their bodies and their clothes smell – they would not be hired by anyone even if jobs were to hand. They could not possibly function in the structural frame of a job even if by chance they actually landed one. Crucially and a yet further fact that lies beyond this: many would never accept the kind of jobs that they have any chance of getting.

The reasons for their not wanting, and their often outright loathing of, these lowest-end jobs are easy to know. In any number of ways they are a thousand miles from the obsequious peasants that bowed hat-in-hand before their landlords, and worked like animals from daybreak till nightfall. Many of them are of course to begin with urban, but they have also grown up with modern technologies and modern ideas, they are cynical, they know about corruption, they know that those who merely work remain poor, and that virtually all of the rich secured their wealth not through labor but through shady and devious means. However, most crucially and most to the point, they in addition to all this despise the trashy, the menial and dirty and out and that extends with full force also to how they feel about jobs.

This has to be added like one more heavy black stroke to our earlier panoramic painting of how the Job System is now breaking down. For years the industrialized West has been flailing with efforts to expand the Job System so that the mass of the excluded would again be accommodated and drawn in. We described the towering prices that we have paid for this, and the utter feebleness with which these efforts have failed to stem the tide of automation and globalization (recall, that the enormous worldwide migration of peasants from their villages into the cities is only one facet of these encompassing changes). What we are now saying pivots this critique of the Job System around a new axle and gives us the chance to see it from a new side. The drama in which we participate is not just ineffectual, wasteful and sad. We are now forced to recognize that it is also ridiculous, clownish and grotesque. For the gamut of these painful exertions were in addition naïve, and thoroughly self-deceived. They were predicated on the presumptuous conviction that providing a sufficiency of jobs would be enough. They leaped ahead and allowed themselves to slumber in that certitude without ever having looked closely at the great mass (at the millions, actually at the close to half of mankind) that they expected to eagerly and gratefully hop into those jobs. Their fantasy was that the building of a pigeon coop with an unimaginably large number of additional holes would be the most that anyone could demand or expect. That is of course a luridly stupid error.

The point is that the Job System fails on a blatant additional count; one could also say that there is a whole additional floor, another level to the calamity of its deficits. On top of the complex pathology that we have analyzed before, there is now the further wall-to-wall fact that the Job System over the years created a vast population that is so constituted and shaped that it could not possibly enter that system even if there were barns filled with nothing but job-hives. It is not only a system into which a great number haplessly cannot enter. It is a system which ordains that an ever-increasing number will become so stunted that the system itself cannot possibly use them.

For once one can justifiably speak of a complex configuration. In the first chapter of this book we wrote about the slums of South Africa, India and other parts of the Third World and proposed that experiencing these places convinces one with an immediate shock that no one in fact seriously believes that all of these millions in any proximate future could be absorbed into well-paying and safeguarded jobs. Now, after many vistas and turns in the road, we once more come to the same recognition. It's as if we have come again to the same view while climbing a mountain, only now we see it from far higher up. And it is precisely this height that allows us to see enough of the panorama, enough of the context to at last see this cardinal fact.

There can be no doubt that the millions that have slipped down into serious destitution are afflicted with shortcomings and disfigurations that for nearly all of them do close the door to the Job System. Imagining them as locked out and barred is still an arrogant and deluded and self-serving picture. That they cannot is in their case inextricably intertwined with their not wanting! (A connection that is of course common.) Many of them would never accept the kind of jobs that someone might actually offer them; not the sort of job that would come into question in the light of their pasts and their current habits.

In this lies the great significance of the sentence that was spoken by the homeless woman who looked like Don Quixote: "They shall sigh with envy at what we are building." The attitude, the posture, one could also say, the high-up aiming determination that she expressed in that phrase runs pervasively – not just like a red thread but like a red carpet – through the mentality of the ghetto and slum-dwellers. Here, therefore, lies the grave or junkyard of countless well-intentioned programs for drop-out youths, for women on welfare, for those who come out of prison, for chronically unemployed, and more generally for the just plainly poor. These programs fail, they waste large sums of money because they hold out the attainment, the gift of a job in return for deference, for regular attendance, for submitting oneself obediently to the proffered training. The kind of jobs held up as lures are not rewards. They are an insult, a slap in the face. Often because of the quality of the work, but also because of the level of pay. Anyone who spends any time at all in the setting in which all of these people live, learns within the very first days that they can earn more money with drugs or through crime than through such jobs.

This throws a quick, sudden light on the bigger picture of how New Work has evolved. Not only some few, but probably the majority of the social workers who work in similar programs would agree with every damning word that I have just said. After nodding their acquiescence they surely would turn and fire back that there is nothing else that they can do! What is the alternative to preparing people for jobs, even if we know that the jobs don't exist, and that the clients of course don't want the jobs that we offer to them. What are we to do? Teach them to stand still in the snow waiting all month for their checks like your Canadian Indian friends? The down and out are not content with the inferior, the cast-off, the second-rate. Part of this alternative includes the important realization that they want things that have quality and give them pleasure. Very crucially they want things that give them the conviction of their own worth – which they, understandably, crave with more hunger than we who are stuffed to the gills with self-confidence.

Distinct from this are the recommendations New Work has made, the projects we have implemented, the policies we at this point propose to various levels of several different governments. The acknowledgment that many of the poor, also those in Third World countries, want exactly the things that we have and that we obviously enjoy is a fact. Distinctive and importantly characteristic – virtually defining of New Work – is that we fully and not begrudgingly, but on the contrary with trumpets and drums endorse this fact. We do not flinch at this juncture, do not raise an eyebrow or wave a gently muting hand. The fact that we do not is for us a matter where a principle stands or falls. Simply one more meaning of our "Here I stand, I cannot do otherwise" declaration: namely, that we are guided by what people seriously and authentically want!

Maybe this should be banal, but it is not. For example, the solar cooker has become something of a legend in the Third World. It is one apt symbol for how controversial and provocative this seeming platitude in fact is. By now this cooker has turned into a joke, but it is only one of a myriad of other similar ideologically freighted examples. For some people the concept of the solar is so very close to the concept of the divine that they distributed this cooker like the Gideon's distribute the Bible. The natural first question which they encountered, however, was of course: is this tinfoil bowl what people in your country use? No? Well, then why do you not give us the same microwave-ovens, with the same dials and bells they have? In the mass-graves of failed programs lie also many whose ideological prejudice is less visible – very particularly to us. How many "workshops" in remote Peruvian villages mindlessly assume that "creating dialog," "raising consciousness," "encouraging more participation," fostering the green seedlings of our idea of democracy is of course and self-evidently how progress and development have to begin. The Peace Corps or NGO worker is often so blinded by his own condition of bliss that he or she never notices how tired, passive and bored the participants look, and with what abysmal resignation one more committee is once more installed.

Despite the great number of clumsy mistakes we have made, on this score we at least always try to be as alert and attentive as we can coax ourselves to be. How the people we are working with react when we present one of the "possibilities" that we have collected over the years – it is a point of pride, perhaps even one of our very few "requirements" to be utterly on one's toes with regard to the nuances and subtleties of how people respond. That means, naturally, that we have learned from experience. There is no mistaking the sudden leap which many slum-dwellers experience when they see and hear for the first time that the manufacturing of genuine "consumer goods" is a "possibility" that is not totally out of their reach. They see a wide gap between the sort of "making of things" that is customarily trotted out: where they can weave baskets, or knit, or make Christmas-tree decorations. That seems miles from being able to make a radio, or a small refrigerator, or a microwave-oven, or an espresso cooker, or one's own fancy and individuated shoes.

The possibility of making consumer goods, and preferably appliances, not wooden furniture or lampshades instantly raises them up onto a different plane. This is one juncture where the startling truth of the possibility of HTSP is especially relevant – simply, because 10 years ago the very idea of trying to manufacture generators or hotplates, or fans, and even more refrigerators, or microwave-ovens in a small shop was utterly unheard of, and would have seemed bizarre. However, that is part of the point. The fact that the design of these goods is "advanced" and therefore far simpler and more elegant (which it must be since they otherwise could not be produced in a decentralized shop-centered way) adds still more to the panache that these things convey. One example are the small refrigerators which operate with a frightfully simple device – consisting basically of no more than two electrically charged metal plates. Here, a touch of sheen is added onto their pride by the knowledge that this technology was originally developed for stations that were orbiting in outer space. That is a fact they love to flaunt every chance they get – that the devices they are making are "space-age."

One suspicion which we often hear insists that ultimately only artists and intellectuals have work that they find fascinating, and arresting, and a pleasure to pursue. One tells us that people are used to drudgery, that this is all they hope for and expect. One then goes on to tell us that this is most particularly true of the down and out: asking them what they really, really want is just a waste of time. To my ears this sounds very like a notorious song that many associate with the old slave-holding South of the United States. The key-line is "that you can hear the Darkies singing," that they are different from us and are therefore happy in their hovels and in their slavery.

The conviction to which I have come is 180 degrees the

reverse: we live in our time, and things in our time have come to an absolute and high-pitched opposition. You can do fancy, well-intended, ultra-modern and fearfully expensive things for the down and out and they will all be a pitiful and massive waste of time if you do not ask them what they "really, really want." It was not always the one inescapable condition. Maybe there was a past in which the handing out of alms was good enough; but that is no longer so. If any upwards movement is possible at all, it must come from their decisions and from their desires.

To be very harsh and very practical: in New Work we have the expression the "Poverty of Desire." That is a mild, almost poetic term. One fact behind it is, however, that in a vast portion of humanity the capacity to want has been extinguished. The "lack of life" in that large mass of people has killed off in them the organ with which one gestates a hope or a plan. We live in a world that creates such passivity in people. Asking them what they really and seriously want might ignite the smallest spark that could possibly squelch the "Poverty of Desire."

Chapter Four

The New Work Economy

From the fact that we help to find people work that they deeply and seriously desire it follows that the sequences of conversations we have with our associates are highly personal and private. Sometimes these sequences continue over many months, they indeed become life-long, but they can also end much more briefly. In each case they criss-cross all manner of divisions, leap from one concern to others, mostly reacting quickly to an intuition, a suggestion or an association. Spontaneity and speed are of their essence, and above all they follow the contours of every individual person. I will, in spite of that, trace here a set of sequential phases. There is coherence and logic to how these phases follow one another, but it must be firmly understood that we do not under any circumstances ever slavishly obey them. They are primarily a device that facilitates the exposition and the explanation of how New Work conversations can be surveyed and structured after the fact. In real-live situations these phases are not kept apart.

Inescapably, after a public lecture I am often asked to give at least some quick but concrete idea of what is involved in helping people in the discovery of what they "really, really" want. It is obvious from how the question is posed that people want a live example, an illuminating short story. It would be absurd and silly to refuse. Before I oblige, I invariably do reiterate that the actual process can be very complex and extremely private but that in the 30 years long history naturally countless memorable stories did occur, and that just as naturally some typical first approaches have evolved that can easily be told without any context or much explanation. One of these is that one can ask a person to run backward through the week they have just lived through. From Friday, back to Thursday, to Wednesday and Tuesday. The recommendation runs further, to do this with great attentiveness and concentration and to make a genuine effort to spot a moment of intense "pleasure." Usually I add a few sentences to make clearer what sort of pleasure we in this case mean. Rather than what might be associated with Schiller and Beethoven, we on the contrary are looking for a very impulsive, physical, instinctive, suddenly erupting "pleasure." However, spotting a pleasure is not enough. Most importantly it must be a surprise! A moment of intense pleasure where one did not expect this at all. Ideally, one should in retrospect be startled, maybe downright amazed, that an intense pleasure was one's reaction under these circumstances and in this moment. As an aside, I usually add: "And please, leave out everything that has to do either with the bed or with the table." That does not help us with the task at hand. We are trying to get some first clue of the kind of work that conceivably might give you a quite surprising sense of excitement. So omit these two realms, and try to focus sharply on just one remarkable experience.

Naturally, there are cases in which this fails. Still, over time there have been many instances when the result was intriguing, suggestive and helpful. To give some idea of how; imagine the case of an extremely shy and reserved, prim secretary who in advance insisted that her "calling" would have to be extraordinarily subdued and quiet, off in a corner, preferably behind boxes, but who to her great surprise discovers that the greatest and most intense pleasure in her last week was the moment in which she indeed wholly lost her temper with a taxi-driver and shouted at him for 3 full minutes in a blast of unleashed exasperation. The fact that close inspection convinced her that this indeed gave her an instantaneous and unexpected rush of genuine pleasure is of course a clue. If one tracks this and several other clues one might discover that the shy secretary in fact has a burning desire to be visible, to stand in the glaring light of full attention, to be perhaps a manager or a performer on a stage.

During the years in which New Work developed I naturally encountered a large number of other similar examples, and it is true that stories of individual people who ended up doing work they really, and in earnest desired often communicate with far greater clarity and force what we hope to accomplish than reams of judicious theoretical discussion. One of my goals would be to publish at some point an entire book filled with nothing but one-page long descriptions of some of the most unusual and strange discoveries in which I had a hand. Usually I tell two other things in this connection: one is the anecdote about the client who has been in therapy for 3 years and who tells his therapist exultantly that on last Wednesday he finally did something that he himself really seriously wanted to do. Also: crucially: a parable – not a story – the very old, 80-year-old servant had served one master since his youth. The flowers. The curtains. The slippers. Then the master died. He continued to perform these services. Meaningless. Pointless. Yet he refused to stop as it was wholly impossible for him to imagine that his master was not there. The meaningless and empty tasks. Someone else comes into his life and finally tells him, with great force, he is no longer here. He died. Has been dead for years. What are you doing? Stop what is pointless; meaningless. What is it that you want to do? Do things for yourself. Not what your master needs, but what you need. Decide all manner of things – ultimately decide your work – the main thing, the big thing is decide what you will do.

I might begin from the very basic idea that work in the past has crippled people and that we are trying to establish a Work System that will instead strengthen and develop people. In most cases I would also allude to the concept of the Job System and to its pathology, but probably as well to the overweening power of the Job-Business-Nexus. Very likely I would in addition sketch our conception of the two cultures, and explain that New Work understands itself as a broad mobilization which attempts to be of help in the transition from the culture that is now decrepit to the new one that has difficulty being born.

Next I might try to convey that though there certainly will be exercises and practices at some later stage, they should settle back and for a start expect that there is a great deal that needs to be understood and learned, and that this in fact has been one of the obstacles with which New Work has had to contend from the beginning: it cannot be compressed into a few slogans. It is intricate, and to understand it at all requires a good deal of patience.

Very near the beginning I also often tell the assembled group quite abruptly that in the 4 years between 1988 and 1992 I pursued an informal, limited, research project of my own. I asked a great variety of different people how they decided upon the profession, or the line of work in which they were engaged when we met. The result was sad, dismaying and in a way disgraceful. For one, the number of those who had made no real choice at all, who were nudged by the tiniest of shoves into the canal down which they floated for the rest of their whole lives, was extraordinarily high (in my little study, in the neighborhood of 70 percent). There was a charming teacher, an unexpected offer, a chance remark that determined the remainder of someone's life. I became convinced that many chose their next meal in a restaurant with more care and attention to the alternatives than they applied to the choice of their life's work.

I was also struck by the extent of the absurdly narrow range of possibilities of which those whom I questioned seemed to be aware. Frequently, there was not much beyond the doctor, the lawyer, the preacher and the fireman. To rectify this particular deficiency or malady became in subsequent years one of the pronounced preoccupations of New Work. One main reason for this had to do with time and change.

In the past, I go on to explain, work was fairly stable. There existed only some fixed number of job possibilities, and many of these were rather similar. That seems now a very long time ago. In our time parts of work are continuously disappearing, like boats that sink. Simultaneously, new previously unknown work opportunities arise. To be cognizant of the totality of these changes is not a part-time task. It requires constant, intently focused attention to be abreast of these developments.

That is how I came to give many talks to career counselors, several times at national conventions. My theme on these occasions was unflattering. I proposed that a new study, a new discipline had emerged. The evolutionary trends in work were every bit as complex and difficult to grasp as those in biology. Therefore, people who had not studied this discipline were not competent to counsel others in the matter of their careers. It was irresponsible! A disgrace! It was like answering the questions of lost tourists without having the least idea of the lay of the roads, only much worse, since not vacations, but life-long work was at stake. In line with this, groups associated with New Work have developed the curricula for courses that would convey this information to future counselors. However, we also wrote similar curricula for schools, and presented these as the basis for full main-subject courses in high schools or colleges. It was a new necessity, one that had not existed in this form before. Students could not inform themselves about the work they should choose on three evenings or in one seminar. The vastness of the relevant material could not be covered in such blips of time. The style of New Work has all along been an emphasis on openness, on transparency, on not hiding unpleasant facts – like the fact that what we have so far experienced of automation is only the overture. There is more than that: conceptions like the idea of the Poverty of Desire, the sense that we are ignorant about our own internal life, have all led us to place a great deal of emphasis on "bringing things out into the open" – into the public space where one can see them.

The rhetorical speech I might make could run like this:

How is it conceivable that anyone could misunderstand New Work so brutally and so completely? The automobile workers in Flint, to take that example, were firmly unionized and General Motors Corporation paid them extraordinarily high wages. New Work would never for one moment propose that a sizable group of chronically unemployed, probably hungry and miserable people should sit down on the floor and spend months teasing out what they most seriously want to do. Do remember the basic approach we take in the Third World? Make your own cement, your own houses, generate your own electricity, grow your own food, up to the making of your own appliances. Of course that does not fit into the Western world, not as it stands now, not at its current level of development, but you cannot simply block it out altogether. The car-workers had 6 months of factory work as a base. Any number of other efforts we initiated had something very similar as a foundation. To ask the question: what do I really, really want with the income of 6 months factory work in place is wholly different from asking it into empty space when I am naked and have nothing.

Before you say: "please, just show us work that we really want and then leave us alone," do at least ask yourself some simple questions. Do you remember the multiple pathology of the Job System? Please, do ask yourself what of that would be repaired, if more people simply insisted on work they really want? Would that get rid of unemployment? Would it lessen the ever-widening split between the rich and the poor? Would it ameliorate the problem of the "compulsory growth," or the problem that we call "The Burning of the Violins?" Patently, in no way. On the contrary, like so many others who pressure people to be more motivated, to try still harder, to give themselves over still more completely to a "soul-sucking" job, it would make the whole ghastly situation even worse! It would mean that some of the best off would now want it still better. In addition to all other privileges, they would still want work they really, really wanted (WRRW)! Or, the other way around, everyone would still be in exactly the same rat-race – only now some would run it in the best air-pillowed sneakers that Nike makes. You cannot butcher New Work down to that one plaintive exclamation! You cannot turn it into a hand-lotion for the millions of galley slaves! Keep rowing, we just want your hands to feel a little better! The prescription to do work that you RR want, compressed into a one-sentence dogma, represents in no sense whatsoever an "alternative." Would it be a way out of the locked train, would it be anything that even remotely could fill the black hole with which the death of socialism has left us?

Cutting still more deeply down to the bone: the enormous power that was unleashed through the Job-Business-Nexus. How in any way does the idea of WRRW by itself set anything against this? How does this create a counterforce that can throw down a challenge to that power and maybe bring it down? If you allow me, I can put it in still nastier terms? How does the advice to find more pleasure in what we are coerced to do, how does that show us a way out of the prison in which we are?

After that sort of shoulder-shaking talk I very often continue in the very calmest, and quietest and detached manner:

We as a culture are in the beginning stages of a surprising and amazing turn. It is the turn toward the next economy. By now most of us have realized that the idea that the post-industrial economy will be an economy of service was a truly ludicrous mistake that soon will be in the wax museum of dead, freakish thought-constructions. Anyone can see with their own eyes that the automation in retail, in banking, in transportation, in travel, in the buying of insurance, in legal services, even in medicine progresses even faster than the elimination of jobs in other sectors. Not to leave out social workers. There is not a single Not-for-Profit organization, right down to the Red Cross, that has not been truncated by a string of increasing budget cuts. Moreover, the very concept of an economy based on the idea that I cut your hair, and you in exchange for that shine my shoes was a Charlie Chaplin pratfall from the start. Or, more precisely, these were sleeping pills thrown down to the poor from the balcony of the rich. The latest version of telling them that they should eat cake. All that is already in the trunk of costumes from 10 years ago. No need to discuss it. Far more important is that we are just around the corner from a new system of production and that of course is what we need. Not service, but production! Growing food and making things, the entire spectrum of equipment that we require for an intelligent, pleasurable and even splendid life – produced in a new, in a post-industrial way! Knowledge of what work will be like in the future has become indispensable, and I will not repeat the false and silly ruminations that one can hear about this on every bus. I will not announce that from here on in everybody will be having seven careers in a row, and I will also not give the advice that the best protection against unemployment is to become computer literate (that is like imagining that "phoneliteracy" will be a great help, that mentioning to a possible employer that one knows how to dial a phone will get one a position). The groundbreaking change in the system of production that is now occurring will have an impact far greater than the invention of the assembly line, or of steam, or electricity, or of the computer. In fact, the great transition into the post-industrial era will not be the shifting into service, but instead the giant step from the outdated to the now arriving system of production; that change will catapult us forward from the industrial into the post-industrial period.

In the years that I spent with one foot in the automobile and then in other industries, I learned the art and science of manufacturing in a peculiarly intimate and intense way. I learned not from books but from hundreds of long conversations with workers who were just making the transition from traditional to computer-controlled machines. The sum-total of these tutorials makes me now very confident that we are only steps from an alteration that is as profound and as utterly surprising as was the change from the agricultural to the industrial mode of production. In fact, in its feel and lifestyle the post-industrial mode of production will be closer to the age of agriculture and the age of crafts than the now passing industrial age has been. To foresee this next phase not just vaguely, but specifically and in detail is all-important for New Work. For one, because to be a midwife to the next new culture is our greatest task, and if we do not see and understand what lies ahead then we cannot assist in its birth. Also for another, equally momentous reason: we were from the very start not a "Protest Movement." We were convinced from the beginning that massive historic forces were pulling in the direction in which we hoped to move. That belief accounts for part of our optimism or as we prefer to say, for our cheerfulness. We must of course understand the dynamic of these giant forces, otherwise we cannot partner with them. On the contrary we might get in their way, and obstruct them, and in the process be trampled by them like a clumsy cowboy by his stampeding cows.

The system of small shop production

Our culture as a whole, and more specifically our economy, is in the early stages of an enormously far-reaching transformation. The magnitude of its implications will exceed that of the introduction of steam, or of electricity, or of the technology of computers. More nearly it will approximate in its impact the metamorphosis from the agricultural to the industrial age. In other words, the difference between this coming form of life and our current culture will be as large and surprising as the progression from the economy based on peasants to the economy based on factories.

The actual picture of what might be next in manufacturing could be very different indeed. Long rows of robots are plainly inefficient. Not long from now we will look back upon this as an awkward adolescent developmental stage. Merely the plain, visual impression should be enough to make one see how wasteful and behind the times this basic arrangement by now has become. A hundred robots on both sides of the line? Each looking like a long-necked bird, or like a black giraffe? Each bending forward as if to pick up a single nut? How could one miss the humor, the comedy, the sheer doltishness in this? From the visual impression alone any intelligent child could surmise that a next very large step is around the corner. Speaking graphically one could say that one robot will have the "intelligence" now possessed by 100, so that one will not have one separate whole robot for each small operation. Instead, there will be robots much more powerfully programmed and far more flexible and diverse than those we have now, so that one robot alone can perform the entire lengthy sequence of tasks that is now executed by an entire "line."

That is exactly the direction in which the evolution of computers occurred. Not toward ever more bulk and cloddish size, but the reverse; toward the miniaturized, the ever more compact, the mobile and the small. It seems entirely plausible that the evolution of factories as a whole will gradually follow the developmental line on which computers are already.

The stereotypical representation of the archetype of a factory might therefore undergo a gradual, but nonetheless wholesale change. Some of this is of course already underway. In the areas of rapid economic development, most of the new, emerging, agile places of production are, as everybody knows, not large but *small*. This evolution might point into the future as it actually will be; not still more gigantic halls, but the opposite. The ideal type of the factory of the future might be a shop, or even a shed or a garage, in which one single machine that is more adaptable, more flexible, controlled by software that is far more advanced and that contains far more information will turn out sets of complete and finished parts.

For many people the image of small, shop-like factory sheds that could be standing by themselves anywhere in the countryside, or also in city neighborhoods, has a powerful symbolic value. The idea of beautifully designed, elegant compact structures – reminiscent of the styles of Fuller or Frank Lloyd Wright – dotting the hillsides, and containing compressed in them enormous productive capacities because they are intelligent, functional and advanced is for them the first suggestion that an alternative to the glass-towers of our present culture can at least be envisioned.

Still, the aura surrounding this is for many still quite futuristic. They probably think that this is 10 or 20 years away, and while they recognize that it is of course intriguing and pleasant to contemplate since it would be so much more human in its size and perhaps even tranquil and bucolic, they are sure that it will remain marginal nonetheless. In many conversations I have been told that charming as this would of course be, it is bound to remain inconsequential simply because it, in the end, cannot hold its own against the great behemoth; the monster of mass manufacturing. There may be strengths and even powers that the dispersed and de-centralized possess, but there is the deluge, the mud-swollen Mississippi of assembly-line production. And it, when all is said and done, is simply cheaper. And cheaper wins! Like it or not, the rest will all be pushed aside.

Ironically enough, there is a quick and powerful retort to this skepticism: Certainly, the cheaper product, or method of production carries the day and on that score we do not disagree. On the contrary, let us write that down in big banner letters, but then let us turn the tables. For the situation is exactly the reverse! Despite much re-iterated and by now deeply imprinted stereotyped notions about the inexpensiveness of mass production, the now coming small shop production with highly advanced technologies will actually be much cheaper and incomparably more efficient than the industrial manufacturing of the last 200 years has been. Indeed, that is precisely one of the main reasons why production in small shops will slowly, in gradual incremental steps, usurp the position that the mega factories occupy right now.

Let me take a lipstick as an example, but bear in mind that we could just as well talk about any of 500 other mass-made trinkets. In fact, in Germany, the case of a cup of yogurt has generated an entire shelf of literature and is now famous. One first issue is simply the difference between the cost of manufacturing a stick of lipstick in the mass system and the price paid for it in a drugstore. The difference is truly huge! The cost of the making of the lipstick may well be on the order of five or six cents, while the price at the point of sale might be 10 or 11 dollars. Relevant here is the fact that the images which persuade everyone of the overwhelming cheapness of mass manufacturing are always images inside the factory, that is, images of the product dropping at a rate of 200 per minute off the "line" into a voluminous container. A first of many rubs is that in the mass-producing system that part is only the opening sentence of a long and protracted story. What is not shown in these pictures are the costs for shipping, and for advertising, and for packaging, and of course a myriad of sometimes hidden costs for the plant, and naturally the costs for the ramified network of distribution, that is, the expenses for the stores in which the lipstick is eventually sold. Missing also are the taxes and the insurance premiums and most significantly the wages, and these not only for the people directly involved, but for the hierarchy above them, and on and on, until we come to bonuses for the upper management and dividends for the investors. The core point is very simple: how many of these additional costs that make the monster difference between the original six cents and the ten dollars in the store could be eliminated – could be saved – in a system of small shop production?

Ever since we were children we of course were told countless times that everyone (with the exception of kings and princes) lived poor and frugal lives until the great onrush of industry made it possible for everyone to own the myriad appliances, and pots and pans, and heaps of other "goods" that define our comfortable modern life. We are now raising a question that is not often asked and we are moving it into a glaring stage-center light: not how ecological, or how wasteful of raw materials or energy is mass production. That question has been asked a great many times, at any rate in recent years. The question we are asking is cruder, and reaches for the throat: what about the expense? The money? The economics of mass manufacturing? How cheap is mass manufacturing when all the cumulative costs have been added? How inexpensive are the products ground out by that system?

Up to now this question could not be even seriously posed because the mass-production system had no competition on its own playing field. Primitive, simple tool production clearly was not in the running, and mass production therefore won without a fight. That is changing. A greatly superior, more intelligent and more advanced system of production has started to develop and for the first time mass production faces a competitor. And, which of the two will win is far from certain.

In some quarters the superiority of small shops was of course realized years ago. Hence we have all become familiar with terms like "outsourcing," with phrases like "flat hierarchies" and with nostrums like companies should do only what they can do well. The very biggest companies like Ford Motor Co and General Motors have by now outsourced so very much into smaller, often independent and more efficient units that management people often ask each other, half in jest: What is there still left? What, finally, does the Ford Motor Co still do? The asking of that question is one of many indications that the giant size is deceptive. The actual work, the manufacturing is more and more accomplished in small, quickly changing places, and the Big Company is not, as one might suppose, the bone-structure that holds these elements in their place. No, even the coordinating is progressively done more and more by the small subunits themselves, and the original company is to a surprising measure only the bell-jar – the brand – under which these pieces lie.

The reaction is a mild surprise. Could this smaller, quieter and much calmer arrangement indeed compete against the system of the mega-towers? If the result will indeed be similar products only manufactured with much less expense, then that question cannot be instantly dismissed. If cheaper, then it is a "lean" and "tough" opponent. If cheaper then it deserves a second look.

The assembling of anything in an airplane-hanger-sized hall is on the face of it far from cheap! Take any number of nearby examples: why have so many of us become used to buying all manner of items unassembled and in boxes? Not only bookshelves, but far more complicated pieces of furniture and a great range of appliances like barbecue rotisseries, bicycles and electronic toys. The answer is straightforward: the assembling of an elaborate entertainment center and the shipping of the complete and fragile unit is another dimension of the old mass-production system that is costly and outdated. It would be expensive even if 1,000 entertainment centers were assembled every week. Therefore, we do it ourselves. Despite all of the frustrations of lying on one's belly on the floor and having no idea where the next part goes, this process pays.

Why? For many reasons. Here is a sampling of a few. Assembling furniture in a factory *en masse* requires a large hall. Halls are expensive. In addition to the rent, there is insurance, lights, janitors and so on. None of this is needed if you assemble the entertainment center in your own home. The space, the lights are already there. Also, and crucially, wages: experience and skill do make a difference. Assemblage, whether of furniture, or cars, or planes takes time. And the time of people who do this professionally for a wage is again expensive, especially if you add not only the insurance and the benefits, but also the cafeteria and the parking lot. Important for this comparison is that we do our own assembling at our own time. In the evening, during the weekend. That again cuts down the cost.

The concept of self-assembling is therefore not unheard of, nor radical, nor outlandish. The truth is that it is so far limited to a restricted number of items that, however, are often not inherently simple. More important seems to be that the assembling of them is a neat and clean process which most crucially requires only relatively few and very common tools. What is now of great importance is to understand the extent to which the two ideas we are discussing fit together and mutually reinforce each other. If one has small, separate standing shops or sheds where each has the capacity to produce between 30 and 50 distinct though similar parts then it seems almost perverse, or at any rate doltish and tradition-bound, to send all these different parts from 100 different locations to one centralized giant assembly plant, where they are then stuck, or glued, or snapped, or welded together into one single piece. If you consider the meandering string of costs entailed by this dubious procedure, and still further the expenses and the clumsiness involved in transporting the hulking finished product and bringing it finally to market then it becomes difficult not to be puzzled or to laugh. Except for the embarrassed shock with which we recognize that this of course is us! That this is our system in the skewed condition which it has now reached.

In short, in manufacturing we have already reached the level on which the making of the parts has been outsourced to China, Indonesia and the Ukraine. That really means that to still send all the parts from every corner of the earth to one huge plant in Alabama or Mississippi merely so that they there can be assembled is anachronistic. One foot is in step, while the other still drags behind.

Relatively few and straightforward steps – none that require dazzling breakthroughs – would put us within reach of a far more intelligent, incomparably more efficient manufacturing system, one that would eliminate both monster factories and colossal assembly plants. One step we already know: we would have to advance from the medium-sized enterprises to which much of manufacturing has already been outsourced, to the smaller and much more elegant manufacturing shops I have just described. Secondly, and this is not easy but challenging: we would have to redesign each product so that assembling it would indeed be a neat and clean process that could be accomplished with very few and common tools. Naturally, this will necessitate a considerable re-thinking of the product, and importantly drastic and major streamlining and simplifications of it. That naturally means that the clutter of luxuries will diminish, and to many this would not constitute a sacrifice but on the contrary a relief and an improvement. Many of the absurdities that are presently designed into our products, that are often not in the least functional, are attached to the items we buy in order to sell them, so that something fetching or sexy can be mentioned in the advertising campaign. Much of that would drop away as soon as we would manufacture directly for our own use, and not *en masse* for the market.

In the third place, we would have to develop the software and the infrastructure that would enable the customer to order the complete set of parts for the products he desires – hopefully, with one single click– from the 30-odd small manufacturing sheds that make these needed parts – and not in Thailand or Singapore, but in the region in which he lives (that is one of the great advantages of small manufacturing shops: they do not require the high-powered infrastructure needed by the mass-factories we have now and, therefore, can be located almost anywhere).

The step toward ordering things we buy with our own laptop over the internet is no longer a new futuristic venture. Far from it! In truth, the groups with which I work are usually already so at home with it, that any belaboring discussion would make them restless and bored. They know it from amazon.com, from Dell computers, and among my acquaintances it is already customary even if one buys a car.

In the great majority of contexts most of the participants at this juncture begin to have some impression of the gestalt, of the general layout and design of this post-industrial production system. It is fortunately straightforward and can be pictured without strain: basically, there will be networks of small and local manufacturing sheds. People will rearrange, and redesign and adjust and customize the product, till it is something they really, really want. Then they will send their order via computer to this network of small shops, who in turn will mail the parts to the neighborhood assembly shop, where one will have access to the required simple tools, but where there will also be mentors who can be of help in assembling whatever one has bought.

Most usually I interject a kind of pause, at any rate a slower, different tempo, around this point to explain that this is only one dimension, one aspect of the system, that a very large and in some ways quite different dimension is still to come.

I also emphasize that the parts so far outlined have been presented in a too-dramatized, too abrupt, too startling fashion, and that these aspects can also be seen in a quieter and calmer way. To be specific: the image of substituting one far more intelligent and flexible robot for a whole row of 100 clumsy robots of the current generation certainly helped to communicate in one stroke the general direction in which we mean to go, but it was of course a picture and one can also make this point in a very different language. The actual development will not be in one jump, and it emphatically will not only deal with robots. More nearly there exists a continuous pressure in this direction in the whole manufacturing community. It has been there for a long time, and it will continue, maybe at increasing speed.

We thus are not discussing the overnight arrival of something that children will watch with their noses pressed against the windows. Not at all. Small manufacturing shops will result from a trend that is not in the least arcane, but from a permanent, ongoing tendency that is utterly ordinary and everyday, that is so banal that one could call it the bread and potatoes of the manufacturing diet. What I mean is simply that engineers who design manufacturing machines have always striven for machines with more joints, so that they can drill, or lathe, or press, or cut in a greater number of directions, and can do this with greater speed and more precision. Among the automobile manufacturing engineers and the car-workers with whom I had daily contact the basic impulse in that direction was a given. It was not debated or discussed. It was self-evident, a reflex, not a thought.

It is, therefore, a fact that the more inventive and imaginative engineers will readily agree that factories as we know them now are absurdly inefficient; and they do not mean in small-scale matters. They are not talking on the level of just-in-time-delivery, or total quality, or lean, or seven other kinds of management. No, they are referring to the more archetypal foundational fact of having a several-miles long line; and along that line hundreds of individual robots that basically all perform one insignificant, limited, Taylorian task. To many of them that seems cloddish and clearly out-of-date. The idea of small manufacturing shops is, therefore, in no sense merely a New Work Proposal. What I have described simply makes somewhat more vivid what many who are working in this field envision as well.

This is not restricted just to engineers. One can equally point to a sweeping trend among entire mainstream industries. Many of them have recently turned a corner, because they have discovered how significant the advantages of smallness can often be. The phenomenon of outsourcing was already mentioned. Companies naturally outsource for many different reasons, but one main reason is the disadvantage, the handicap of their hulking size. In the last 20 years a growing literature has endlessly pointed out that companies need to focus, that they need to concentrate. Few slogans have been quoted as tirelessly as the mantra that companies should only do what they are able to do well; which means that they should get rid of everything in which their competence is thin.

In my 20 years of working on the edges of the auto-industry I saw how that idea was branded into many people's flesh. Endlessly, anecdotes were circulated about managers of any of the Big Three (Ford, GM and Chrysler) whose ideas and energies to somehow produce a change were defeated and smothered by sheer size. In contrast to that, anyone who visits a really agile and quick small company is bound to get an immediate first-hand impression of an enthusiasm, of an immediacy of communication, of – most importantly – a level of high-spirited motivation that no large company anywhere can match.

Separate from this general broad trend, though of course related to it, is a deep division that is of special importance to New Work. It is odd, but nonetheless the case, that in many seminars and conferences, one perception hovers palpably in the air: the conclusion that giant companies were more comfortable and at home in the past age. The culture of most of the colossal companies, with their elaborate hierarchies, their stiff formalities, their awkward modes of communication and, as a result, their slow reaction times, demonstrably no longer fits the now prevailing tempo, but more than that, really the whole of the now existing business culture. They seem uncomfortable, old and out of breath.

Any effort to comprehend the contemporary world of work must put this profound split into whatever map it hopes to draw. The industrial complex is not one coherent and unified single block. Far from it! The differences between the old industries (auto, oil and steel) and the new industries (computers, software, biotechnology and chips) divide two starkly opposed worlds. This can be seen at a glance. The new industries, which are also the ones that evolve in small plants and small organizations, often call their sites "campuses." In that one word a great deal is summed up. The ratio of PhDs among their employees is much higher than in oil or steel. Their connection to the academic world is vastly closer, so close indeed that one could now speak of an academic-industrial-complex. As a consequence their entire culture, right down to the modes of speech and dress and casual behavior is naturally very unlike that prevalent in the old and "heavy" industries. The new ones are distinctly "light," and therefore quick and agile and adroit. Which means that the struggle between these worlds is one more version of the David and Goliath story.

Beyond the sheer depth and width of this division, there is an aspect which makes it particularly painful for the "old" and especially hopeful for the "new" industries. In brief, the powerful just now developing technologies are clearly on the side of the "new" and small-scaled companies, and just as clearly unfavorable to the "old" and large. What are the three most contemporary pieces of technology? The majority of people would agree that they are the internet, the cell-phone and the laptop. A moment's thought makes it evident that all three of these encourage the dispersed and the decentralized. Think of the young entrepreneur who sits high in the mountains in the back of his pickup truck and phones while he is writing his email from there.

This bears on the cardinal issue of power. Nothing is more common than the view that the struggle against the giant companies is doomed and hopeless from the start. Both the division I have just described, and also the just mentioned fact about the new technologies undermine that old-fashioned conviction.

We might indeed be close to a drastic turn toward the small and the decentralized. Crucial for the achievement of this turn will be that some of the most modern and potent industries are small already, and that the newest technologies favor the small and the decentralized in this struggle (IBM and Microsoft are exceptions in the picture as a whole). So, if this turn will be attained then partly it is because the arrival of new technologies helped to tip the balance. The old Babylonian organizations cannot put the new technologies to their best use. Indeed the new technologies run against their grain, and disarrange and weaken them. In contrast to that, these new technologies are the natural food for the small and agile companies. They invigorate and strengthen them. It is, therefore, these technologies that could be our allies in the making of this great historic change. Which means that the methods and specific tactics that might help us to achieve this end may be wholly different from the methods and tactics of the politics of the now passing age.

If the struggle in which we are now engaged were indeed a struggle of the poor against the rich, or even of the mass of humanity against a unified and single corporate complex, it very probably would be hopeless and in vain. I have no faith at all in the shopworn political organizing processes of the past. If our hopes depended on them, I would have wandered off into a desert and become a hermit long ago. The odds against the poor, against the mass of humanity, would be too overwhelming. If there are bright spots on the horizon, then it is because of the split I just mentioned, and the trend of the decentralizing technologies.

To put it into farcical language: it was one of Marx's most fatal mistakes that he said loudly at the very start that all the rich would be expropriated. That was the very worst "PR." It united the propertied so firmly that no force on earth could ever have prevailed against them. Fortunately, the strategy can be smarter now. If there exists a split between the old and the new industries, then the last thing we should do is close it! Anything but. We should put it to the most strategic use, and pull the "new" industries cautiously over to our side. With that alliance, the pendulum of power will swing in the direction of the culture that is struggling to be born.

This last point could be put much more provocatively, by using language that I most of the time deliberately avoid. One could say that capitalism has itself produced the technologies that now have the power to render it obsolete. Towering hierarchies were integral to the power of the capitalist system. Information technology makes these hierarchies unnecessary and puts more efficient and faster horizontal structures into their place. Again, the new technologies created an army of very different workers, workers that are in their mentality so close to that of artists or intellectuals that issuing commands and insisting on obedience no longer works. Companies with a large proportion of PhDs require an organizational and personal culture wholly different from the one which capitalism fostered. This explains why such a large number of the most talented, and frequently most successful younger people rebel against the old, encrusted structures, which in turn means that the old and mighty companies much of the time cannot attract the smartest and quickest people. The entire scene is reminiscent of the late Middle Ages when knights were raised with winches onto the backs of their horses, in armor that made it hard for them to move, and fearless peasant youngsters managed to make them crash down to the ground, where they would suffocate in their own helmets.

There is more: not only these specific technologies weaken and erode capitalism. The entire battery of conjoined technologies that made automation possible in effect decimated the army of workers who *en masse* obeyed the orders of their manager-generals. The very automation that capitalism created killed off these armies, just like the Russian winter froze to death the soldiers of Napoleon and those of the German army before Stalingrad.

One could put it into these terms, but "capitalism" is no longer the appropriate word. We have allowed ourselves to descend into a condition that is more nearly a "Robber-Pimpdom" in which vulgar and brutish toughs call the shots. This Pimpdom is above all self-destructive! Occasionally a wild sow bears young that will tear into the mother and eat her alive. This is what some of the new technologies do. And this is one great reason for hope: the Great Turn toward the new culture may indeed happen, and not least because so much of the old culture is on our side.

Predictably, numerous people have told me that chronically unemployed, or otherwise down and out people would never listen to the description of these trends. "This is not concrete enough; it does not address the interests they have. It is too difficult, too academic, too remote!" That turns into another juncture where the volume of my voice is apt to rise and a little drama is played out. After pacing the length of the room once or twice, I might propose that we better have a "crystal talk" right here and now, and the opening of that might be that I say:

You could not be more wrong, or more mistaken! Do you not realize what these people are forced to listen to hundreds of times, at meetings which they are commanded to attend? Go to one of those official meetings and listen and look around. Even those who are on nothing, act at these meetings as if they had been drugged. Endlessly they must suffer through the same drivel of old lies. "If you only try hard you will find a job. All you need is to be motivated and to have persistence."

Merely the fact that what I am saying is different is already an enormous relief. Quite a few are always startled into paying attention just on that account alone! Yet you also misjudge their intelligence. They have heard the slogans. I always start with a 2-minute summary of the quintessence of the totality of New

Work. I know that this is risky. It does not matter whether I am in Detroit, Calcutta, Chemnitz, Kiev or Johannesburg. Everywhere the suspicion of ideas could not be more intense. People have been abused and lied to so many times that anyone with an idea makes them instantly skittish. The last thing they want is hot air out of a hot head! Not to be used as cannon fodder yet one more time, is one of their instant reflex reactions. And that reaction is of course wholly and utterly justified – given what they have been through.

Still, they must know where I am going, and where I am asking them to come, otherwise they put on their coats in the first 3 minutes. So I do the slogan part out of necessity, but I do it just as quickly as I possibly can. After that, make no mistake, it is the other way round: you harangue and you preach, you give them big words and a few tricks, and their eyes will shut and their heads sink down on their chests. NO and No and No; they want details, they want to understand, they want clarity, proof and facts.

It may require many repetitions and much patience but it is wholly crucial that one understands that there is a massive confluence of trends that flow in the very direction in which we (NW) are struggling to go. If you cannot convince them of that, you are wasting your breath. They'll think of you as just one more street-corner preacher. Maybe they will smile, maybe they will drop a few pennies into your hat, but they will walk away and not take you seriously for one moment.

This relates back to the basic puzzle: how does one "arouse" the poor, how does one pull them out of the crater-hole of the Poverty of their Desire? What is the ladder on which they will climb out of their apathy, their disillusionment and their despair? Understanding these trends is one small but significant hand-hold for this upwards climb. They must, however slowly, come to the conviction that they are part of something powerful, and impressive; part of a determined effort to make a vastly superior world, that is not just a whistling in the dark, but that lo and behold, surprisingly, could indeed succeed!

There is one further mountainous fact: from the first beginning we made it difficult for people to put us neatly either into the box of the left or that of the right. Clearly, we have all along been on the side of the low and the poor. Far more so than many who think of themselves as left, for we did not want to only calm the poor with small gifts or with band-aids – especially, not across their mouths. We have been trying to rouse them to become self-reliant; not to plead, not to remonstrate, but instead to struggle upwards, and by no means only to the level of subsistence, but much higher; to raise themselves up to an exuberant and a cheerful life! We have cajoled and hectored and again and again put the tools and the technology at their disposal so they could rise and become vigorous, strong, creative, independent and yes, yes even competitive. Obviously, those are the very words, the very values, the very incantations that have been monopolized by the "conservatives" and the "right."

So we are 50:50. On the one hand fiercely for the down and out, but on the other hand we put into actual practice what those on the right merely preach for a small, select elite. We try to put their rhetoric into practice for the great mass of the poor.

So, how can the conservatives oppose us? We take the words right out of their mouths – we only address a different audience, one which they could never reach. This split, this division – half left and half right – is not only a tactic, or a trick. If it disorients and confuses those who oppose us, all the better. Wonderful as a by-product. Yet that is not our goal. Both halves together, is quite simply what we "really, really" believe. We believe that those who are now down and out should become the kind of human beings that Whitman, and Blake, and Thoreau and Emerson dreamed about. They should not be only fed and clothed and housed, though that too, but they should have the chance to become splendid, effervescent fully human individuals! Yes, nothing less will do!

In practice this has of course meant that the unions were always in two minds about New Work: some members were sure we were from the devil, and others were just as sure that for the unions we were the last still remaining hope. Similar, of course, with management. Except that this was decisive for our own development and for the issue of power. Always and everywhere, in every context and in every country some of the most inventive, successful, forward-looking businessmen and executives were on our side. They believed in what we were doing. They too wanted the sort of world that we were struggling to achieve. They found far more creativeness, and inventiveness and optimism in the Network of New Work than in their own mega-corporations with their Babylonian Bureaucracies.

New Work thus was always a mix, a far-flung network that cohered even though it encompassed people from all backgrounds and all walks of life. That must be part of the picture if one is to understand New Work at all. The extent to which we have been welcomed, and sometimes have managed to succeed, always reflected the fact that we were not only working class, that we spoke not only for the seriously poor, or the unemployed, or the low. People always knew that we also walked in and out of the doors of Fortune 500 companies. They knew that the proposals we advanced, the ideas we advocated also evoked genuine empathy in some factions of the management hierarchy.

This was true from the start in Flint right through to the much more recent and difficult work with the Hypobank. It is true of our most basic proposal that people should do WRRW, and it is also true of our current attempt to connect the poor in the Third World with advanced technologies of self-providing.

The cohort of successful, imaginative, advanced businesspersons on our side, who agreed with our ideas and encouraged us and opened doors while also giving money – and here and there even practiced what we had proposed – naturally shaped the history, and the development of New Work in countless ways. That fact also has to be connected with the image of the locked train. The numerous groups who are appalled and disgusted by the direction in which we are moving but who feel themselves locked into a downward rushing train include also this far-flung array of different, but often most talented and most imaginative executives. Some have left the companies in which they had dominant positions, or even the companies which they evolved and then led, and have become New Work Associates. The confluence, or the partnership, or coalition which we have started to fashion, which is working toward the achievement of the Great Turn, very much includes and counts on them. They contribute greatly to our optimism, and our confidence, to the quality that to us is so precious: to our "cheerfulness."

In my efforts to communicate, and to teach New Work this partnership with a most talented and advanced wing of the business world plays a leading role. Otherwise, outdated, romantic images of what we are doing sneak into our thinking; we toy with fantasies of conspiratorial meetings in musty basements, or of training camps high up in the mountains. The crucial, pivotal point that those who are forming an association with New Work must understand is that we do not need this! We are far, far stronger and far more advanced than these adolescent self-pleasuring daydreams assume. The foundational idea, that technology can be developed in an intelligent and sane direction (not deeper down into the self-destructive idiocy in which we have been trapped) and that this means the development of technologies and of products that foster self-reliance and self-production, makes excellent business-sense to many business people! It also makes the same immediately convincing sense to droves of government officials in the Third World, and gradually, but of course much more slowly even to some politicians in the West.

To fully assimilate that recognition right down into the flesh of one's instinctive and reflexive thinking is a must. It is a rite of passage. One must traverse it in order to grow up, to not remain politically a thumb-sucking toddler who mules about "changing the world" without seeing the levers, switches and dials that can accomplish this end. Even though there is this complex and multifaceted dynamic exerting great forces in the direction in which we are trying to move, we of course do not believe that the Great Turn will occur automatically, by itself, of sheer "scientific necessity." Far from it. All manner of efforts from every one of the host of different groups that want it to happen will be required. New Work thinks of itself as merely one of these very many different groups, and accordingly we have selected a number of sharply circumscribed tasks that we are currently addressing in the hope that these will be the contribution we are able to make.

Among these are an array of efforts, some of which exist in the United States, while others are located in Guatemala, Belize and Brazil. These do not harness technical prowess to manufacture in a small space, instead they make use of the technology of the internet to realize the ancient dream of eliminating the middle-man, and to establish the most direct possible relationship between the solitary craftsman and her or his customer who may live on a different continent. In the development of some of these New Work played a role, others were initiated by one or another of the quickly multiplying NGOs. All of these are representative of developments that are now in the air, so that examples of them sprout out of the ground in a host of climates and regions. Slowly, connections are being made, a mutually supporting web of similar efforts is gaining strength, and distantly the outlines of larger possibilities are beginning to take shape.

Well known, for instance, are groups of small, village-based projects, which often invite or address individual women who weave rugs, or make pots, or baskets, or carve and solder and assemble jewelry. In the past these women were exploited and abused, and the intention of the projects is to enable them to sell the products of their craft or art directly, say in New York, Paris or Berlin. Again, what is of cardinal importance from our view is that the technology of the internet provides the space for an "end-run" around the territory and the power of the big corporations.

The somewhat larger picture is, therefore, that two very different developments converge as it were from opposite sides. On the one hand it is factories that are becoming smaller, on the other hand the shops of individual craftsmen or women become small independent stand-alone business enterprises. Nonetheless one oddity in regard to the whole endeavor of HTSP that has dogged us from the very beginning, still even to this day persists. This paradoxical quality is that even people who have been associated with New Work for a very long time still thoroughly misunderstand the entire thrust of main-truss practice and idea. Half-humorously I associate the birth of this by now long-lived project with the years I spent living self-reliantly in the woods of New Hampshire and specifically with my not having a chain-saw, but only a bow-saw instead. The original impulse was to assemble, or also create and develop technologies that would enable one to live a free and self-reliant life but without the sweat-producing and spirit-destroying hard labor for which the bow-saw has become the symbolic representation. In other words: technologies were the whole point! We did pursue this through a meandering long row of projects (some of which I described earlier in the section on "WRRW and the Seriously Poor"), and admittedly the progress was like walking through very deep snow. In our own eyes the much-publicized project in Vancouver, BC in which street youths ended up growing food on the roofs of high-rise buildings was a step toward becoming more HTSP. Both the technology used and the degree of self-reliance achieved were many miles from the goals we envisioned. The same was true of the projects in New York City, or also the one in Ann Arbor, MI, in which homeless people participated in the building of their own homes. Partly, no doubt because of this very slow start the one dominant misunderstanding persisted. Like with much else, we have our own somewhat tongue-in-cheek name: we call it the "Jam and Tomato Syndrome." It means what it says: relentlessly some people insist on thinking that we mean something like making one's own jam, and raising one's own tomatoes by HTSP, which is of course grotesque. For if this has any relationship at all to what we are trying to achieve, then it is what we want to leave, what we want to put at a distance from us.

Perversely and even to the point of exasperation, the Jam and Tomato Syndrome has persisted in spite of our determined efforts to assemble far more advanced technologies and to of course come much closer to a semblance of economical, material independence. Also, of course, very much the other way round: quite without any connection whatever with New Work all manner of technologies have in the meantime developed which have given us enormous and unexpected support. As we are beginning to see, nothing less than the internet and even the computer itself could be included in these technologies that now aid and abet self-providing. The broad evolution toward the whole new system of manufacturing in which the factories will be small and the assembling will be done in a neighborhood center, that could even be a Center for New Work, is of course one more such large and groundswell development. Ineradicable the Jam and Tomato Syndrome persists! Even long-term Associates of New Work in a remote corner of their otherwise brilliant minds, preserve the fantasy that we want people to inflate their own bicycle tires because that is HTSP while using the hose at a gas-station would be a capitulation to the corporate world.

This comical misapprehension has persisted for years, and some remnants of it are still afloat even now. However, there was a point in the history of New Work – roughly in 1996 –

where we engaged in one of the most ambitious projects that ever came our way, and one, though by no means the only, reason for our accepting the invitation to join it was the Jam and Tomato Syndrome. We were approached to participate in the designing and developing of an entirely new and very different car. Frankly, we pounced on it because we believed that if we could, even in an extended sense, show that one could build and assemble one's own highly elegant looking car – then gradually our friends would begin to understand that we meant the making of one's own electricity and the building of one's own house, but eventually also beyond this the making of one's own radio, or TV, or micro-wave oven, or even cell-phone, or laptop by the HTSP that we were struggling to achieve.

One other reason for the purpose of the New Work Car Project should be mentioned before I give a sketch of how it evolved. One taps right into the core of the New Work philosophy. We were determined not to remain an "enclave," not to address only a small and fastidious group but to make an attempt to reach what David Thoreau called: The mass of humanity. Obviously, there were many connections to Flint. One of them was that we had learned in our long apprenticeship that nothing would make quite the same impression on the consciousness of Americans as a car! (Admittedly, this is more true of men than of women.) Still, if we wanted to reach beyond the usual coterie of opposition groups, the demonstration that one could produce a serious looking car with this new Small Shop Manufacturing system would convince people, like nothing else could!

The New Work Car Project

Without a clutch of personal connections, some of which had their roots back in Flint, this project would never have been conceived. The fact is that some of the top management people in the car industry had all along been intrigued and favorably disposed toward New Work, and conversations took place uninterruptedly from the early eighties on, and some leading executives had become personal friends. In 1994 I was approached by three business people – all three luminaries, legends in the car industry – they proposed I should write a concept paper for a dramatically different car – the more different the better – a car that fitted in with the intellectual world of New Work. I do recall the opening sentence of the three pages I wrote: "The very first reaction upon seeing this car for the first time should be: 'Ah, at last. An intelligent car!'" At the risk of sounding presumptuous, I will emphasize that the three who approached me were indeed "luminaries," the names of each instantly recognized by anyone familiar with the American car industry (somewhat like the name of Juergen Schremp in Germany).

The three who constituted the core were Dwight Carlson, who for many was the very embodiment of the successful entrepreneur, and who at the time was president of Michigan Futures, the organization to which the most forward-looking and ambitious business leaders from Michigan thronged. The second was his close friend, Dr Thomas Weber. What Carlson was as an entrepreneur, Weber was as an engineer. At different times he had worked for each of the "Big Three," and also, as he never tired of reminding us, for Porsche. He was a specialist in baffling manufacturing problems. When something in any plant resisted fixing, then Dr Weber would be called. Incidentally, he was the very first person to ever receive a PhD. in Manufacturing from the University of Michigan. The third was Heinz Prechter. If Carlson was the entrepreneur and Weber the engineer, then Prechter represented capital. He was in every detail the true American success story. From the German exchange student who he was at his arrival, he had risen to become one of the wealthiest men in the American automobile industry. He was president and CEO of AC, one of the largest supplier corporations.

One should recall that one large component of the Small Shop Manufacturing System is technologically unproblematic. It could be easily and quickly realized, for it is primarily a matter of *starting* from a different organizational design. Conceptually, it is the simple, straight-line extension of what we know already from the case of the large factory, and also from the example of the lipstick. Central to both of these analyses was the concept of a very large gap between the very low, very modest manufacturing cost and the enormously higher cost one pays in the store. With lipsticks this gap extended from a few pennies up to between five and ten dollars; the point was made that the images of the goods as they tumble from the assembly line always signify an unbeatable cheapness, which, however, is an illusion, because it leaves out the long line of super-added costs (rent and electricity, advertising and transportation, and as a summary of all the rest: bureaucracy, administration, levels and higher levels of management.)

The Small Shop Manufacturing System had naturally been discussed for many months, and in these long discussions, the elements just reiterated played a key role, but it is cardinally important how the three as leading edge executives and entrepreneurs saw this matter, and how their perception differed from the one of New Work. They saw these matters not primarily through the lenses of cost and waste – the inefficiency of long lines of robots, the emphasis on leaner cheaper, more ecological, less transport requiring, direct, and self-assembly. Their crucial term, unsurprisingly, was the economists and key manufacturers' term: namely the phrase "adding value." One much-cited jibe at the US Army is its notorious ratio of front-line soldiers to support personnel. Supposedly the ratio is one to ten. Nine people give support, so that one soldier can move into "harm's way." That became a mantra in the group that worked on the new car, though it was applied to economics, and the art of making things. Led in this regard by Dr Weber, the guiding concept became that in traditional manufacturing only one out of ten workers actually adds value. The other nine, just as in the US Army, sit behind desks in the hinterland. They are responsible for paper and administration and management, but they do not actually "make things." So, for the core of this group a leading question became: how could one eliminate the high heap of additional costs? Through what alterations in the structure of manufacturing could one peel away the nine-tenths that (in the eyes of this group) were essentially camp-followers; groupies that sponged on the splendor of manufacturing (again, that is how this group saw it), but did not really contribute to the creation of value? How could one bring manufacturing back to its essence, to the grit which it originally possessed and clean away the muck and dross that was weighing it down? That was the question they posed.

To them, in their different terms, this question also raised a possibility with great power and daring, and the élan and excitement in this group was as high as can be imagined. All of the people involved had been associated with New Work in different ways over periods of time, and they, therefore, immediately understood the connections; they recognized that this was a far more dramatic, more flamboyant version of minimal cost manufacturing than anything now on the horizon. (We also started to use terms like 'digital manufacturing' and 'decentralized manufacturing.') They also grasped from the first moment that this moved manufacturing as a whole far closer to the idea of becoming HTSP, which we had been discussing for months, if not years.

There was one additional dimension: everyone was fully aware that proceeding in this direction meant not only a plummeting of the cost of the finished car (or washer, or television set), it meant also that the hours of labor needed would fall down right through the floor. For our purposes it is decisive to realize that the "experts," who in this case were legendary in their specialty (in Detroit parlance they were real "car-guys") saw no technological difficulty in the way of this new manufacturing system. The obstacle was something entirely different; their cover word for it was "culture." What they really meant was that the Small Shop Manufacturing System would be resisted intransigently because the loss of jobs entailed by it would be too great! Of course they were correct: in our current culture, that is, in the culture based on the foundation of the Job System, the resistance would be intense – though, judging by past experience, ways would be found around the resistance, and eventually the jobs would disappear. Nonetheless this was their perception of the partnership, of our intriguing alliance that they proposed. They saw themselves as each making a one-third contribution, but they acknowledged that a fourth contribution was needed, and they made it quite clear that they expected that contribution from me. This contribution was no less than the entire intellectual framework, but also the track record, the history of New Work. My task, differently put, was to tirelessly and in a host of situations explain that this new manufacturing mode would not inescapably lead to high unemployment, but instead was one important step in the transition upwards from a culture based on jobs toward a culture based on New Work.

No one imagined that this task would be easy. On the contrary, in various ways we agreed that the United States was not ready for the idea of a new and different culture. It was too soon. We were now in the second half of the nineties, and the dot-com bubble was still large and glittered enticingly in the sky. Talk about alternatives, or anything like a Big Turn would have to wait, particularly for those who lived lives high up and secure. That, indeed, led directly into the second guiding thought: one was the thought of a manufacturing system stripped down to the essentials, the other was the thought of a new market, of customers quite unlike those in the Western world. In short, we started to think of this new car with one eye on the Third World.

This meant that we were now asking two questions, which in our minds superimposed themselves upon each other, and thus merged into one: how could one manufacture a car in a no frills, no waste, no fluff system? Also, might this be a car appropriate for the "other four billions?" The "other four billions" in fact was a phrase which Dr Weber used in the title of many papers he wrote. The combining of these two into one double question greatly reinforced our determination to get rid of waste. In addition to being incomparably cleaner, and also lighter, a car for the market of the Third World would necessarily have to be less expensive by several orders of magnitude. In our minds this meant that merely pinching pennies would never be enough; that would only result in a shoddy product but not make a large enough difference. Thus that line of thought also brought us back to our evolving conception of a new approach to manufacturing.

One additional element congealed into a firmer shape, as we focused more sharply on the conditions in much of the Third World. We had been thinking in terms of small, shop-like manufacturing sites. We now added explicitly that these should be *dispersed*, that there should be a network of 30 or 40 smallish plants and each of these would produce one set of components for the car, and only all of them together would manufacture the totality of the needed parts.

The first advantage we noted in this idea was the much smaller infrastructure that would be needed. A factory in the old sense requires high amounts of electricity. Dispersed, each small manufacturing site might generate the electricity it needs, with one of the relatively inexpensive micro hydro, or bio-gas, or wind, or solar plants that recently came on the market. This means that these factories could be in a host of different places, and conceivably could even be mobile. We also thought that such a network would be more flexible and adaptable to sudden changes, and that this would be an advantage in areas with weak and unstable central governments.

Weightier even, especially with my colleagues, was the concern with bureaucracy. The introduction of computers made some levels of management already obsolete through the course of the nineties. What buzzwords described as the "reduction of hierarchies" and the striving toward "flatter organizations" would have been unthinkable without computers. (The principal task of middle-management in the car industry is to collect, organize and consolidate information and then to pass it on to the center, in this case to Detroit. Computers send the information directly from the local level up to headquarters.)

The combination of computer technology with small dispersed plants would rid us of bureaucracy. If the plants are electronically connected in a sophisticated way then very large parts of the hierarchical structure can indeed be dispensed with. That relates back to the general advantages which small plants possess. They need less bureaucracy simply because of their size. So, if one pursued the path that we now call outsourcing very much further, and if groups, or networks of small plants, ended up manufacturing cars, then their autos could easily be a great deal less expensive than those turned out by GM or Daimler-Benz. The sharp curtailing of the entire complex involved in the advertising, selling and distribution of automobiles seemed to us like a second hefty saving that one could perform. Dell computers is a model from which much can be learned. The selling of cars via computers, despite initial difficulties, is in any case gaining ground, which means that the entire expensive apparatus of dealerships with their showrooms and employees will grow leaner. Similarly with advertising: using the internet could save much money that is still spent on TV commercials. Here we come once more to a structurally isomorphic point: naturally, much can be saved *within* the current system. Still, that misses the point. We wanted to show that the system itself was inherently monstrously wasteful, and that with two or three small steps *outside* the system savings of a wholly different magnitude would drop into one's lap.

Needless to say, designing a car in such a way that assembling it would indeed be manageable, that it could be done in one's own garage and with inexpensive, simple tools would be a daunting challenge. Even so it seemed as if Dr Weber had been waiting for this kind of challenge most of his life. He bounced with pleasure at the thought of trying his hand at it. If this could be accomplished, then the entire landscape would indeed change with a single stroke. No more bureaucracy, no more dealerships and advertising, and also the end of the large assembly plants. All of that would disappear, and with all that wiped away, the final cost might really be a third, or a fourth, or even less, a fifth of what it was before.

This last feature, that it would be a car which, in addition to its other qualities, could be self-assembled, added in our minds greatly to its appropriateness for the Third World. In truth, this was an element with which we had a long row of previous experiences. As early as 1986 (roughly 12 years before the work on the car), while we were developing projects for homeless people in the city of New York, the cardinal double-fact that they had no money, but that they on the other hand had a plenitude of time, had "time to *kill*," played a crucial role: the group working on these projects decided that this excess of time should be used, that it should be traded in for money. Not by selling time in the framework of a job as that was not an option for the homeless of New York, but by assisting with work on the places in which they would live, by reducing the cost of their housing with their own "sweat equity."

The same thought made sense for the Third World. There, too, lived many millions of people who were drowning in a quicksand of unused time. Would engaging them in the assembling of their own cars not have a multitude of benefits? Importantly, it would bring down the price, but in addition, it would motivate and teach, and perhaps help with the one most disheartening task, the task of helping them to climb step by step up the ladder out of their paralysis, their stupor, the sandhole of their passivity, the Poverty of their Desires. Imagine a group of youths in a neighborhood in Sao Paulo, or in Accra, or Bombay assembling their own car! Significantly, their own *new* and elegant and zippy, but also very sturdy jeep-like car!

This harks back all the way to the image of the train and of there not being an alternative. There are hosts of ideas afloat in our culture. They are all like remonstrating fingers, they wag their warnings, and their good advice, and their hind-sight corrections in front of our eyes, till our lids droop. They are NOT "alternatives!"

Socialism was an alternative. That, I believe, everybody would concede. Liberalism, or ecology, not to speak of smaller groups like New Age, or Voluntary Simplicity, or Tibetan Buddhism for Americans – none of these are alternatives! They may be wonderful in ways, and deserve support. Certainly, they can have the support, the partnership, even the solidarity of New Work. Nonetheless, they are not alternatives. They are ameliorations! Gentrifications! Ways to manicure the claws of our present system, ways to cushion, to retard, to soften, to put fig-leaves into the appropriate places. To say it one more time: the crucible of our current situation is the job-arrangement that in alliance with the corporate complex keeps the locked train on its downhill tracks. An alternative must be completely different *to that!* It must be a replacement, an improvement, a superseding, an arrangement that transcends and surpasses and leaves behind in the dust of the dying past the system we now have!

HTSP in the Third World

As the work on the new car progressed and decisions needed to be made to solve a series of problems, we gradually realized that somewhat unbeknownst to us and under our hands, the shape of this project had changed. Originally we had thought loosely about any number of possible markets, but the lines converged, the focus narrowed and eventually it became firmly established and explicit among ourselves that our goal really was a car for the Third World. One point on which I personally insisted – sometimes, I am sure, to the hair-tearing exasperation of my good friends – was that the automobile could not simply be "cheap." This was one lesson that I had learned in my years with the "seriously poor." They would not bow to the ground and with many thank yous accept tawdry trash! That had been one of the worst mistakes of the countless failed efforts at "Aid" or "Development" so far. The basic manufacturing concept had to be the exact opposite of that of the West: not expensive, highly automated machines and as a result ever fewer hours of work, but the other way round. A superbly designed product, attractive and manufactured with superbly designed intelligent equipment, but one that would take maximum advantage of the one resource all of these countries have to abundance: people famished for work.

The Small Shop Manufacturing that seemed in the future went half the way. Certainly, manufacturing in small shops, shops possibly owned by the local co-ops of villages, yet equipped with tools and machines that on the one side would cost much less, and on the other side demand many hours of work. Simply, so that the vast numbers standing now on street corners, or dozing in the slums would at last have a chance to engage in work that was on the way to being meaningful and productive.

Oddly, as it turned out the New Work Car project did not play a role in the Big Change we had worked on and anticipated for so long. Why? Because in spite of the juxtaposed differences between them, all of these countries without exception follow the same "single rule politics" that has been the hallmark of the Post-Cold-War-Era. The rule to never resist any demand made by Big Business no matter how outrageous it is. The country is to always lie before it prone on the ground, with one's face in the dust. As we discussed earlier at length, this same rule is also obeyed in the United States and Europe, but the "Business-Job-

Nexus" has of course the same irresistible power in the Third World. If anything, its power there is still more relentless, for these countries suffer from far higher unemployment, and their wish to create development, economic growth and jobs is even more desperate.

To take the example of South Africa is particularly instructive. South Africa fought and won a revolution against white dominance. The whole world watched that revolution with breathless attention till 1994, and the country has now had a mainly black government for almost 20 years. However, despite its revolutionary tradition and despite the complexion of its government, it has at every turn done the bidding of the Great Corporate Powers. Is that not shocking? Is it not what one formerly might have pronounced to be "a contradiction?"

The subservience to Big Business politics is sometimes masked with terms like "Neo-Liberalism," or also "Free Trade." They have nothing to do with Freedom, either of trade or of anything else. Nor do they have any connection to liberalism, new, middle-aged or old. Grand ideas of whatever description have no bearing on these politics. Words like Free Trade, or liberalism are only used to distract and confuse the great mass of the by now hapless and discouraged people. It is also an error to imagine that the World Bank or the IMF are responsible for the enactment of these politics. Governments in every corner of the earth would still follow this single rule political directive, even if the World Bank and the IMF ceased to exist tomorrow. These governments believe that they need economic growth in order to create jobs, and in their minds there is only one way in which this can be accomplished, and that is through Big Business. Therefore the subservience – even in the face of a revolutionary tradition, and even in the face of the color of one's own face!

We are back inside the locked train. There are many people in these countries and also many officials in these governments who see fully and clearly and with horror where the continuance of these actions is taking them. No insight or wisdom is required for that. In virtually the entire Third World the last decade or two have been a series of disasters. Even in the Ukraine they now speak of the "good old days" and they mean the days of Breshnyev, and in South Africa one meets many poor blacks, who are the first to say that their lot was better in the days of apartheid. Slowly, many people the world over are waking up and are seeing with clarity how very much worse things have become since the dominance of Big Business began. Yet still we are in the locked train. There is no alternative visible anywhere in the sky. Which is why governments everywhere follow this one rule politics: simply, there is no alternative! What else is one to do? One grows ever more desperate for growth and wealth and jobs – and so one meets the Lords of Big Business in sackcloth and ashes, with the keys to one's city around one's neck.

That situation has had a decisive impact on the development of New Work. From all of the countries in which I have begun to work in the last 10 years invitations arrived, and fundamentally all of these invitations were alike. More or less explicitly each of them said: "We have read about your work, in books, in journals and on the internet. Apparently you have been developing an alternative during the course of the last 20 years. We very urgently want to have more information about this. Could you send materials, come for a visit or receive a visit from us?" In the case of South Africa, the approach was most direct. The person who traveled all the way from Johannesburg to Ann Arbor, MI was Langa Zita. He is a ranking Member of Parliament and Special Assistant to the Minister for Social Development. He was very blunt: "You must come to South Africa. South Africa is the only country in the world that very possibly will soon pursue a different direction. It possesses two attributes which other Third World countries do not have: it is wealthy, and it has a revolutionary tradition. So come, better today than tomorrow."

I have been traveling to South Africa at irregular intervals ever since. From the perspective of New Work the great step forward can be summed up in one word: policy. While we tried to explain the idea and the practice of becoming more HTSP to a host of small dispersed groups in our earlier phase (from the case of growing vegetables on the roofs of Vancouver, to the building of their own homes by homeless people in Ann Arbor, MI) we were now in conversations with the representatives of governments! The question invariably has been the same: is there any hope that the government might change its policy away from the subservience to business – even if only by one or two degrees?

Part of what has made the experience of the last years for me personally quite astonishingly wonderful were the oft repeated "five minute conversations." Wherever we were, 5 minutes was enough to present the essence of our case. The opening always was the question:

How much money does it cost you to create a job? Can you roughly estimate how much your government is spending on subsidies? What conceivably might be the sum-total, if you make an addition of all the different kinds of support given to businesses of every sort? Do count the payments in cash, but also tax abatements, the expenses involved in creating a climate attractive to business and to the international investor community, etc. – all the different blandishments of every sort. What is the number of jobs that these sums have produced for you?

Let me give you a single micro-example, just to abbreviate the process, as I could easily give hundreds of examples like this one. One of the ministers of the South African government had to give the celebratory speech on the occasion of the re-opening of a small mining operation. He knew that over 100 million dollars had been spent, but just as he was reaching for the microphone, he in a whisper asked the person next to him: how many jobs are there in this mine? The answer was 18! Needless to say, this is just an anecdote, but it is representative enough to give some approximate first idea of the ratio that is involved.

With that said I launch into the second part: I propose that New Work receive only 1 percent of what is now spent for a single reasonably secure and well-paid job, and that this 1 percent will be used to make available to 1,000 people the most important technologies of HTSP. This ratio of 1:1000 is of course the core and substance of our entire case. What we offer to 1,000 people can be regarded as more than a job, even for the 1,000. For we will do our best to enable them to create their own electricity with generators they themselves will manufacture, in a small shop that they will own cooperatively. (Part of the raw materials will be recycled plastic from milk and soda bottles.) We will do the same with food (using perma-culture) and water (using a filter, that they again will manufacture for themselves in a small shop) and the building of their homes (conceivably using a small mobile factory in which they can make their own cement) and beyond this for the making of their own stoves and their own kitchen utensils (out of recycled aluminum) and onwards along these same lines – as close as we can get to the 38 products that constitute the platform for a pleasurable human life.

To my own amazement, and also to the same amazement of any New Work Associates traveling with me, the response so far has uniformly been: why did you not come 5 years ago? When can you come again? Can you stay here and start tomorrow if we assemble a team and the rest you need?

The exuberance of that response is of course one thing. The actual implementation, quite another. As anyone with any experience in Third World countries would fully know, it is slow; there are politics, there is corruption, there are established interests, contested territories and God knows what else. On a deep-down level we are in spite of that calm and of good hope. Why? Because the pressure is enormous already now, and it is growing by the month. In a great number of countries the rage of the unemployed and destitute has become a factor. The spreading of terrorism is one first indication of this. Many members of these governments did not want to walk down the "surrender to business" road. They only did it because an alternative to that was not even conceivable. There was not even a vague idea hanging somewhere in the air.

Thus even a wispy notion that there might be an alternative makes a big difference. Many who are members of these governments naturally know their own countries very well. Especially in Africa, many of them know that if the conditions continue to deteriorate as they have in the last 1 or 2 decades, then they will not only lose their seat in parliament, but they will likely lose their life in a painful and blood-spilling death. Many in the New Work community are therefore quite convinced that the news that there is an alternative will spread fast indeed. If that should happen, then the rest is largely a question of exactly where and when? If a tentative, pilot program of changing the policy direction does not happen in the next month and not here, then assuredly a few months later somewhere else.

The turn in the use of computers

There is, however, one other development underway which has a very different trajectory. This one has its origin at the extreme opposite end of the social polarity: not in a response to the great mass of the down and out, but as far from that as possible, among the "most advanced," and possibly among the most advanced of the most advanced. The background to this mighty development is nothing short of the sea-change in the global "labor force." This came about, on the one side, through the elimination of many millions of mind-extinguishing jobs through the successive and still continuing waves of automation. The other side was the creation of almost as many millions of jobs that were intellectually far more highly placed. Jobs that some identify with the label "systems analysts," jobs that account for the far higher ratio of PhDs in many of the smaller new business organizations. Jobs that have changed the appearance of our airports: for on every second bench you see a person oblivious to her or his surroundings, because their entire attention is riveted on their laptop. The net effect of these two changes has been a huge upwards shift. The profile of the sum-total of those working is dramatically new. By some estimates close to one-third of the total require an entirely different culture from the organization by which they are employed, closer to the culture of universities and research laboratories than to the culture of steel-mills and assembly lines. Their demands are not those of the workforce 20 years ago, and most importantly for New Work, what they expect and want from their work is miles from the "mild disease," and is far more proximate to our conception of WRRW. One much-publicized episode in the recent history of the legendary Silicon Valley gives a particularly vivid impression of this. It also shows in what surprising ways New Work has progressed among those who are at the very top of our current social hierarchy.

In all of the United States, but particularly in California and most especially in the magic circle of those who had managed to get seats on the roller-coaster of the e-business wealth, a jubilant air had lasted for several years. One basked in the extravagance of life, and poured money like wine out of a shoe over one's head and face. One walked into the future as if it were an orchard: all ready and ripe and begging to be picked. The fantasy of "limitless possibilities," the idea that everything and anything at all can be achieved if one only tries, lies in the USA always just under the surface of consciousness. And that idea had managed to become king of the hill for 10 years. All this, however, represents only one side. For many it was a carnival that had lasted too long. There had been too many drunken nights in a row. So – and that is a first major point – when it stopped overnight one also heaved a sigh of relief. Thank God, it was over! One could leave the party and make one's way home. Thus, indeed, the mood was nothing like despair; more like a sobering up, more like Ash-Wednesday after a string of masked balls that had begun to get on one's nerves.

That relief was only one part: there was another part that had roots that went further down. One has to know a little bit about the history of the computer community to understand this. When I taught at both Stanford and Berkeley a good number of my students played some role in the initial phases of that industry, and through that connection I know this history rather well.

Some of the fables that it all started with kids who tinkered in the garages of their parents were indeed true. Numerous books have been written about this early period and it was very distinctive and had enormous charm. The culture, the mindset and much of the ambience reminded one far more of an incredible productive group of artists than of business, organization and law. The terms "geek" and "hacker" early on were coveted terms of high praise. They signified acceptance in a marvelous clan. Very like artists the members of that clan cared more than anything about one measure: the esteem of their peers! What counted above all was that one was "good" – "good" at writing software in the typical case. To emphasize a main point: money was not an overriding concern. If one had it, it was fun, it was a joke, but all one really needed was some love if possible, and some good wine. For many of these people their work was far and away more important than anything else, and in the early period they managed to arrange their lives to fit smoothly around that overriding preoccupation. Caring about their work very like artists, they also worked very much in the rhythm in which the creative have always worked: when the blessed demon goaded them on they would work 3 days and 3 nights without sleep, but they could also feel dull and would then not go near their work for a week.

All that of course changed. What happened was like an invasion, like being occupied by a hostile army. In this case by the army of the business culture. Many felt that their ideas had been stolen from them, worse that their ideas were put to uses entirely adverse to their own intentions. Retreating from one ditch to the next they surrendered ever more of their lives. The image that summed up what they most loathed was finishing a piece of code under insane pressure, sleeping on a blanket under the desk in one's office, and having to search for a spot in one's little black book if one wanted to sleep with one's partner.

Naturally, they were not heartbroken when much of this came down like a house of cards. Yes, many no longer sat in their manager chairs, and had to vacate their fancy apartments, but they were in spite of that gleeful. They had woken up from a nightmare, and soon after they had taken stock of the pieces, many decided that perhaps this was their second chance. They could start over again and this time without losing what was important to them. Not by any means all, but a good number decided to venture out into a field which had been the subject of speculations for a long time. Their mood was far from depressed. More nearly venturesome, vigorous and brisk. The talk was of new enterprises, new products and of a whole new approach.

How very new that approach in fact was cannot be grasped if one is not at home in that community. Yet there is a way in which it can be suggested. The implications of the turn they were taking was so radical, the consequences of this turn would be so broad, that one can easily imagine how a group of youngsters 5 years from now, after these consequences have taken hold, would look with bemusement at one of our present-day laptops, and in the light of the new developments would find that even our use of the term "hi-tech" had been presumptuous and premature. Given what had evolved by 2008, our current electronic toys would look like dated experiments to their eyes. Mere early attempts that were preparatory; leading up to the actual start of the computer age, that was initiated only by this new turn. This conceivable and imagined reaction of youngsters in 2008 would have its cause in one quite extraordinary and astonishing fact. It is a condition that exasperated and irritated some in the computer community already in the very late nineties. One first way to name it would be to say that it turned on the way in which the potential of computers had been enclosed and imprisoned in the pigeonhole of "information." The crux of it was the absurd identification, the marriage, of computers with information to the exclusion of everything else.

It is patent, if one looks back at the last 20 years, that the use of computers from the very start actually had a radically different orientation. Roughly, in 1980, computers were for the first time massively introduced into the domain of manufacturing. Those were the years in which I helped to evolve the first Center for New Work in Flint, MI. Nothing then could have been more palpable and self-evident to any 6-year-old than the fact that computers started to appear on both sides of the much mystified "line." These computers were "making things," they were producing or manufacturing *objects*. They were not printing documents, or organizing files of information in 20 different ways. They were making parts and products that were three-dimensional, and solid, and could be picked up and moved. Computers were cutting metal in breathtakingly complex and stunningly precise ways; they were grinding, polishing, welding, drilling or whatever else the blueprint required. What makes the monomaniac identification of computers with mere information all the more amazing is the timeframe that has been involved. Computers moved into factories long before they began their migration into offices and cubicles. The difference was as long as 10 whole years, which measured in computer time is an enormous span. By 1982 (when I began to work in Flint) one could easily find rows of computers on both sides of the line, not just in the automobile industry, but also in factories that made TV sets, or radios, or calculators, or also elsewhere, in factories that produced cups, or chewing gum, or handbags, or belts, or

Christmas wrapping paper. In contrast to this, one did not find anything like the full wall-to-wall coverage with computers, with a machine on every desk, in insurance companies, or banks, or hospitals until about 1992! So, one could say that computers had a 10-year lead in the great realm of "making things" over the realm of information. In these 10 years a frenetic race was continuously run both in the design of chips and motherboards and the other components that make up computers, but also, and no less, in the development of software that would allow computers to direct and guide and control manufacturing machines.

Once we free ourselves from the *idée fixe* that weds computers to information, we shall see that they can be used for the purpose of making things in quite unexpected and novel ways, ways that are no longer connected to factories or to global corporations.

One statement can be made quite unequivocally about the present time, namely, that we are at the very threshold of escaping from this temporary blind alley, to return back into the realm of computers "making things." Most crucially, we are beginning to use computers for the making of three-dimensional products, and we are doing this no longer in the factory, but at home, or in the neighborhood copy-shop. A whole spate of minor but not inconsequential developments have occurred so quickly and so peripherally that we have accepted and grown used to them without understanding their larger significance. Among these is the developing of our own (digital) photographs, which includes emailing those of our children as Christmas cards to our friends. Within the matrix I am trying to suggest this represents only one small step beyond the mere reproduction of a typed text on a page. Similarly, it has of course also become possible to reproduce and then enlarge and maybe frame a broad collection of very heterogeneous works of art. Not very different from this is the possibility of transferring images and patterns onto cloth. Right now this is much used by teenagers who in this way can make their own unique T-shirts.

Another development that was assimilated so quickly that the novelty it represented was hardly noticed was the self-burning of CDs. For a short time one did this in separate small boxes. One inserted the blank CD and could inscribe anything in music from Bach to Hip Hop on it. Of course, relatively soon that changed, and was simply included in the computer. Still, one might have assumed that the introduction of an attachment to computers that in effect manufactured a round shining disk instead of mere print on paper would have caused more of a stir, that the issue of using computers for domestic manufacturing would have been raised, but this hardly occurred.

Nonetheless, all of this made an impression on some in the advanced computer community, which in the United States is not only in Silicon Valley, but also in Boston (Massachusetts Institute of Technology,) North and South Carolina and near most other important universities. A handful of researchers began to work on other attachments, and soon on whole groups and families of attachments. This was only to be expected. The pressure that had been building up was irresistible: For 10 years computers had been right in the center of most homes; computers that self-evidently were capable of driving hundreds of different machines. They had been doing this in factories all along. And yet, perversely, masochistically, during this lapse of time, a whole generation linked them up with only *one* attachment: printers were the solitary outlet, monotonously and unimaginatively paired with computers in homes. Everywhere else, computers controlled shelves and rows and warehouses full of different machines – but in the home, only one, and that one prim and dull: a mere printer! How closeted and blindfolded could one force oneself to be?

One handsome, small attachment that an acquaintance of mine has developed to a point where he is not far from introducing it onto the market is a Lens Molder. Part of the background here is that for a number of years a company called "Lens-makers" had made glasses to order right in their own shops. Suggestive was also that a great number of people had begun to wear contact "dailies," since trying to wear them for months never became comfortable for them. On top of that, copy shops for a long time had already used devices that enclosed photographs in plastic. Also, contact lenses needed to be perfectly precise, which computers achieve with ease. There were no bubbles, no flaws and no imperfections. One of the nicest aspects of this situation was that the little "Lens Molder" hardly needed much adjusting. Once you had set it correctly for your vision it could stay that way until your eyes got worse.

The difference in cost will of course be fantastic. Apart from the cost of the device, which probably will be less than ten dollars, you will be able to mold yourself a new pair of lenses for one-fiftieth of a penny. Naturally, we (that is, the New Work Associates) hope that some people will conclude that commercial mass-manufacturing prices are outrageous, and that some will move one or two steps closer to a mindset that will open them to the practice of HTSP. The group working on the development of the "Lens Molder" also expects that some who will soon realize that the computer is a natural for making lenses that are absolutely precise will want to go further, and will want to play with the making of other lenses, different sizes, different purposes, every kind of curvature.

In their view it is likely that some people will soon make not only their own glasses but also their own designer frames – which is bound to have consequences for the airport stores that sell only extravagant frames for extravagant prices. And their hopes go beyond this, to the idea that some will soon make their own binoculars and cameras, and that the differences in the prices will again be grotesque. Clearly, once one has made the breakthrough in this direction there are no obvious borders at which one is required to stop. Domestic manufacturing is in principle merely a matter of miniaturization, which patently has become one of our main strengths. To take the process out of the factories and into one's own home or into a cooperatively owned neighborhood shop one only has to make the many different kinds of mechanical machines which computers can drive very much smaller. With that done one can manufacture one's own jewelry, one's own accouterments, also one's own lampshades and knick-knacks, perhaps one's own silverware, bowls, kitchen utensils and beyond that, conceivably even one's own transistors together with the spate of electronic toys which are based on them.

Put one additional ingredient into the picture. Think of these attachments as located not in the home, not in the living room or the bedroom next to where most PCs are now, but assume that they are grouped together and located in a shop. For everyone to have his or her own complete set of attachments would in any case be too expensive and too absurdly wasteful. The best analogy might be to a copy-shop: some machines stand in an open space and everyone walks in and uses them for a fee, others stand behind a counter. Only people who know what they are doing get to use those, and there is usually a consultant or a mentor close by who can supervise, give advice and instructions. The fee for using those is slightly higher.

Several New Work Associate Groups have been discussing these developments. While they feel that they are almost certain to soon occur, it is less clear how important a difference they will make. After all, we are already self-providing in a vast number of respects – from the printing of our own train tickets, to the serving of our own salad at salad bars, to the pumping of our own gas, and the fetching of our own cash – but our attitude has if anything become more passive and dependent than it was before.

One product is in this respect an exception. It must be admitted that with our customary admixture of humor, the New

Work community has begun to attach some hopes to it. That product of all things is the ubiquitous jeans!

Some New Work Associates take the view that making your own clothes will be quite different from making your own glasses or lampshades, partly because clothes are more intimate and in the case of jeans almost your second skin. The forerunner to this was, appropriately enough, hair. For years it was possible to walk into a hi-tech beauty salon and pick out of a catalog the hair-do that one wanted to try. Trying it in the flesh on one's own head can be dreadful if one loathes the result. So a technological device scanned your head and face into a computer and you could then press a few keys and see what you would look like with any one out of the 500 hairdos pictured in the catalog. A marvelous invention! Saved no doubt great quantities of bitter tears! Via several intermediate steps, exactly the same thing became eventually available for clothes.

At one stage you could have it done only in the fanciest department stores. They would scan your whole body into the computer when you arrived. You could amble through the different departments and make your selections and then have your three-course lunch. Just as you were drying your lips with a napkin someone would hand you everything you had picked out "made to measure." At another stage (in the summer of 2001) the fabulous Levi-Strauss Company announced the "mass customization" of their legendary jeans. One could have one's lower body scanned into a computer, and specify down to the last detail what one's dream-jeans would be like, and they would be delivered exactly as requested 10 days later to one's house.

That made an impression and it became one more of the many sorcerer's apprentice stories that accompany this entire long development. It seems likely that Levi-Strauss underestimated the symbolic, mythic power of their own astonishing product. This is one example where the transition between the dying Job System culture and the New Work culture becomes luminously clear. Focus on the utterly unbelievable success of the blue jeans! What is McDonald's compared to that? Sure, it is worldwide but it is low-end, low-class, low-nutrition, low-taste, low-expectation food. Not so the jeans. They, too, are worldwide, but far more impressive and significant is the egalitarianism that they proclaim with every behind! From the billionaire to the homeless person, everyone in jeans! Did the French Revolution achieve anything that is more impressive than this? Consider the significance of pants in history! And then burst into jubilation: one pair of pants challenges all class distinctions! Which is precisely where Levi-Strauss made their mistake! They had no inkling of what they had in half-blindness chanced upon! They ignored, and abused and, above all of course, exploited the marvel that had dropped into their lap. Like so many other great discoverers they denied what they had found! They resisted it! If they were catholic they would have exorcized and excommunicated it. For in the face of a grand symbol that at long last proclaimed the equality of humanity, and proclaimed it in ever so bodily a way, they introduced differential prices! Differential cuts! Differential buttons, seams, insteps and what not. That, in our view, was close to sacrilege. To bring humanity with a pair of pants so close to the fulfillment of one of its oldest dreams, and then to scorn and destroy the just glimpsed great possibility. In the view of some New Work groups this called for retribution, for punishment. They, therefore, decided to make an example of those very jeans. Much like a conspiracy they teamed up and focused their energies on turning jeans into one of the products that one would be able to make oneself. The technology seemed ready and waiting, and it suited their project to stunning perfection. For with one computer scanning one can literally take 1 million measurements, and the "fit" of jeans made in this way is obviously not to be surpassed. At the same time, one could reduce the price of even these superbly customized jeans to such an extent that they would again become the symbol of equality that they once were. That reduction could be achieved by adding the making of jeans to the extensive menu of already existing offerings for which the Centers for New Work have all along striven. If one could walk into a center very much as one walks now into a copy-shop and with the help of advanced computerized sewing machines (and, naturally, also the help of a Mentor-Associate who can assist with the use of these machines) make oneself the exact pair of jeans one really, really wanted, and do that in less than 20 minutes, then their price would come back down to what it had been, before designers and fashion consultants muscled in.

So far this scheme is far from fully realized; it is mainly a plan. Everyone understands, I assume, that it is one more attempt to tweak the nose of a world-class corporate giant, very in the spirit of Napster, of Linux and the Open Source Movement. No one seriously believes that being able to make one's own jeans will convert great numbers to the mentality and the practice of HTSP. We think of it as an analogy to an "educational campaign" in politics. The point is not to score a victory. The hope is to take some people another few steps away from the solid molds of the job mentality in which they were stuck for so long.

It would be natural to add the computer attachments that will be developed in the next 10 years to the computer training and equipment that the Centers for New Work already offer now. The fit could not be better! The growth could hardly be more organic! From the technological side, the computers are already there. The new attachments could be plugged in. More importantly, the people associated with these centers are intellectually, emotionally and also culturally prepared. That the Job System must be overcome cautiously and gradually is an old and familiar mantra for them. The *idea* of HTSP is for them a very old acquaintance. Many of them chew their lips, impatient to finally get their arms up to the elbows in it. For these groups associated with the centers the coming of these machines would, therefore, be a welcome, maybe a jubilant release.

Also, access to the technologies that make HTSP possible will be quite inexpensive. In general everyone will have a chance to go to the shops or the centers where one makes things for oneself. Remember, that in these centers we will not only manufacture. Food also will be grown, and as we said before, somewhere near 80 percent of everything needed for a comfortable modern life will be available there. Therefore, virtually everyone will have *at least* the goods and products of their own HTSP.

Personal Fabrication

If we step three paces back we can see the larger pattern. One element has been that factories will become small manufacturing shops. The second element moves in from the opposite side: the very small, personal computers will be combined with attachments, and the result will be Micro- or Mini- Personal Factories. In centers or copy shops could be computer-controlled miniature versions of some of the machines which we currently use in factories, and all manner of products from lenses, to watches, to cutlery and jewelry could be turned out in these Mini-Factories. However, there is a third, far more radical and future-directing phenomenon, one that will truly upset our traditional economic ideas. I always present this particular technology with great caution, when I teach future New Work Associates or some other group in a corporate or some other setting.

I prefix a warning: the two elements so far discussed are mild compared to what you will be encountering now. The next step has a different status: it has been worked on for years and it was hypnotic or mesmerizing from the start. It is so simple that any child could instantly understand it, but it is at the same time so dramatically different and new that all manner of fables and legends were spun around it even while it grew. Some people talk about it, almost as if it were magic or somehow surreal.

It is a technology that embodies the "New Turn" in the use

of computers (that is, the use of computers for the "making of things") to a far greater degree than computer attachments. I, therefore, remind the group with whom I am working of the youngsters who perhaps 5 years from now would not even want to call our current laptops or cell-phones "hi-tech." They would consider this premature, because they will associate serious hi-tech with this next step in the making of things; the mere reformatting of information will in their eyes be only a preparatory finger-exercise game. At issue is not one single device or one machine, but a genuine "technology," a "field." For a number of years, one heard reports about experiments and isolated efforts, until now it has turned into a publicly recognized and acknowledged area of research and development, with an extensive literature, and distinguished professors (like Andreas Gebhardt at the Technical University in Aachen and Neil Gerstenfeld at MIT, and many others). In spite of that, as a field it is still not yet fully in the limelight of attention, not if one compares it to the work on the human genome, or hydrogen fuel cells, or the sterling engine, or thin film solar technology, or to nanotechnology. All of these have received more media attention, and compared to these Personal Fabrication, or Generative, or also Direct Manufacturing as it is sometimes called is still relatively unknown. Many of the people involved in it have a sense of its extraordinary future potential, but for many complex but also easily understood reasons they keep rather quiet about this dimension. I will describe what it is and how it works in very nontechnical language.

Imagine to begin with a box, in size not very different from an aquarium, made out of very thick and super-hardened glass. The glass must meet these specifications because inside the box is an intensely rarefied vacuum. Next to the box is an array of computers. Incidentally, not hugely powerful but rather normal, average capability computers. At the heart of the idea of this technology is an incredibly fine powder, or a variety of different powders, made from different materials. These powders are fine not just by ordinary measurements, but fine on a level that suggests the dimensions employed in nanotechnology; so fine that 20 or 30 grains of one of these powders piled up in a heap would still not have the height of the diameter of a single human hair. The quintessence of how this technology works could hardly be simpler: there are devices, you could think of them as miniaturized funnels or chutes, with which this powder is laid down in extraordinarily exact layers, which are also extremely thin. These layers, each shaped to enormously exact specifications, are laid down, one on top of the other. Each, after it has been laid down, is then welded onto those already there. There are many ways in which this can be done, but for our purposes think of it as glued and hardened into place with a laser beam. The crux of the matter is that one can "make" or "model" any, even the most twisted, complex and inverted, object out of these layers in one single process! The computers control the exact shape of each of the super-thin layers. No two layers need to be the same. So as in geology, for example, in a lime-stone cave, the most fantastic shapes can be built up by patiently and systematically adding one layer onto the one before. One of the showpieces of Generative Manufacturing (incidentally, the relationship to rapid prototyping is very close) are models of human skulls. These are incredibly more complex than any part of any imaginable mechanical device. They are highly irregular and the channels and openings running through them are immensely involved. Nonetheless, it is possible to make the exact likeness of a human skull in one single manufacturing process. For our purposes this falls still one dimension short. Models of human skulls, for medical teaching purposes, are made out of one single substance. Most mechanical devices clearly are not. Still this does not constitute a major hurdle. In principle there are no reasons why one could not use five or six different materials or powders. There could, for instance, be several kinds of plastic, plus copper and aluminum and brass. The state of the art is not quite at this level yet, but in a foreseeable time one will be able to scan the exact blueprint of a mobile phone, or calculator, or of course a silicon chip, or almost any part one requires for an automobile or a plane into the computer, and then each of the needed parts can be "built up" out of sufficiently complex layers. Some of these might contain only one of the available plastics, but others might use a combination of several plastics and also various metals. It is crucial that anything can be "built up" in one single operation, and for all intents and purposes with virtually no human labor. One much discussed and often vaunted advantage of Generative Technology is that it is far more frugal, or conversely, far less wasteful than manufacturing has been in the past. If you observe the many stages, the turning, and the cutting and the drilling and the sanding with which a block of steel is slowly machined down into a crankshaft, for example, you are surprised not just with the doltish cumbersomeness of this serial procedure, but also with the amount of waste; with how much of the initial block is, in the end, not used. None of this happens in the generative process. One only needs the precise quantity of the materials that are actually used. It is of great importance that there are no principle difficulties which block the further development of this technology. On the contrary, compared to issues like the further increase in the speed of computers, where the theoretical limitations stand out very starkly, the further progress in this form of manufacturing does not face a wall. Further materials almost certainly could be added to those used now. In fact this is one of the most intriguing aspects of Direct Manufacturing. Since the raw materials will be entirely ultra-fine powders that will be laminated together, the idea of developing entirely new materials, some of which may be renewable since they will be derived from plants (for example, from corn or rapeseed), is much discussed. Tellingly, the difficulties at the moment seem financial rather than scientific or theoretical. That of course could change virtually overnight if the economic potential of this technology becomes publicized. So far its potential is still boxed up in one corner, which is actually paradoxical, for its impact could be amazingly broad, far broader on the face of it than that of its current main rivals. The impact of deriving electricity from hydrogen decidedly would be anything but narrow, and nanotechnology, too, might have applications beyond the medical "miracles" which are the showpieces which it likes to parade at the moment (the possibility of making nano-sized carriers of oxygen that would perform the task of red blood cells, only so much more efficiently that one's heart could stop for a whole hour without this causing great damage). Still, neither of these could be compared to the domino-series of effects that this production method could entail.

Admittedly the cost at the present time is still prohibitive. If the use of these machines became widespread their price would obviously drop, and then one could imagine one of these in many neighborhood community centers, or of course Centers for New Work. (Naturally, they could also be mobile, so that 20 or 40 centers could time-share one of these.) Clearly, there can be no question of anything like a complete enumeration, but perhaps an impression can be conveyed by mentioning a few of the applications that are being worked on already right now. The possibility that this machine could by itself manufacture much of what the other so far mentioned attachments have the capacity to produce is a first point. Evidently, a generative machine could make lenses out of plastic. The technology is perfectly suited for this particular task, since they need to be made to exact specifications and without flaws. It could also make jars and bottles out of any material you might want to choose. It could also make the frames for eye-glasses. Again, the building up of these out of excruciatingly thin layers would be a natural thing. Similarly, one could make rings, but there is no need to stop with them! It could really make jewelry of all kinds! Also, all manner of tools or kitchen utensils such as garlic presses, espresso makers, toasters, mixers, knives, forks and spoons. Again out of different powders the whole range of plastic hardware that comes with electricity, from simple plugs to surge protectors, transistors, cell-phones, the cores of radios or TV sets, but again vases, knick-knacks, little statues (three-dimensional busts of one's children). Also the gears for bicycles, some of the parts needed in making generators, a great range of small parts crucial in automobiles: carburetors, distributors, piston rings, but also elements for the interior of the car: dials and gages, knobs and handles and the like. In Japan, the idea of robots making robots has been developed for some time. A natural next step would be the idea that generative machines could manufacture computers – in one single action, and with virtually no use of human labor.

Again, there is no reason why the glass-boxes of this technology would have to be roughly aquarium sized. Surely, they could be larger, and then one could take waste-wood, or remnants of plants (chaff, for example) and grind these down into ultra-fine powders. That would open the door to making everything that we presently make out of wood (and not waste-wood!), tables and chairs for example, in a generative way. For the reduction of waste, but also for the reduction of cost (which is crucial for New Work) the capacity to manufacture virtually every kind of spare part, whether this is for a car, or a washing machine, or a locomotive, or a crane has great potential. This is frequently mentioned in the context of the developing countries, but there is no need to restrict it to these. In the last few years many New Work groups have discovered that many people in the West would like to live less income dependent (that is, job-dependent) lives, and significantly prolonging the lives of everything they own might help them to quit what Arthur Miller (in *Death of a Salesman)* called "The Race with the Junkyard."

For the sake of contrast, let me add one further, admittedly somewhat nasty, twist: in his book *Business at the Speed of Thought* (Warner Books, 2000, p. 115), Bill Gates wrote:

The internet is enabling a new way of life that I call "the Web lifestyle." The Web lifestyle, like the electricity lifestyle, will be characterized by rapid innovations in applications. Because the infrastructure for high-speed connectivity has reached critical mass, it is giving rise to new software and hardware that will re-shape people's lives. Intelligent devices such as the PC are becoming more powerful and less expensive. Since they are programmable they can be used for many different applications. Within a decade most Americans and many other people around the world will be living the Web lifestyle. It will be a reflex for these people to turn to the Web to get news, to learn, to be entertained, and to communicate. It will be just as natural as picking up the phone to talk to somebody, or ordering something from a catalog is today. The Web will be used to pay your bills, manage your finances, communicate with your doctor, and conduct any business. Just as naturally, you'll carry one or more small devices using a wireless connection to stay constantly in touch and conduct electronic business wherever you are."

I do not quote this in order to single out the world-famous CEO of the world's most powerful software company. Precisely the opposite! Bill Gates' projections for the future of computers are typical. They are representative. In fact, if anything is surprising, then it is the unanimity, the monotony, the utter lack of imagination with which virtually identical statements are repeated by a whole herd of writers. There are virtually no exceptions. The imagination of the people writing on this subject seems to be amputated, so they think only in terms of the still faster, the still more ubiquitous, the still more boundless, the still less discriminating flow of information. They do not think. They follow the lines of past development and merely extend them 3 inches further.

The contrast could hardly be more extreme: the area of having computers provide solid, graspable objects, which we seriously need, is virgin, is unplowed, rudimentary and still full of weeds. In the area of information we chase after frills. Typically we "invent" refrigerators that announce to us that we are running out of milk, or we simply put the same information on a still smaller disk. With great effort we achieve nothing impressive, nothing useful, nothing in any genuine sense new. Only a twist, another bell, another whistle here and there. Some people blame the recession partly on the slump in the computer industry. Others speak of the age of computers already in the past tense. It has crossed its zenith, is on the downward arch of its decline. Sales have dropped since the euphoric bubble burst. That is the frustration of working in the area of information. In the area of making things, not in factories, but of making them directly for individual people in homes and shops, we are at the very foot of a Mount Everest; and the top of the mountain is still shrouded in white mist.

This difference could not be more provocative and inviting. To make progress with the manipulation of information, we are reduced to scratching with the fingernails an inch here, a twist, or a spin over there. We are desperate. What can we promise the jaded customers to perk up their interest? Nothing truly exciting is coming down any of the proverbial pipelines. In the area of making things not in factories but at home or in shops we are still doltish. We are just beginning, and a mountain of unexplored opportunities stands there, right in front of us! It is ironic that Gates used the title: *Business at the Speed of Thought*.

Business without thought might have been more appropriate. I would like to reiterate: his book is not exceptional. Far from it. It is the rule. Virtually the whole literature about further developments in IT does nothing more than extrapolate from the immediate past. At this point this is great folly, for there has been a major collapse, and a huge challenge with roots to the more distant past rises up right in front of us. There is no reason to think that some of the best and brightest will not rise to this task.

The Portfolio of New Work Products

I tried to explain in the first chapter that the Business-Job-Nexus has dominated our economics and our politics since the end of the Cold War. It resulted in the Blackmail Economy of the last 20 years. How can one break out of the stranglehold of this grip? Not with protest marches, not with the boycott of sneakers or grapes, not with the old method of "Organize! Organize!," least of all with writing letters to one's congressman. To break this hold, or to get out of the locked train, a whole new economy is needed. And the backbone of this new economy is nothing more than that we will relentlessly, step by step, advance in the direction of making our own products! Not only our tomatoes and parsley sprigs, but also our own refrigerators, TV sets, microwave-ovens, cell-phones and laptops. Instead of bribing large companies with opulent subsidies to please settle in our town, or region, or state we will say:

We no longer need you! That you do not create jobs is in any case a known fact. You eliminate jobs, you do not create them. We also no longer need you for your products. We have learned how to make these in small cooperatively owned shops, with small mobile manufacturing rigs, with computer attachments and progressively more with an even more ultimate technology, that of the Personal Fabricator. We will make your products in neighborhood community centers, or in Centers for New Work. You can no longer blackmail us with the threat that you will go to Brazil. On the contrary, the sooner you leave, the better we will like it, for the air will be improved once you are gone. And by "air" we in this case mean many things. Do go! We will help you to pack, and carry your suitcases for you. Go and manufacture under the thick ice of Greenland – the cool climate is just what you need!

The technology of the Personal Fabricator is still in its infant shoes. We are in continuous conversations with the scientists and engineers who spend their lives developing it, and we, therefore, have probably a fairly accurate sense of the timeframe in which the next few stages will be attained. It is a matter of a considerable number of years; not whole decades, but certainly several large portions of them. We, thus do not suffer from the illusion that even most of the products we mentioned will be directly or generatively manufactured by 2018. From our perspective, however, that is not at all the main point.

The enormously important role which Personal Fabrication will play in the next years will not be on the pragmatic stage, but one level higher, on the intellectual plane. Exactly which products will be turned out by exactly which date is far less important than that the conception, the idea of this technology, the vision that this is indeed possible and in fact on its way becomes known! What is urgent right now is something like a media-campaign – and New Work can of course be of assistance in this. Why is it important that the evolution of this technology enters into the mainstream of public and even popular thinking? Ultimately, for a pivotal political reason. Focus on a fact to which we are completely inured, though the monotony, the repetitiveness, the unabashed shamelessness with which it is used is actually astounding. I mean the one and only ploy (it is not an argument, but a ploy) that the Blackmail Business System tirelessly invokes: all we need is for the economy to turn over faster, then everything will return to normal and bliss will spread through the land. Yes, there is poverty, yes, there is unemployment but just move the obstacles out of the way so we can push the gas-pedal down to the floor. If only the graphs of the stock-market and the profit margins go up all our problems will dissolve in cheer. The idiocy into which the hypnotic power of this mantra has mesmerized people beggars comparisons. That conceivably could be the great function of spreading knowledge about the direct manufacturing technology. It might be the snap of the fingers that wakes subjects from their hypnotic sleep. The conception, the idea is the compelling thing. Seeing vividly that making anything whatsoever with virtually no labor at all – recognizing finally that this is the direction in which we are going – the encounter with that image might be enough to wake people up.

In other words, these machines express simply through their astounding technological capacity an aspect of the ethos which very likely will prevail in the next new culture. Merely by observing these machines close up one cannot help but see that they inaugurate a new era. The quantum leap between the amount of labor that was formerly required and what becomes possible with the use of these machines simply is too great. The idea that we are merely going through some minor adjustment finally collapses. If one takes note of how these machines minute by minute perform one cannot help but acknowledge that unbelievable quantities of what we in some former time did with our hands and our backs have now been usurped. We come face to face with a wall: we can no longer dodge the conclusion that we must find an altogether new direction, a new outlet for the energy for work which we possess. For the tasks that these energies have in the past accomplished, they are now no longer needed. Therefore we must aim at higher and so far barely dreamed of goals.

Possibly this picture would finally trigger a counter thought in people's minds; namely that the faster the economy moves the more quickly will we reach the new forms of the mass-elimination of labor which we have just glimpsed. Or, translated down to another level: the more money we give to the big corporations, the more quickly they will buy the machines that enable them to eliminate jobs.

Raising people's consciousness about the technologies that are to come is, therefore, an important political action. In this respect, there is much more to be done, and the Network of New Work Associates and Groups is engaged in a great arch of different pursuits. One of these is an umbrella project, which we call the Portfolio of New Work Products. This is the complementary other half to what I have so far described in sweeping terms as whole new approaches to manufacturing; it is the slow, painstaking, on the ground development of one individual product at a time. All of these have a set of shared characteristics: they all contribute to the audacious hope which we call HTSP. Each of these products represents one further small step toward assembling the sum-total of technologies and tools that will enable people to produce for themselves everything that they need for the leading of pleasurable and fulfilling lives. Half-whimsically we have been saying for a long time that this sum-total needed is only 38 products. The point of saying this is that there is indeed an upper limit, and that it is far more easily reached than we often imagine. Whether the figure is exactly 38 or not clearly depends on the circumstances and on the individual people. Still, the goal itself we pursue with resilient determination.

It would serve no purpose to here list and describe every last product which we presently have in development. Such lists we must create together, keep expanding them and make them accessible to all. The aim here is to give an impression with a few representative examples. One especially dear to the hearts of many associated with New Work is a remarkable water filter developed by Ulrich Weise, who is now the CEO of the small company that manufactures this filter. Basically, one can pour almost anything into the top of this filter, and water that is either much cleaner or even drinking water will come out at the bottom. The device is small, about the size of a night-table and not too expensive. We have approached Mr Weise with the proposition that his company is evidently too small to introduce his filter effectively into the African or Asian market, while New

Work has the competence and experience and also importantly the connections for this task. In addition, the market in Central Europe for such a filter is clearly very limited since most people (still) have access to clean water more or less at will. We stressed from the outset of the negotiations with Mr Weise that to simply assist with the marketing of his product was not the topic. From the perspective of New Work, it was a firm condition that these filters – which in Africa could save literally millions of lives – would be manufactured locally, and that they indeed would be manufactured in one of the small manufacturing plants we have been discussing, where this plant in addition would be owned by a group of people now living in a slums. One of the many uses for this filter (there are far too many to enumerate) always causes special excitement when it is discussed so I will mention it. Currently, in some undeveloped places, great amounts of energy is spent, washing clothes, because it necessitates carrying large amounts of precious water, sometimes great distances. An alternative idea is to use the filter to recycle the water that comes out of the wash tub, and wash ten loads of laundry with the same 4 or 5 gallons from which you start. Imagine the amounts of backbreaking labor this will save! Possibly this will give mothers more precious time to spend with their children and on small business industries of their own. Something else that is currently causing excitement is the possibility of making a generator for oneself, with relatively simple tools in a small, conceivably even mobile shop, and making a good number of the parts out of recycled plastic that could come from bottles and wrappings. One remark made by the young highly placed person whose mandate it is to "eradicate poverty in South Africa" (that is the officially prescribed expression) throws a shaft of light on a telling point. He said: "The more hours it takes to make one of these generators, the better the government will like it." Part of the background to this is that the cost of the wages in South Africa is of no concern. The crucial goal that is incredibly difficult to attain – hugely more difficult than those who have never experienced these situations first-hand could ever imagine – is to by one means or another lure a group of long-term unemployed people out of the despondency, the meltdown of their own poverty of desires, and to bring them to the point where they will wind copper wire around an iron core.

In a closely related effort a group of New Work Associates are trying to work with a firm that is developing the design for a dramatically simpler diesel engine which again could be manufactured with relatively simple tools, in a small manufacturing shed – once again with "the more hours of labor the better." (This ultra-simple diesel engine is of interest to us because we are somewhat more skeptical about solar technologies than most others who work in the field of development. Solar technologies are as everyone knows expensive, but they are also fragile. Panels break when they are struck by a thrown rock. The so-called thin solar technology seems like an enormously promising start, but at this juncture it is still too expensive, especially for the Third World. The diesel engine is decidedly just a stopgap for the time being.) The one technology that in our view justifies the highest hopes is the legendary Stirling Engine. This is one other technology that seems to border on magic: the engine drives a piston with hot air. This engine has been legendary for many years because anything whatever can be used to generate the heat. One could use goat-turds, peat-moss, refracted sun-light, all forms of remnant wood and oil and so forth. Groups of New Work people are in discussions with various firms that have developed models of the Stirling Engine to the point where they are almost ready for the market.

On a different score, years ago it struck us as an oddity that in the area of air-cooling the equivalent of the mobile, practical small space heater cannot be found. Many have asked themselves, why is it necessary to cool down a whole house, or a whole apartment? A space heater goes under a desk. It keeps one's feet warm, while one's head stays cool. Clearly, this is wonderful for writing. Why is it impossible to find a small air-conditioner, the size of a thick book, that one could attach to the ceiling, so that the cool air could naturally descend and with a gentle erotic breeze waft the heat away from one's body. We worked on this for a long time and eventually discovered that small refrigerators did exist, and that for us of even greater value, the device that generates the lower temperature which they employ is incomparably simpler than the clumsy and outdated mechanism that we still have in the refrigerators that we use in our kitchens. Amazingly, the device consists of nothing more than two metal plates that both receive a very low electric charge. In the meantime, this small refrigerator has become one other item that we are moving toward producing in small manufacturing shops in shack-settlements. It should be easy to form some idea of how very differently a group of the down and out react if on the one side one tells them that they can cut lawns or clean side-walks, or, if in contrast to that, one tells them that they will be able to manufacture new, cutting edge, space-age refrigerators.

Other products that are presently most in demand in the Third World are hotplates manufactured in part out of clay. Such hotplates are urgently needed since many of the shacks are built out of cardboard and sheets of plastic, and the sparks from open fires can turn these shacks into a torch in an instant. We initiated developmental work on these because the very impressive organization of the International Network of Slum-dwellers offered to distribute them in the slums of many parts of the world. Our Center for New Work in Gotha, East Germany, has been at work on the development of building materials made of clay for several years. Of special concern are roof-tiles made from clay. This is difficult since dried clay normally cannot withstand rain, but they are nonetheless very much needed since the roofs now in use, which are made often of corrugated metal, turn shacks into baking-ovens in the hot sun. Our plan in regard to these tiles is of course not to sell or export them to the Third World. The center in Gotha, rather, is working on the development of small, mobile machines that will be manufactured in the Third World, and could then travel on the bed of a truck from village to village so that people could make their own tiles for their own roofs. One especially exciting project is an effort to introduce the small manufacturing shop in which these tile-pressing machines would be produced into a Ukrainian prison, with which the center in Gotha has been evolving a relationship over several years.

As I have explained before, we ensure any new group during any first meeting that we unlike other agencies do not come with answers and expertise, and will not tell them what to do. Instead, we will display many possibilities before them and then ask our question, namely, what do they "really, really" want. One of the most memorable answers to this was given by young people in Kabul. They answered they really wanted two things: no more bombs for one and music CDs for another. This response was particularly revealing. Yes, of course, one does want electricity. Yes, one does want to build and to grow food, but access to the internet and to computers, to music and indeed to an internet café are invariably among the highest priorities. That is why we now have several groups of New Work Associates who are specialists in Information Technology. Arn Gehrke, who lives in Berlin, is among the most talented of these. He has devoted some of his impressive expertise to the development of IT technology that would be especially adapted to the conditions of the Third World. One of these is his attempt to design walkie-talkie technology that would not require the extravagant infrastructure of our current mobile-phones, but would nonetheless function over much larger distances than walkie-talkies do now. Another is an effort to create ways of accessing the internet that are cheaper and more widely available than those currently marketed; the project of his that I personally find most useful. Also charming is the idea of a mobile phone that would no longer have the jungle of confusing functions in which one becomes perpetually entangled. It would be the "lean," stripped down version of a mobile phone, one with which one could phone and nothing else.

There is yet another line of products which we are gradually developing forward in cooperation with a whole network of other organizations. These are the small, mobile manufacturing shops that of late have almost become an aspect of our identity, of the "brand" of New Work. Our closest partner in this is the Technical University in Chemnitz, and most specifically Prof Enderlein and his co-worker Thorsten Hildebrandt. In the very specialized branch of the design of small, mobile factory shops the University of Chemnitz seems to be far in advance of most of the rest of the world. At the present time a considerable number of possible small, mobile shops are under discussion. For example, one in which one could melt recycled glass but at the same time form it into the plates, or glasses, or bowls that are needed. Similar with plastic. Instead of merely collecting these things and sending them back to a mass-manufacturer, the people in a village would collect glass or plastic in advance of the arrival of the mobile factory, and would then make for themselves the item they need. Other possibilities along similar lines would be small, mobile shops with which one could produce every kind of hardware from nails and hooks to hinges and drills, or again shops equipped with all the materials and tools needed for every conceivable repair in a home. One variation on this theme took shape during one of my stays in Haiti. Since virtually all manufacturing in Haiti has come to a complete stand still we explored the possibility of collecting aluminum cans and making from these a variety of different products. These ranged from spare-parts for refrigerators, to microwave-ovens and espresso coffee-machines. These last items were once more examples of our conviction that the down and out are not satisfied with the primitive and second-rate, but "really and seriously" want the very same items that we enjoy. In general, the quality of all the products of High-Tech-Self-Production will be elegant but stringently simple. This is in part because that is what the manufacturing process in small shops calls for. That is all that this process allows. There is also directly the desire to be inexpensive and simple and never to be wasteful and plush. Still, most importantly of all: the products for self-production can afford to be functional and plain. We make them for our own use, for the use of the group that immediately surrounds us. Things end up with a clutter of elaborations when they need to appeal on the market, when they need to capture an idle, roaming eye. That is not the problem of the products of self-production: they fill a need, they are desired, therefore they do not need to be fancy.

From the beginning, it was the lightness of HTSP that was the guiding concern. The deep, underlying desire was to have more time, more energy for what one seriously and deeply wanted to do. The activities of self-production were therefore intended not to take too much time, but to be light in that sense. From the Bio-Blocks and the Ability Blocks all the way up to the small refrigerators, and even the Ferrari-like erotic car – all of these were products that were intended not to take much work. Distantly they all reflected back upon the spirit-killing cutting of wood with the small bow-saw in New Hampshire. All of them embodied a: "Not this!" and a "Not too much of the biblical sweat." Yes, we do want excellent quality, but manufactured with technologies that ensure that it can be done quickly and with ease, that the whole of HTSP can be done "with the left foot" that maybe even one finger of the left hand is enough!

Given that I explain all of this most usually in the context of training, and therefore to people who are so to speak "in training," who are already interested in the process of becoming New Work Associates (as in the context of teaching the seminars in Emmendingen, for example) there occurs usually a kind of explosion, a burst of excitement. In the context of teaching, any number want to know more about one or another of these products; they want to become more involved. Often their questions are specific: what company should they get in touch with for the making of refrigerators, or for the recycling and the "direct," the "generative" manufacturing out of aluminum powder? Invariably there always are some – given the generally high spirits, the exuberant mood of New Work – who have an idea for a new approach, for a new product, for one or another way of advancing the frontier of High-Tech-Self-Production. The mood surrounding this is often so high that it is easy to slip into a fantasy where one sees many hundreds of companies each advised by a handful of associates, and where each of these companies makes yet another product that advances HTSP by yet one further step, and all of these companies are somehow connected in the network of the New Work Enterprises.

In moments like this it is important to remember that none of the product-examples is the actual issue. They are all part of one larger Declaration of Independence. Whether this is expressed through a neighborhood manufactured air-conditioner, or refrigerator, or radio, or television set, or a self-made suit, or pair of glasses, or camera, or for that matter through a house that one has built oneself does not finally matter. The items themselves are marginal and circumstantial. Crucial is that each additional product that we bring to the point where it can be self-made with a minimum of mind-dulling work represents one additional step toward freedom from the servitude to the Job System.

The "fixed costs"

One objection that is most often and rather naturally raised by women advances the question of the regular, monthly bills. People agree that the new manufacturing technologies, in particular that of the Personal Fabricator, are very impressive.

Still, they will say that some of this seems showy and beside the point. The daily economic realities do not hinge on this or that fancy contraption. They are cruder and have more to do with maneuvering past the first of each successive month, and of how one could do this if one indeed adopted a New Work life- and work-style. Personally, I am filled with delight when this issue is put on the floor, for this is an area in which we have done a great deal of careful, hands-on work and we therefore are in a position to be of genuine help. Our procedure in regard to these monthly bills is plain and home-spun. We start from the top, and go one by one down through the stack, commenting on each in turn until we have leafed our way down to the bottom.

1. Phone

For very many the phone represents a sizable portion of their expenses. We can begin with a fact. One of the best-known colleges in the United States – Dartmouth College – has installed a telephone system that channels phone calls over the internet. The technology is similar to that of email, and most important, the cost is also not very different from email. One upshot was that the college decided not to send bills for phone calls to the students, because the expense of mailing the bills would have been greater than the cost of the calls. Since most everyone knows how interminable the phone calls of most college students are, this is an impressive statistic.

In broad terms this is another example of where the intelligent use of a novel technology can reduce a cost that seems non-negotiable and fixed. Still, it is also the case that very many people do not know how to make use of this technology, and that this is also in a number of ways quite complex. This means that giving assistance to people so that their phone-call costs will drop to one-tenth of what they formerly were is yet another task that New Work can perform. It also means that having the use of a phone is one of the "38" – a phone is one of the requisites for a pleasurable and acceptable life. It is understood that the phone is only one member of a larger family. The costs associated with cable-TV, with the renting of movies and the purchasing of music are all members of this same group. Many feel they are needed for an acceptable life, and reducing the costs of all of them is at the same time one of the political tasks of New Work.

2. *Rent*

A fascination, perhaps more than that, an obsession, with building the space in which one lives runs through the entire history of New Work. Exploration of alternative building became a strong focus from the very first project with homeless people in New York City. It was agreed self-participation in building their own housing was an important factor, and that "alternative" building "systems" that would be very friendly to people with no previous experience and no developed talents played a great role. The domes that have become one of the emblems of New Work are themselves an example of this. (You remember they are constructed by blowing up with air a thick bubble and then simply spraying a mixture of clay, or of light cement, onto the outside of that skin.) There are a great number of additional ways to build beyond these. Most crucial in relation to the high cost of rent is the basic realization that we are all very much less helpless in this domain than we allow ourselves to imagine. There are a myriad of ways to reduce this cost. Each of these is different from all the rest, and in each case a careful choice has to be made as to which of these fits your situation and your special needs. To acquaint people with these many possibilities, to supply expertise and support so that an intelligent course of action is followed is again another task for New Work. The fact is that with a knowledge of these available systems and, very crucially, with the support of a network of people like the New Work Associates, the exorbitant sums most of us pay out now could be very greatly reduced.

3. Transportation – Car

Nearly everyone in these training situations has long known the story of our New Work Car. So we do not have to explain that. What we are in a position to say is structurally the same that we can say about housing. Namely, that there are of course a proliferation of small measures with which one can save so as to reduce the size of that item in one's monthly budget, but that these are more or less trifling and do not produce a decisive effect. There is, however, an alternative to this. Just as New Work can facilitate the possibility of building one's own living space in a dramatically different way, so we are also at work on the Car Project and hope that before long a similar alternative will exist there. Here, too, the alternative turns on the further development of new technologies. Still, our goal is to create in the foreseeable future a situation where one could choose to have a New Work Car instead of one that is mass-produced. That would mean that one would have a very high-quality car, but one without the luxurious and infantilizing frills – no pre-warmed seats in the winter. Importantly, it would be a car that one to some degree might have built oneself, that would be incomparably less costly, and that quite possibly might be a car that one drives for a "life time," since the spare-parts for this car could be manufactured individually and with very low expense. Manufactured with the "Generative Manufacturing Machine" or the "Personal Fabricator" that exists in one's own or the next neighborhood.

4. Health

Falling ill has become the nemesis. One serious sickness of one child can ruin a family for life. The costs of health insurance constantly rise, and so does the insurance of physicians to protect against malpractice suits. There are a great number of approaches that when bundled become effective:

(a) Part of the cost is due to high salaries for physicians

and nurses. At the same time these professions are fearfully overworked. A great number who now cannot afford the training clearly want to work in this field (or, would want to work in it if the conditions were saner). Many of these should receive fellowships, just as this should be the case for teachers, so that we would have a profusion of labor instead of a shortage.

(b) This is of course an area where the state should intervene. Monies that are now spent to prop up the tottering Job System should be spent on reducing the cost of health-care. This is part of encouraging the shift from the Job System to HTSP.

(c) It helps to be part of a group that might create its own emergency health fund, that might give support in a crisis and so on.

(d) Technology can also help. To walk into a doctor's office informed, and not as a helpless, desperate infant is possible by informing oneself about everything up to and including the most recent research before one sees the physician. Technology can also amplify preventive medicine through more information.

(e) Deal with the large pharmaceutical corporations very like we propose to deal with the rest. Some breakthroughs have been achieved (cutting the price of drugs for Aids in half in the Third World, partly through generics). There is much more to be done along these lines, so rich opportunities for innovation.

(f) Have access to medical para-professionals in each center, and use the centers for support in all medical matters.

5. *Education*

Early education could be drastically different from what it has been. Young children would spend a great deal of their time in the neighborhood center and would therefore learn in part through participating in the whole spectrum of activities in which their parents are engaged, from raising fish to manufacturing espresso machines, to art, to using computers for the making of clothes, DVDs and so on.) Naturally, there should be life-long universal learning, but how to deal with the expense. Part of the answer here too, is that there exists an enormous pool of gifted people who really, really want to teach! Large numbers of them should receive fellowships. They would be fresher, less jaded, not as preoccupied, not as exhausted as teachers are now. The high expenses for books and materials could be reduced through technology. (Make use of the technology of publishing "books on demand.") As in matters of health: some of the monies that are now spent on desperate measures of support for the Job System should be spent instead on the entire expanse of these educational facilities. Major funding should come from new corporate taxes, and from savings on corporate welfare. (I want to underscore that these improvements in matters of health and of education can be achieved only if we achieve the advances in manufacturing that have been described. We must produce a range of goods in our own small manufacturing shops, so that we can lessen our dependence on the big industries, and only then will we be able to tax them in an equitable fashion.) The same network of foundations who sponsor fellowships for WRRW should also give fellowships for university attendance, and this on a very generous scale. The widespread phenomenon of parents having to remain in a spirit-killing job so as to save for the college education of their children – often from the time the children are 4-years-old – could then stop!

6. Retirement

On the basis of HTSP we can approach this topic in a wholly fresh way. Central to the current state of the matter is for one thing that the security which many pay for during many years of their life is anything but secure. In the USA many thousands have lost their retirement benefits often because their company committed a sequence of frauds. Some additionally went bankrupt because of mismanagement (for example, Enron) or because the stocks and bonds they had bought lost a large part of their value. In many countries, and especially in Germany, the discussion around how these benefits can be curtailed is in full swing.

There also is a different side: New Work has carried out many projects with older people. (We think of them as "ripe" and therefore as juicy and sweet, like fruits and of young people as green and hard, like apples when they are still small.) Many of these "seniors" dread the hollow emptiness which they face, and leaving their jobs is for many of them like falling off the edge of a cliff. To establish a connection with a community center, or Center for New Work and thereby enter into the practice of HTSP is at this juncture safer than depending on one's pension plan. It is also superior in a great number of other ways. The "ripe" woman or man can continue to participate in the myriad activities the center offers. There is no reason to be terminated or to be dismissed. It is in the nature of HTSP (just as it is in the nature of housework) that it is not limited, but infinite. These activities range from spending time with the children of the group, to gardening, to all kinds of art, to teaching, to the making and manufacturing of the products which are emphasized in that center, to much else, and these could naturally be pursued with less time and energy as the person grows older. Again, once the ripe person becomes seriously frail, the horror of banishing him or her into a Home for the Dying need not occur. Both the care of the children and that of the truly elderly are tasks which the group could perform as a whole. In the present condition the pressure of the Job System on many in the younger generation is far too great to allow time and energy for the care of parents who have become frail. That pressure would obviously subside.

There are other fixed costs that could be discussed, but this should suffice as a first sketch. The feasible goal in all of the six categories upon which we have touched is of course not to wholly abolish this concern or this cost. The aim of the New Work approach would be to greatly reduce the coercive power of these costs. In particular to ensure that the fearful apprehension which these items create does not force people to stay within the Job System, when they would prefer to leave.

The media

Frequently I encounter someone who flatteringly explains to me that he is greatly impressed with the battery of factors which New Work has assembled that supposedly all pull our culture toward a major turn. From small-scale methods of manufacturing, to a whole stream of simplified products which facilitate self-providing. Together with a host of projects engaging people ranging from fancy corporations to the seriously poor. In addition the powerful gut-appeal of enabling people to do work that they actually want to do – for seconds one could almost believe that it might actually occur, that is what some of these people say. In reality that is of course fantasy and wishful thinking, they continue. There is not one snowball's chance in the hottest hell that these changes will happen on a major scale. And the reasons for my cynicism are not the financiers, not the chairmen of various boards, not all of the politicians that are for sale. Against those the emerging movements which New Work is attempting to bundle, possibly could prevail. However it will come to nothing, because of the power of the now unified, centralized media. Nothing hopeful could ever occur. The possibilities may be legion and they may be close. One vigorous reach of a hand might be enough. That vigorous reach is exactly what will be prevented.

The really controlling power emanates from the little screen that mesmerizes, hypnotizes and lulls into sleep the great mass of the people. Famously, wars were fought so that one small nation (the English) could permanently drug a far larger people (the Chinese). That is the comparison to bear in mind: in objective terms the structure of the old culture may be a shambles, and enormously exciting new possibilities may be sprouting out of the ground. Yet there is the opium of the media, and as long as nearly everyone gets their daily, regular hit, nothing will change. Sleep will prevail.

My usual first response is that I thoroughly agree. If the media remain as they are now, then no matter how many other forces are trying to pull the ship of our culture into a different direction, that ship will continue to drift exactly as it does now. That is the major pivotal point, as in much else: the technology used by the media in the last few years has developed by leaps and bounds to the point of where a 180-degree turn in their use, and in the control of them could, take place. The situation is oddly parallel to that in manufacturing: There has been the succession of leaps away from the colossal factory to the small intimate Personal Fabricator. Surprisingly, an analogous succession of bounds has happened in the very different world of the media. There, too, new technologies were invented that led away from the massive and centralized toward the individuated and dispersed. It is, therefore, true, there are the Murdochs and there is Fox and CNN, and many cities have become one-newspaper towns, and of course the owners of the big conglomerates are becoming fewer, and the advertisers speak with ever louder voices in the editorial rooms. All that is granted. However, simultaneously a wholly opposed development has also occurred.

Since discussions of that sort happen most often in the context of teaching, I sometimes seize the chance to act out a short monologue: I might say, yes, there are the fortresses of the Business-Job-System, the high-rises in every down-town, towers of international finance and of bureaucratic control, and there are also steel-mills, and oil-refineries, and auto-assembly plants. If any of you throw up your hands in capitulation when you confront these, then I of course disagree, but I understand. In relation to the media, such an action would leave me baffled and very upset. The reason being the excuses that once existed have evaporated in the last few years. Just as in manufacturing, there have been technological advances in this area, advances that bring the media within our reach, in fact they are within inches of switching sides, and of coming to our aid.

I then go on to explain that our present conception of the media is so engraved, so imprinted in our minds, that a patient, piecemeal process is required to break free from these ideas, and build up a juxtaposed view. One fact from which I often begin is that it is now possible, and indeed rather easy, to publish one's own manuscripts thanks to the technology of the internet. Indeed there are now quite a number of colleges in the US, Oberlin College in Ohio is one example, which create an entire information web as part of what they offer to their students. This makes it possible for a sophomore who has a gift for poetry to disseminate the poem that she wrote 2 nights ago to an audience in Asia and Africa. Within 2 days she might get feedback, or criticism, or applause from ten different countries. This is a miniature example of a massive phenomenon. It applies to the distribution of writing, but also of films, videos, music and more. The foundation of this phenomenon is the technology of the internet. There happens to be a whole literature on the early Utopian expectations that many attached to the internet. This, in sharp contrast to these premature hopes, is a straightforward fact. If a school in a remote impoverished Indian village has access to the internet, the children in that school can potentially view everything that has ever been recorded on film, or on video tape, or is included in the collections of one of the world's great libraries. That a great deal has to be done to put this access to use goes without saying. Access is now possible, and this in itself is a transforming accomplishment.

One especially crucial aspect is that the young author at Oberlin College need not wait until she is "discovered." The harrowing process of first having to convince an agent, and then having to please a publisher, who is more likely than not a small piece of a multi-media corporation, whose interests may be totally opposed to those of someone just starting to write, is circumvented in one elegant step. The actual self-publishing of a manuscript, the turning of it into a perhaps splendidly crafted book, requires additional arrangements that might include someone who assists with the design of the cover, and of someone else who does the physical binding. Still, apart from these minor gaps, the entire process can be one's own.

An equally powerful groundswell change has in the last few years occurred in the realm of film. 'It may sound banal, but the most upending innovation in that realm has been simply the cost! The equipment with which one now can make a high-quality video or film costs a small fraction of the price it fetched just years ago. It is also far more user-friendly, much smaller, far easier to use in difficult locations and the result again has been similar: that much is still needed to put this technical possibility to good use need not be said. Still, as with the internet, the potential domino effect of this new situation could clearly be stunning.

The possibility that films which small groups make on a shoestring budget are quite capable of achieving high excellence is no longer a controversial subject. One would have to go no further than to a list of the films that won prizes at the Sundance Film Festival, though one emphatically could go very much further. The number of artistically first rate films made in remote Third World countries has become truly legion. If anyone attempted to argue that the whole machinery of studios with their star-systems is needed to achieve results that are really great, many with gusto would turn the table, and propose that it is exactly the other way round. To create a superb work of art in the corrupting context of the large studios may if anything be more difficult than to do this with one's own improvised crew. Ask anyone with integrity and standards who works for a newspaper, or a television station, or one of the huge media concerns! It is in those contexts that quality is hard to maintain. Meanwhile, we now have the opportunity to create literature and art and works of music, and works of journalism and entertainment that communicate directly with the audience for which we think and write and compose. In addition, we can reach an audience of an unheard of size with an immediacy that no one dreamed of 20 years ago. Many of the woeful complaints are, therefore, self-pity, excuses for lack of talent, and laziness. It would be easy to put together a voluminous list of musicians, artists, journalists and writers who work almost entirely alone and create their own labels, or publishing houses, or website magazines. (Let us create such a list on our website!) The idea that we are utterly helpless and stand by with tied hands while the mass media pour cow-urine into everyone's ears and brains is now a silly and obsolete whimper. We have such possibilities now and this is a very significant change which has occurred in the last 10 or so years.

Just as with books and other texts, some years ago it became possible to burn one's own CDs, and this communicated a symbolic message: CDs are a serious expense, especially in the lives of most young people. To burn one's own CDs is a way around the big music corporations; it is a highly publicized route and has led to a battle now still in progress and still undecided. Napster became notorious almost overnight. Not least because it was the perfect story for our age. A single college kid threw a gauntlet down in front of the giant music corporations. Napster made it possible to get one's music without cost, to get it for free! Of course, Big Business howled loud enough to shake the trees, and in no time the whole world knew about it. Legal smoke- and stink-bombs were let loose from both sides. The battle has raged back and forth and the lines have become unclear. At the present moment a diverse and colorful band of websites make offers very similar to that originally made by Napster, but the final exact outcome, where precisely the cost-lines will be drawn, seems unclear.

Looked at from the perspective of New Work, Napster represents of course a spoof, a send-up, a thumbing of one's nose that should be praised and celebrated, like other giant-slaying deeds. After the applause, a discussion in a different voice needs to ensue. To make the music available for free, for nothing, free for the taking, seems to me like a large and clumsy mistake! It is on the face of it something of a grand, but utopian and foredoomed gesture. It certainly was an exuberant beginning, but there has to be a re-grouping, and re-thinking, and then a new assault. That could start from the recognition that it is not at all obvious that music should be "free." There are people who make it, and it requires talent and a lot of training to create music that is good. Even those who are not street-wise know that on the whole musicians have a hard and up-hill battle in life, though there now are a number of staggeringly rich exceptions. If anyone at all can claim with a straight face that he is creating something of "value," then musicians may have one of the very best and most defensible of claims. (If pleasure or satisfaction is a measure of value, which has certainly been much reiterated in economics, but also in moral theory, then Mozart with his single quill created far more value than any 50 corporations!) Far from not being paid at all for the music they create, musicians should receive more money than the music corporations have allowed to trickle down so far. In one of the Centers for New Work, the one in Asheville, North Carolina, we established a small business with the title "Musician's Gate." Asheville as a town is blessed with an abundance of local musical talent. In the past, many of these fretted their time away on efforts that for the most part were half-hearted, until they gave up and remained undiscovered. Those who succeeded were abused, squeezed dry and exploited. The great corporations forced them to jump through endless rows of hoops, their best art became breathless and exhausted in the process, and then the corporations took the crocodile's share of the profit (usually around 85 percent!).

After that, the musicians were dismissed, and sent back to their village. In contrast, the Musician's Gate was designed to provide a straightforward service. Anyone from the town or the region could come, either with a tape, or a CD, or with a group, or band and could arrange a contract: Musician's Gate would help them to disseminate and broadcast their music, with the help of a website on the internet. If it turned out that people liked the music, then the musicians would receive nearly the whole of the money they had earned. Subtracted from that sum would only be the relatively minor fee (7 percent) for the service which Musician's Gate provided. So that we do not talk at cross-purposes, I must add that nothing hinges on the "originality" or on the success of what that center did. On the contrary, similar efforts are underway in a growing number of communities in many countries. The point is a difference in principle, in the fundamental design. There is no hint of stepping out of the economy of money if one steps through the Musician's Gate. Far from it. The central purpose is precisely to ensure that the musicians *are* paid, and are paid comensurately to the value they create.

Here then is the sharp difference from what Napster tried to do. It aimed at furnishing the music for virtually nothing. Leaving all other questions that could be raised aside, that seems the wrong approach. To put it harshly, the opportunity provided by the technology of the internet was wasted, or at any rate, only half-employed. Half of the opportunity consists of curtailing the exploitation practiced by the corporations. That half was at any rate engaged by Napster. The other more explosive half Napster forgot. It consists of using the technology of the internet to ensure that the musicians who create the music are decently and promptly paid.

We have the technological prerequisites for a turn in the field of the media quite as startling and dramatic as the turn now possible in the very large arena of "making things." How drastic that turn could be is best expressed by saying that "the media" as an "institution," as a distinct "industry," would no longer exist. That, naturally, is how most cultures existed until roughly 120 years ago. The picture that in retrospect might emerge is that soon after the invention of the radio, recorded music, film and TV these means of communication were captured by commercial firms. Advertising played a key role in this usurpation. It was relatively short-lived, and eventually these means were integrated into the everyday natural expressions of the culture. Just as people used to write letters, and played music, or danced simply to express themselves, so many people might film, or broadcast, or tape, or burn CDs. It is evident that in many ways we are already headed in this direction. It certainly would make a great difference to the quality of our lives. The increasing pressures of Job Work have in the last few decades extinguished a great deal. (The "burning of the violins.") That could now be reversed. As a greater number begin to practice HTSP and Job Work recedes, many will again have the energy and time to make use of these technologies and create for themselves thereby a far richer and more attractive life. (One of the functions of the Associates is giving people a sense of the enormous wealth of material that now exists. We are trying to train people to become DJs who could play any song that was ever recorded, or show any movie, or video out of the utterly incredible number that lie in different archives, collections, cellars and libraries. Part of the aim is to wean people away from the monotonous idiot diet to which they are presently accustomed.)

There is, however, another function which is deeper and of greater moment that the centers on this score need to perform. This is the bundling, the combining, the connecting, the integration of the many different strands, all facets of the new, coming culture, all more dispersed, decentralized, less hierarchical, more individuated – and because of that more person-developing, more life-enhancing. It is crucial that they are combined, interconnected, blended together. This has to happen because they only become visible as an alternative once together, access to all of them in one place, only once bundled and unified in and through a center. Only then enough economic difference, difference where one day Job Work and one day HTSP and all of the rest of WRRW becomes possible. Not otherwise and not without this.

In every center there is also a "media-shop" in which those connected to the center can learn about media, and have opportunities to practice and experiment. Beginners are encouraged to make use of the equipment for their own purposes, very much in their own small world, to start with tapes of family celebrations, and videos that tell the story of their own family. People used to write letters as a matter of course, in the same way they should make videos and CDs. One of the functions of the Associates is giving people a sense of the enormous wealth that actually exists. We are trying to train people to become DJs who could play any song that was ever recorded, or show any movie, or video out of the utterly incredible number that lie in different archives, collections, cellars and libraries. Part of the aim is to patiently wean people away from the monotonous idiot diet to which they are presently used.

The corporations

Since the end of the Cold War, our political life has been dominated by "the Business-Job-Nexus." The rapid progress of automation, as well as the introduction of other more efficient procedures of management and production, has created a steadily growing chronic shortage of jobs. Since business is universally perceived as the only source and provider of jobs this has placed the business sector by degrees into a position of nearly absolute power. All political parties have again and again capitulated to this power: in effect we have all acted like the citizens from Calais in Rodin's famous sculpture: wearing sackcloth and ashes and the keys to our cities around our necks we have approached every kind of business, begging them to please, mercifully settle down in our walls so as to bestow upon us the jobs we so desperately require.

All those associated with New Work have pointed it out in countless lectures, seminars and workshops that doing the bidding of Big Business is a hopelessly failing strategy. That in any case Big Business does not create jobs, but on the contrary eliminates them. If at all, then jobs at this point in our development are much more created by small companies. Worse than that: the strategy not only fails, it increases the plight! For in a vast number of cases one can show that funds given over to Big Business were used not to create jobs, but the reverse. They allowed the company to buy new machines which required fewer workers than those employed before.

This horror story can be told more or less starkly, and with smaller or larger embellishments; still one thing is clear. That story by itself, though ever so true, is as ineffectual as tossing dried peas at an onrushing tank. The reason for this is plain: one can shout many times over again that this strategy is not working. People will answer that there is no alternative, that there is nothing else one can do. One has no choice. No other strategy is visible anywhere on the horizon. One therefore slouches forward on this same path, even though one full well knows that it leads one downhill. In short, we are back once more in Hitchcock's locked train. The possibility of an alternative is the axle, or the Archimedean point, around which this whole drama turns.

What renders the Business-Job-Nexus so paralyzing is the fact that it is two-pronged: we need both jobs and also products, and business controls one as well as the other. This is a measure of how dominant the power it holds has become.

This is why New Work has addressed both: the issue of how to create an alternative way to structure work, which would be superior to the organization of it into jobs. Also the issue of an alternative mode of production; of another way of making the products we need for a pleasant and acceptable life, so that we are not dependent on business for these, and cannot be blackmailed by having them withheld. The importance of HTSP lies in part in the fact that our life does not fall into an abyss if a group of businesses announces that unless we oblige they will move to Brazil, or to the Ukraine, or to China. HTSP has put us into the position where we can reply, well and good, go! In a pinch we can make our own refrigerators, and microwave-ovens, and TV sets; and given provocation and time we can also make our own mobile-phones and laptops and cars. Flinging that sort of remark on the table in a moment of empty bravado would obviously be a meaningless and ridiculous gesture. Therefore we demonstrated this in detail and in careful small steps: one manufacturing process after the other, and one product at a time. Having done this we can now say calmly and in full earnest, that we will not yield to extortion; that if some businesses do want to leave then we will not hold them. Far from it. We would be delighted if they went to Greenland, and established their business there deep under the ice.

However, that is still far from enough. Most people have been convinced that there is no alternative ever since 1989, and that is why "taking the media back" in the same sense in which feminists speak of "taking back the night" is politically such an important task. Clearly, lectures, seminars and some books will not change the mindset of the mass of humanity. To bring large numbers of people to the conviction that there really is an alternative will require a throng of videos, films and CDs and also many sites where one can study New Work in depth, similar to the one we are now developing in Emmendingen, near Freiburg. What we face is an immense pedagogical task, and without full use of the media we have no chance of succeeding in it.

The range of topics that such a media-driven re-educational program should potentially address is virtually boundless.

Clearly, each of the issues that we have raised in this book from the pathology of the Job System right to the advantages of small-scale and personal manufacturing should be included. Nonetheless there are two subjects which deserve priority: the first of these is films, videos but also posters and songs that convey how very much we have done to refurbish, buttress, prop up and somehow invigorate the deteriorating Job System. How we have been like a desperate tribe that in desperation brings fruits, sheep and cows but also cart-loads of young virgins, and for that matter young boys and feeble grandmothers to the altar of their angry god. The actual cash payments made to entire caravans of different businesses are only the merest beginning, the tip of the iceberg in this. Even in this most people have not the vaguest idea of the frequency with which such payments are made, and of the size of the sums involved. (On this point New Work is far more in line with "Free Trade" than those who preach this idea. Sick companies would be allowed to die. Saving the jobs would not be the pretext with which great transfusions of cash would be pumped into their dried up veins.) More publicized are the utterly scandalous sums that are doled out to farmers in virtually all Western countries – quite often as a bribe so that they will not plant wheat or potatoes – and also the notorious payments made to some of the old sectors, most notably in Germany and the US, to coal and steel. All of these are still merely part of the tip of this iceberg of money that has been squandered on keeping supposedly sinking jobs afloat. There is no reason not to count as an example the towering tax-cuts that Bush has enacted. Compared to others this is a relatively transparent instance: in this case we are literally talking about trillions spent to stimulate the economy, with the immediate explicit justification that this is being done to create jobs. While these astronomical sums are handed over, most of the country stands by humbly in the posture of the Citizens of Calais. There is much more that an intelligent use of the media could show to be part of the Business-Job-Nexus that has been the scourge of our lives since 1989. The myriad measures that are all herded together under the heading of "creating a business-friendly climate," the huge panoply that stretches from handicapping the unions, to permitting outrageously low minimum wages, to allowing companies infractions of laws that protect the environment, since obedience to these laws would diminish profits, the entire array of these manipulations are all part of that same floating mountain. They, too, are offerings that we place prayerfully on the monstrous altar of business, invariably with the petition that this god may trickle down jobs. So far we have placed only the crudest items into this enumeration: if we decided to move downwards into the subtle, a whole additional realm would come into view: consider the "budget cuts" now even shamelessly called "reforms." Someday the history of this will be written and people's heads will drop onto their chests in dismay. This field is truly enormous: hospitals are organized along corporate lines, physicians are supervised by accountants. Why? Ultimately to make hospitals less expensive so that the government can afford the tax-cuts for business. Same of course with educational institutions from kindergarten up to universities, and of course further downwards from there. The case-loads of social workers are increased, orchestras and theaters are allowed to go bankrupt, museums are closed – in effect a wholesale looting of what formerly was our culture. I have called this the "burning of the violins" because we so clearly are not to be stopped. We will stuff our last treasured family pictures under the kettle of the Job Machine because "there is no alternative," because its wheels at any price somehow must turn!

One task which the newly independent media should try to perform is to convey the sheer mountainous size of the prices we have paid. What would be important here, too, is to come in closely on many details and at the same time portray the big picture, the panoramic context into which each of these details fit. (The example of reports on the contortionist efforts made by a particular city in its campaign to attract one particular plant of one particular company, contrasted with a careful analysis of the precise number of jobs they got in return, was mentioned before. What I am adding now is that the Network of New Work should be brought into play to ensure that these vignettes are interconnected and eventually become a mural-sized tapestry.)

The presentation of this would put exactly one-half of the quintessential New Work-case on the table. The juxtaposed other half would be a confrontation of this with the New Work alternative. The core of what we are saying in regard to the corporations can thus be compressed into one essential contrast: take stock of what you have lavished on business and compare it to the jobs you got in return. In other words, get some idea of the approximate cost of a job. There is of course the basic investment, and virtually everyone knows that the increasing costs of technology are raising this cost every year. We now have some rough sense of the stunning additional payments that have to be put on this scale. Regard this as one side of the equation, and compare it now to the other side.

One way of expressing the point graphically is as a ratio of 1 to 1,000, or even of 1 to 10,000. We propose that with the amount of money that is now paid out for one job, we can assist 1,000 or even 10,000 people up to the level of a pleasant and acceptable life. Spend what you are now spending on one single job on technologies of self-providing instead, and we can help with that same amount a whole neighborhood or a whole village. More likely than not, money will be left over. With the surplus we can fund fellowships that will pay people to do work they really, really want (WRRW). So we can assist them to reach even higher levels than that.

If the media effort in support of New Work develops further then some films and TV shows should put special stress on the implied disclaimer. Our proposition is so limited that one could think of it as a slice, a pittance, a splinter. We are not proposing a Long March across the expanse of China. We are merely suggesting the re-direction of some sums of money. Not more, or new money; but a different channel that will funnel some already spent money into a new direction.

This is true also of our larger posture toward the corporate world. We are miles from any grandiose and bombastic declaration of war. Apart from its being in any case doomed from the start, it would only turn away people who could be our allies. Crucially it would also be utterly out of keeping with the spirit; the "light," the Mozart-like spirit of New Work. If we had been around in Cromwell's time we would have said: "For heaven's sake, don't cut off the king's head. That will only ensure that there will be a Restoration. No. Condemn him to selling ice-cream on a tricycle, instead." Similarly, all we want to bring to an end is the absolute rule of the corporations. The begging, pleading and bribing that has to stop. We are not "against" them. They could become very useful if they were put in their place. We hope to accomplish this by manufacturing the things that we really want ourselves. We do want to be in the position to tell them that they can go to Greenland as soon as they make unreasonable demands. There they can produce all they like, and occasionally we will even buy something from them, but at prices that reflect their marginal and limited position.

Chapter Five

The Structure of the New Work Economy

The first and most fundamental fact about the New Work economy is that everyone without exception will be able to work. They will not by any means only do stone-pounding and spirit extinguishing work, but instead work that will be challenging, self-developing and purposeful. HTSP will be available to everyone and will have much in common with what was best about farming. It will be work that immediately provides for my own sustenance and that of those around me. So it will be meaningful in this very strong sense. At the same time it will exclude what was worst about farming, namely the steady, gradually stupefying exhaustion that comes from laboring from sunup to sundown for years. To participate in HTSP will involve one in a great diversity of activities, which will be requiring judgment as well as taste, and in the process one will acquire a large range of skills.

The academic discipline of economics defined labor throughout its history as an "externality"; as an addendum, as not properly part of the subject, as of no consequence. It seems to me that is its most damning disgrace. New Work takes the exact opposite as its starting point: if there is to be any subject like economics at all, then its most basic concern is naturally the devising of ways in which people can provide for themselves; it is the designing of ways which will give people the opportunity to develop and become full human beings instead of "dead baby's fists." The Centers for New Work will provide the tools, the support and the infrastructure that will introduce anyone who asks instantly, on the first day, to do this kind of work. Hence, the down and out will not only be fed and clothed. HTSP will help them out of the Poverty of their Desire. From the very start they will be on their way to "becoming somebody." They will become confident, more cheerful and strong. We know from thousands of examples that the down and out do change in these ways when they are not only given the opportunity to cut Christmas-tree decorations out of tinsel paper but are instead given the chance to make their own stoves and their own refrigerators. This will be more than the "eradication of poverty." It will be "the rise of the poor." In each center they will have the chance to create for themselves the base for a pleasurable and acceptable life. (They will be making the 38 components needed for this.) They will be on their way up to the base-camp at the foot of the mountain. The climb up higher comes later. They will not all look happy and glowing like all Chinese children on a Chairman Mao poster. Nonetheless, our cities will look very different from now: the slums and shanty towns will disappear. There no longer will be clusters of young men on many intersections, trying to clean windshields, or sell oranges, or chewing gum. There will be no one to wait on us in the public toilets, and the people riding the buses and subways will not look like prisoners who are being transported to their next camp. The constant pressure to push the economy to higher and still higher speeds will not only abate, it will be reversed. For those who need sustenance now have no alternative: they need a job. In the face of the continuously progressing automation, new jobs, therefore, must be forever created. That will change. Many will recognize that they have a choice: gradually they will do less Job Work, and more of the work of HTSP. In short: we will be able to allow the Job System to shrink, because the work of HTSP will expand. It will be like shifting one's weight from one foot to the other: as we take weight away from the Job System, we will place more weight onto HTSP. (HTSP will put a floor under the down and out, and this will narrow the now widening split between the haves and the have-nots. The pressure to grow will cease, meaning that the "burning of the violins," and the ravaging of our natural resources can be brought to an end.)

The lightness of HTSP

The quality of HTSP that we extol beyond all others is the "lightness" of it. For the impulse that originally propelled us onto the pursuit of this idea was the fact that most people are crippled by the excess of drudgery they have to perform. That is the misery that we set out to erase. The root idea was childishly simple: if we have been able to develop technologies that allow us to perform surgical operations at a distance via TV, and to build engines one molecule at a time, and to send rockets to Mars then it is laughable to suppose that we cannot assemble the contraptions that would allow humanity to achieve a moderate, acceptable level of life without work that would maim and stupefy three-quarters of them. Maybe that proposition was worse than laughable, maybe it was perverse and grotesque. Our capacity to produce excess meets us on every side: we pay farmers high sums so that they will not plant their fields, the nightmare of the car industry is that they can produce far more cars than they could hope ever to sell. In spite of the rhetoric of the "free market" we have laws against countries that sell goods too cheaply (we call that "dumping"). The grimmest sign of our capacity to produce excess: we have millions who cannot find work. With these streams of profusion flooding through all the windows and doors, is it not possible to imagine that a moderate level for all can be achieved with a minimal effort, with an effort that corresponds to 6 or 8 hours of work per week?

We decided a long time ago to make the case against this not just in a few general words, but through a step by step process of material demonstration. We identified one technology at a time, fitted each one like a building stone next to the others, until we by now have parts of a configuration: a conjunction of technologies that allow anyone to make the most of the products needed for an acceptable life in very few hours of work per week. Our initial efforts were clumsy and crude. We found systems of building materials with which homeless people could build their own homes, we helped untamed street-kids to grow vegetables and flowers on roofs. Many years later, and on a far more advanced level, we integrated the development of Small Shop Manufacturing, and still later the evolution of Personal Fabrication into our ongoing effort. At this point it has turned into a many-faceted project in which groups of associates in many countries have become involved. They are working on an enormously extended range of different endeavors. They design new products and devices, but also develop new ways to grow food, while they at the same time breed new plants and crops that are especially adapted to Urban Agriculture. (Breeding new crops is of course entirely different from achieving new crops through genetic manipulation.) Not only that, they also search for new possible uses of plentifully existing materials, such as sand. It is an enterprise that could not possibly have existed even 10 years ago, since a global network of hugely diverse people all engaged toward the achievement of one single goal was then still beyond our reach. Still, this is now in the process of formation. The enthusiasm and dedication in this network is probably unparalleled, because there has never been an equally intoxicating and thrilling goal: namely to assemble the technological wherewithal that will enable people to themselves produce all that they need for an acceptable life. (One has to understand how very much this excludes. HTSP is not an attempt to reach the point where everything and anything can be manufactured in small shops, or with Personal Fabricators. Boeing 747s and oil-tankers certainly will never be made in this way, but they are not among the products (the 38) which comprise the base for an acceptable life.)

HTSP for the laptop people

In the present phase the practices of HTSP are spreading most quickly on the two opposite ends of the social spectrum. That it "makes sense" for the 70 or 80 percent who are poor is becoming more evident with every day. It is also sending down roots and growing at the opposite end: among the most advanced, that is, especially among the highly gifted who work in research laboratories, universities and the computer industry. These live in *oasis* all over the world, though there are of course far fewer of them in some very poor countries than in the countries that possess the greatest wealth. In the United States these, by some estimates, are now close to one-quarter of the total workforce.

They are attracted to HTSP for reasons very different from those of the poor. What is decisive in their case is the passion with which they want to pursue their own work. For many of them this is their one most supreme value. The life-experience of virtually all of them is the perpetual subjection to pressures, the unending need to accept prostitute compromises. For them HTSP spells an enormous relief, something close to redemption. For their decision to establish a connection with a Center for New Work and to engage in the practice of HTSP releases them at last from that pressure. It removes the cluster of obstacles that perpetually stand in the way of the one thing they love, which is to pursue the work that they really, really want to do!

To formulate this in still more practical terms: clearly HTSP imposes some sacrifices: it requires some work, though that is challenging, meaningful and diverse. It also requires that one live with simpler, more functional, less luxurious and fancy products. (This will be true right from the Handy and the Espresso machine, to the furniture and the car.) What emerges from this is that for a large number of this group, the burdens and miseries which come with their jobs outweigh the loss of income and luxury which would come from not doing this work. Many, therefore, make a straightforward decision: for material security, for a life-base they choose HTSP and for that they achieve far greater freedom for their work! (As a footnote, to avoid a misunderstanding: many of them of course still earn money with the lectures they give, or the discoveries they make, or the software they write. The difference is the degree of dependence. They no longer receive their sustenance from their work. What they earn with their work is a welcome bonus, an addition, cause for a party or celebration. Again, the similarity to how artists have lived for generations cannot be missed.)

The jet-stream of ideas

Throughout history there have been astonishing bursts of creativity. Very often these occurred because the members of a group were able to work with great freedom at something they very much loved. This may have been the case in Athens, in Renaissance Venice and in Elizabethan England – and oddly, in the early phases of the computer industry. Since the collapse of the "New Economy" many of the most talented have begun to leave the Job System and are now in search of the next thing they want to do. The New Work network of associates connects some of these people across all international borders and offers them the opportunity to work at something they love. We have the hope that this will help to turn the so far sporadic bursts of creativity into an ongoing and permanent jet-stream of new ideas. This would create an enormous forward propulsion, so that regions or countries which adopt a New Work economy would soon be far in advance of countries or regions who do not. That same jet-stream would be also of very great value in reaching the goal of HTSP more quickly than would otherwise be the case.

The Niagara of human energy

In the New Work economy the majority of people will be working between 3 and 5 days a week on something that they really and seriously want to do. What will they accomplish? Many will want to do creative and useful things, which frequently translates into activities that will improve the lot of some group or other. What tasks can be performed with that enormous quantity of human energy? Differently asked, what would be the results if approximately 70 percent of humanity would not pour their strength into the useless grinding of stones as they do so far, but if they instead could perform work that served an intelligent purpose in which they believed.

I would suggest that any effort to describe the upshot of this would be a mistake. It will be a jump perhaps almost as large as the leap from the caves to the first cities. Even the smartest Neanderthal man could never have formed a conception of what the land of the Pharaohs, or Athens, or Greece would be like. We are at a similar point. The birth that is now underway will be as startling for us as that transformation would have been for the creatures who still struck each other's heads with large bones.

The wealth of the New Work culture

Economists sometimes compare societies in terms of the hours needed to earn a pair of shoes or a loaf of bread. The inordinate wealth of a country that had adopted a New Work economy would be demonstrated by the very small amount of time needed for the building of a life-base. At the very most 1 or 2 days a week would be sufficient even in the earliest phase. To discover additional raw materials, and additional ways to manufacture, and still further devices, tools and machines that would reduce this amount still more, till it would descend down to perhaps only some few hours per week, that is one of the visionary tasks in which the Network of New Work Associates is already engaged.

The state and taxes

Many of the traditional and current tasks of the state will be rendered unnecessary. First and most patently of course the whole system of supports for those who are unemployed. If we reach the point where everyone has access to a Center for New Work and can there participate in the rich offerings of various kinds of work, the financing of make-work programs and the distribution of paltry alms will be able to cease. Similarly, with the expensive apparatus of a great portion of what currently constitutes public education. Much of the learning will happen in the context and also the physical rooms of the centers. (This, too, is a subject on which far more information is posted on our website.) The same will be true for the administration and the subsidizing of retirement benefits and rent, since the alternative of doing this through the centers as well will be far superior, and will above all offer far more security than the payments on which older people have depended in the now ending phase. There also will be new tasks for the state to perform; needed above all will be support for the development of the technologies of self-providing, and for the establishment of foundations that could finance WRRW through the awarding of fellowships.

This shift in tasks and obligations will be naturally reflected in an analogous shift in taxation. New Work believes above all in the importance and the value of work. In line with this the details of taxation will be guided by one preeminent rule: no taxes will be levied on any income earned through work, that is, work will be encouraged and the rewards for it will not be cut. The opposite should be the case for all other incomes that are acquired not through work but through other contrivances and machinations. This of course includes incomes from windfalls, from winnings in lotteries, from inheritances but by the same token also incomes made from sitting on real estate, or from the investing in and the holding of shares.

The New Work culture as a whole has two levels. There is first the base. Through the intelligent use of the appropriate technologies the establishing of that base can be reduced to a 1-day-per-week or also a 1-finger task. The base is mandatory for otherwise people starve. Still the base is no more than the foundation; the floor. The ascent into the tall building in which the living of life takes place is not achieved through the work, or the economy of HTSP. That upwards climb is possible only through the work that we really and truly want!

Chapter Six

Discovering the Work We Really, Really Want

The history of New Work has been the history of one protracted conflict. From the very first the question, what is it that you really, really want? was invariably welcomed with acclamations. Certainly, in the early stages this was a surprise to us. The reaction was more avid, hungrier than we ourselves had imagined. It did not seem to matter much in what context we posed our query. In the realm of the business world, whether we were talking to large corporations or to small or medium-sized organizations, they all greeted the notion that we would help people to discover the work that they really, really wanted with immediate, never reserved, applause. The tone was always, why did you not come a month or a year ago? What kept you? Now that you are here, please unpack. The more you can give us of this precious stuff the better we will like it. That first reaction was the same also when we were working with seniors, or with chronically unemployed people, or with "at risk" youth, or in a prison, or with an Indian tribe, or, for that matter, anywhere in the Third World.

That this should happen with business enterprises is of course entirely natural. Why should any manager not be delighted? What more could he possibly ask? To have the people in his plant or in his organization believe that they love their work, that their job is what they really, really want to be doing, that would turn the managerial task into child's play. All the usual difficulties would be wiped off the slate. However, there is already the first indication of the rub, of the conflict or the arm-wrestling that has accompanied us, maybe stalked us at every step we took.

In the case of business enterprises, the problem is patent.

Naturally it has great advantages for the company if the workers believe that they are pursuing their calling, but ultimately the company of course also wants their workers to perform the tasks that benefit the company, which crudely is often the profit line. Certainly, these must not inevitably be juxtaposed, there is room for win-win strategies, but looked at sharply and in cold blood, the result is nearly always at best a compromise: a compromise between what someone RRW, and the pressures of reality, the demands of the objective, material situation.

To tell the truth, we never stopped chafing against this. We resisted and bucked, and never made our peace with that "middle of the road" solution. There were a multitude of reasons for this. One was the philosophical base from which we began. In the version that became popular among New Work groups this was compressed into the adage that you do not give a vegetarian much freedom by giving him the choice between pork and beef; that is, between two options neither one of which he wants. That did set the tone for much that was to come. It laid into the foundations on which we built the arch contrast between a deceptive, misleading, ultimately tricky use of the idea of freedom, and the genuine reality, which for us was always tied to the idea of having the option to act on something that one seriously, deeply and authentically wanted. In other words, we had from the beginning a high stake in taking the notion of "really, really wanting" not loosely and not lightly, but on the contrary, in giving it weight, and in giving it a meaning that we could defend in earnest and that was tight.

The dynamic was similar in the whole very large spectrum of our projects. Whether we were involved with a group of seniors, or chronically unemployed people, or members of an Indian tribe, or for that matter students in one of many different schools: there invariably was the issue, how close to the "really, really wanting" do we in this case actually come? In the background, was always the concern that we were not "doing enough," that we were falling short of our own goal, but also of the claim that we had staked. Which meant that we perpetually reiterated the question: how far from a "vegetarian choice" have we in this or that situation advanced? Were the members of this group, or the students in this school, still merely drifting? Were they only coasting between an array of options for which in the end they did not care very much, so that they merely slouched toward one or the other of them in lethargy or indifference? Had they only shambled in a certain direction but were nonetheless afterwards told that they had had a choice, that they were now responsible for the consequences, because they after all had been free!

To put it in still a different way: we hectored ourselves relentlessly with the question: how far from sham, from mere window-dressing, from the use of the idea of freedom as a bait, as a self-justifying rhetorical platform had we managed to move? How authentic and genuine was our own effort? Had we pushed it as far as the seriousness of what we were trying to do demanded? Were we coming close to something that deserved the word "emancipation," or were we only changing the words or the costumes as countless previous attempts?

This should throw one more shaft of light on the 20 years in which we gradually assembled the wherewithal for the practice of HTSP. In general terms we believed that there could be no end to the compromises, to the half-way houses built out of mutual concessions, until and unless that practice has been attained. In every situation everyone will be compelled to yield to the "necessities," to the "constraints of everyday life" unless we create a new situation in which people will be economically or materially independent. HTSP is a deliberately non-rhetorical, non-ideologically obfuscated synonym for this material independence. Only after that base is in place will people be in a serious sense "free" to do what they really and in earnest want, and not, as is so common, to be content with a toned down and tepid semblance of that. Still more compressed: HTSP is the material prerequisite for freedom: it liberates us to do what we seriously desire to do. Without that foundation, freedom is bound to be less.

This puts the matter abstractly. Let me now also express it very concretely, since the abstract is so often the language of the dead. Consider a woman who is working in a supermarket, who is punching out groceries at a cash-register. You ask her: how do you experience your work? Are you enjoying it or not? Her first response is very likely to be: sure, I am enjoying it. I am dealing with people. It's fun. If you persist, and push and ask again, she is extremely likely to change her tone quite abruptly. She will tell you to leave her alone, and a moment later she might raise her voice and suggest that you get lost.

It is important to understand the superb economic intelligence that is embodied in that response. The boredom, the socially distasteful pressures of her job keep her at the very brink of what she manages to endure. She is in a precarious position, close to the edge. She must hang on to the belief that what she is doing is "fun." If she adds to the weight of what is on her back already the admission that she dislikes it, if she repeats to herself even just once a day that she hates her work, her situation will have become very much worse. Now imagine that she allows more than this to occur: she opens herself up to a series of New Work conversations and in the process discovers how intensely and deeply she loathes her present work, and still beyond this, she forms an idea of what she would seriously like to do instead. The result is apt to be grim. This may be the additional rock – not the straw – that breaks her back. She totters and collapses onto the floor.

Asking the what do you "really, really want" question in earnest, thus entails a risk. One needs to be careful and cautious, or more to the point, one must be prepared to follow through. That is a major part of what we have done from the beginning. Admittedly, never adequately, never to our own satisfaction, but all the same with strenuous efforts. Seen in one light, this has been one reason for our establishing Centers for New Work whenever we could. We wanted to be in a position to say: we are not asking idly. We have a place, here in the neighborhood, which is designed to give you support. We know the risk you are taking by talking to us, we have known this well in advance, and we can be of use to you in the difficulties that lie ahead. Setting up the centers has of course been only one of many things we have done. Very in the same spirit, always against the backdrop of the question: how much is needed to be serious in this? Are we still only dealing in trinkets or not? We also established the Network of New Work Associates. That too was of course not enough. Therefore, we also started to work on the political and the public relations plane. For instance, we tried to soften and maybe erase the absurd prejudices against part-time work, and more recently we also advanced the idea that there should be "Fellowships for the Unemployed." It of course is a fact that what is needed to help people through this transition has no definite borders, but is open-ended. Which meant that we in some centers also assembled data-bases of what new jobs exist, and developed beyond this all manner of connections to local business companies which might offer internships or the like – all this always with the idea that the possibility of doing what one really wanted to do was difficult, and elusive and needed all manner of assistance and support.

We are of course often asked whether we have "a method" or "a recipe" to help people discover what they "really, really want." The answer is neither a simple yes, nor a simple no. We certainly do not have a surefire, four-step catechism that we lay out in every case, but, on the other hand, we do have a very clear idea of a general procedure, of directives and a sequence of phases. In that looser sense we are firmly committed to a first phase for which we have even a name. We call it:
presenting possibilities.

Presenting possibilities

Frequently we do explain half-jokingly at the very beginning that one approach that most certainly does not work is to look intensely into somebody's eyes, and then right at the start ask: "What do you really, really want to do?" My standard little joke is to say that this is very like looking at a person midway in a conversation and saying out of the blue: "Now, say something intelligent!" There is no surer recipe for an absolute, embarrassed silence. It is close to the worst, clumsiest thing one can do. Naturally, the settling down of a dead silence is not always quite literally what occurs. There is the illiterate 16-year-old street-boy who says "I want to be a surgeon," without having the least idea of what the steps to that goal would involve. That street-youngster is the exception. The most typical response, especially if one is asking among the down and out, is: "Any kind of job, I don't care," where that is accompanied by a despondent shrug.

Behind our approach lies not only a long line of experiences, but also one of our central ideas – the idea of the Poverty of Desire. It is a great folly to ask people in this fashion partly because that is in fact how they will respond, but also, more deeply, because they are miles from knowing the answer, and also, and perhaps still more deeply, because that is the exact opposite of what our belief in the Poverty of Desire suggests. To suffer from that poverty means that finding the answer will not be easy, it will require patience and time. That same conviction also predisposes us to be very critical of much that is the standard practice of counselors, coaches and social workers. They talk in encouraging, rosy generalities: "If you only fix firmly in your mind what you want to do, the battle is already half won. Your thoughts have power and can change the world." Or, "You only need to try, to be motivated, to aim high, and you are bound to succeed, to get that job, to come out on top." I must have listened to thousands of such secular sermons. Eventually I made a practice of observing carefully the bodily reactions of the unemployed, or of the at risk youngsters, or of the new-hires that were being addressed. One could easily see how every still more glowing announcement brought their heads yet another notch down; how their despondency grew with every reiteration of just how promising the world they faced really was.

The core of what we have in mind when we say that the presenting of possibilities has to come first lies in the contrast, in the sharp reaction, even in the rebellious revulsion against anything that resembles these mindless ways of talking. The backdrop to our insistence on possibilities is that they must be specific, they must be concrete, above all they must be possible! Which means that they must be in touch with the real world, they must be realizable, and they must be a first step out of the black hole of someone's depression and Poverty of Desire. Maybe it is not presumptuous to claim that some of the examples of our own projects – say, the example of the youngsters in Vancouver, BC who ended up making Bio-Blocks and placed these on the roofs of high-rises, or the example of the youngsters in the maximum security prison who assembled motorcycles – give an idea of how very demanding and inordinately difficult it is to reach the standard that the word "possibilities" is meant to suggest. Which makes it needless to emphasize that we have of course countless times failed, and just as often fell short.

Precisely that difficulty suggests yet another connection to the pursuit of the goal we call HTSP. Think of that goal as a wide, maybe even an enormously extended, "niche." The idea of developing sophisticated and advanced technologies with which one can manufacture impressive and elegant products in small shops not automatically, but instead with a great deal of labor is clearly still in its infancy. At the same time numerous New Work groups have collectively accumulated an inordinate level of expertise in this domain. Beyond that know-how we have also evolved a great number of personal connections, which are indispensable if one wants to advance in this field. Added together this means that along the very long line of this entire frontier we are in a position to suggest genuine "possibilities" and not just glittering bubbles of false hope.

Included among these possibilities are naturally further work on all of the products we listed before, so that the project of developing a generator that can be built in a small village shop largely out of recycled materials, or the idea of building a similar refrigerator, or again the effort to design a safer stove made largely of clay, all of these and of course many more, right up to the so far still unfinished New Work Car, can be presented by us as "possibilities." In our practice we describe these, putting much emphasis on the fact that they are all "endeavors in process" that someone who is searching for something she or he seriously wants to do could consider joining. All of these thus represent an invitation that we extend. Naturally, this applies not only to discrete physical products, but also to the gamut of pedagogical, political and social programs in which we are engaged. One aspiration on which we have only recently begun to work is the idea of re-manufacturing computers out of used, recycled or discarded parts. Since many firms get rid of computers that are still of quite recent vintage, some of these could be of great value in the Third World. However, this is one instance of many where the element of teaching is particularly significant. How to re-assemble, but also how to use these computers, has to be taught. Which in turn means that a large range of teaching tasks are among the "possibilities" which we hold out. From there it is only one step to what we earlier described as our efforts to reduce the "fixed costs." You recall, these include among others the costs for the phone, for insurance, for medicine, for education. Each of these areas again represents a field in which those who want to associate themselves with New Work could conceivably find work which is more meaningful, closer to the level of the talents which they possess than the Job Work which they do now. Again, there are a large variety of political tasks which someone could address here at home. The range of these is particularly large. A very great deal of educational work needs to be done just to explain the pathology of the Job System to the great numbers who still cling to that institution like a drowning person might cling to a tree. It goes without saying that this is equally true for every one of our constructive proposals.

New Work is complex, surprising and hard to grasp. Therefore, an enormous quantity of teaching tasks need to be performed on that score. To spell out in detail the kinds of changes and programs we are trying to foster in countries like South Africa, or Morocco, or India or Kazakstan, even though some of these are still in a quite fledgling state, would greatly enhance the understanding of New Work. So would, of course, detailed explanations of how and in what form Hi-Tech-Self-Providing might eventually be introduced for the down and out in the First World. One indication of how very urgent and numerous the tasks that involve teaching have become is our effort to establish the Center for New Work in Emmendingen, near Freiburg, specifically as a Learning Site.

All of the Centers were from the start intended to be different from one another. There were a host of reasons for this, but one was that they would be able to supplement and complement each other. In that spirit, we are trying to develop the Center in Emmendingen as the one site in which the teaching of New Work in a sequence of seminars will be most emphasized. In Emmendingen the connections between New Work and the growing movement of Alternative Schools, but also the connections between New Work and the many different forms of "Body Work," as well as the concern with a more focused and intensified awareness which includes and extends to meditation will be fostered and taught. This means that the area of these topics, too, can be offered to newcomers as "possibilities" they could consider.

Again, we are in the early stages of establishing a Center

for New Work in Wuppertal. We hope that there will occur some parallel development between that Center and the one in Emmendingen, with the difference that the Wuppertal Center will focus on teaching especially young people the Hi-Tech-Self-Providing use of film, video, music and of course of mixed media along the lines we described before. This, too, in our perception of it, opens up a range of new possibilities. Teaching young people how to act in front of a camera is maybe one of these. As I indicated before, the production of numerous films and TV programs are urgently needed as well. Since our goal in this area is particularly ambitious, and is in the end nothing less than a kind of "taking back of the media," the number of exciting, creative, possible tasks in this domain is quite especially large. Several full-length documentaries about individual people who actually practice New Work have been asked for many times. It is odd, even after long question and answer-sessions, and many detailed explanations, that people who have only participated in some seminars still cannot imagine how a New Work Person actually lives, what they do, especially what the work they really want is actually like. Most especially how they pay their bills. Even if we made as many as 20 separate such films, they would not be useless, it would not be an excess. Similarly all the many aspects within the centers: how decisions are made, how the finances are arranged, what a single day from sunrise to sunset is like, how all the different activities, from manufacturing to theater and sports, to growing food and having children learn, how all of these together with the 15 others all fit under one single roof, many have to see this spelled out slowly on a screen before they feel that they have got it. So there is masses of work to be done with media, just among ourselves. Still this omits what no doubt ultimately will turn out to be the bigger part, namely the explaining of the difficult complexities of New Work for those who have heard about it from far away and are naturally as skeptical as they are curious. We are fortunate to have some of those who are carrying out different aspects or expressions of New Work filming every step of the way so that we may watch, understand and learn. Marcin Jakobowski has been tirelessly recording the ventures of his HTSP prototypes, as well as the groups of participants and some of their processes. There are bound to be others, and the importance of such recording efforts for our future formulation of the New Work economy cannot be underscored enough.

It would be an absurd and laughable misunderstanding to imagine that all of the possibilities we offer are in some way or another connected to New Work. Or worse, that they are limited to possible work that could be turned into a calling, that is, into work that someone might do with extraordinary commitment or passion. We insist strenuously and emphatically and if need be even theatrically that the exact opposite is our practice and intention. When we begin a sequence of conversations with someone and first of all propose possibilities he might consider, we by no means exclude ordinary jobs. Certainly, not arbitrarily, not dogmatically, it all depends. If the person is employed, but we know of better opportunities for him within the Job System we are apt to recommend, to assist, to spread out what information we may have. Our general picture is that our culture is in the process of going through a wrenching and traumatic transition, that if it can be compared at all has its equal only in the transition from agriculture to industry. Given this fact, we think of a Center for New Work as an institution that should offer whatever support and aid might prove useful in this great turbulence to anyone who comes to our doors. That, naturally, requires far more than we have any hope of actually giving, but our attitude is that if we must fail, then we will only do this after our strengths have been exhausted. Therefore, we try our best to keep informed on what old jobs have vanished, and on which new jobs have most recently appeared. Of course, not only this. If a set of conversations take a turn that requires this, then we may also bring in expert consultants that can discuss the latest developments in microbiology or macroeconomics with one of our present or would-be associates. It is important to us that the choice she or he makes is properly informed. Or, to give a different example: among many other things we have spent much time and effort combating the prejudices that surround part-time work. That by itself is for us a large and fertile field. From the beginning we pointed out, especially to the big, multinational companies, that the very best universities give every few years a whole year off to their most productive faculty, and that this pays in countless ways. They are refreshed when they return, they teach with more motivation and in higher spirits, they may even return with one or two new ideas, which is what universities should be about. That is where business with their big bag of antiquated notions about the grit, the high-quality, the seriousness of full-time work should learn from universities. This is not widely known, but one organization located in San Francisco with whom we have co-operated for 20 years calls itself "New Ways to Work," and it is marvelously focused and splendidly organized. Their special forte is to help upper management women to negotiate elegant and fancy contracts and only for part-time work – part-time CEOs and CFOs.

We know of course that this creates impossible demands, but we make an effort not to draw boundaries. We are in an enormous transition, as I mentioned before, comparable to the transition from agriculture to industry, and there is no end to what is useful, urgent, helpful and important. We would much prefer it if some other institution performed these many services. As long as they do not, we will try to fill the gaping hole. Much of this should of course be done by the schools, by career counselors, by people working in "Human Resources," by institutions like the German "Arbeitsaemter," importantly by the labor unions. For years we have tried in different ways to encourage them to take some of this work away from us. So far this is happening only to a small degree, but we are confident that it will soon expand.

It might suggest more of the spirit, the mood, the feel of the actual practice of New Work, and in particular convey a snapshot of how I myself am working (if this is permitted) if I give one more illustration of the degree to which we try to be specific, concrete and hands-on. Quite often I myself have gone so far as to actually travel to the lectures or the seminars I give with a large, cumbersome suitcase. During a workshop I never open that suitcase until after I have in some sketchy way given an impression of "where we are coming from." Some things of course the group would be told when they were invited, but I try to make sure that some of the basic philosophical concepts, such as that work can cripple, but that it also can give life, resonate in the room. Also, before I open my box, I explain that our approach is drastically different from what they might be expecting. Then in small bits and pieces, I try to indicate that we have been working on a grand and ambitious, but to our mind a very basic and commonsense alternative to the economic system in which we now live. Around that time, I open up the trunk next to me, and from then on my plan is to mix the general, somewhat philosophical and visionary ideas with pictures and models and examples and, frankly, numerous toys. The contrast and the interplay between these opposite extremes functions sometimes with real elegance. Nearly all of the photographs, or slides, or actual objects which I show have some connection to one or another of the New Work projects. During the long stretch of 20 years there naturally have been major changes and developments in this regard. One of the most important is the deliberate and continuous shift in the direction of HTSP, but also our movement away from one-person micro-enterprises and toward larger business enterprises, till we are now in the process of bundling all of the business endeavors which deal with the Third World into one comprehensive New Work Enterprise.

While I explain these weighty matters I produce one after

another of the products, or toys I have brought along. All of these are surprising, intelligent, often with a humorous touch, and all are also ecological, simple and rather easy to produce. For a time one of my favorites was a pair of strange looking rubber gloves, that in my long experience no one had ever seen before. A bit in the tone of a magician I would say that these gloves had the power to turn one partially into a duck. Then I would put one on and point out that there now were large black rubber webs between all of my fingers.

Invariably everyone was amused (which is crucially important, especially if one is working with the down and out, who instantly respond with gratitude if anything lifts the gloom of their everyday lives). I would continue and explain that one could paddle much more efficiently with these gloves than with one's bare hands. The point was not only the cheerfulness that trying the glove on generated. Doing this also opened a spate of interesting topics, from why the marketing of these gloves had been so badly bungled that no one had ever heard of them before, to the "stupidity" of the usual fins, worn on one's feet, which are far worse for the small of one's back than these gloves.

At various times I carried in my suitcase devices that had to do with gardening, with painting walls, with shingling roofs, with cooking, also very much with bathrooms, with repairing cars, and more. All of them were, I believe, intriguing, clever gadgets, each ultimately was part of the effort to show that our "possibilities" were not vague, not nebulous, but immediate, graspable and real. Naturally, I produced not only products, things, but also gave reams of descriptions of small, surprising services that New Work had initiated or invented. In this context, I often mentioned that one of our successes was the introduction of a service that was founded on one simple observation: clearly there are some people who are extraordinarily gifted at having full-fledged conversations with 4-year-old children. The misfortune is that often these gifted people are not the parents, with whom every launched topic immediately stalls. What more logical than to arrange for a visiting service for the children of such parents and call it "toddler-talkers"?

It would be hard to count the total of all the different service ideas that I suggested in the hundreds of seminars and workshops I have given. One I do want to mention is the "assembling" of store-bought furniture or contraptions, since it certainly had some connection with the much later idea of self-assembling items that had been produced in Small Shop Manufacturing.

The difference between suffusing a workshop with a generally optimistic mood and presenting in it real-live possibilities is far larger than those who have not tried it are apt to imagine. The quantity of concentrated labor needed for the assessment and collecting of possibilities is surprising. There is no hope of "inventing" such examples under pressure on the spot. Each has to be researched, maybe tested, and then it is still difficult to select out of those the one that is appropriate for this small group, or this individual person. Our aim was to never give the impression of a limit, of an "impossibility" that someone encountered. Our ambition was to have a concrete, workable, positive suggestion, not just for the first question, but for the next question after that, and once more for the skeptical and yet hopeful glance that met our eyes right after that.

In our practice, as we try to perform it, but also as we envision and further plan and develop it, the gradually accumulating mass of possibilities functions like a foundation, like a heavy, thick and steadily solidifying base. One could also say that the totality of these intriguing, intelligent and luminous possibilities envelops us, a little like a sphere of light which travels with us and proves especially useful in the grimmer regions of the world. Quite irrespective of whether we are working with a business enterprise, a government agency, an NGO, an informally gathered group or a single person, we always refer to the greatest spate of possible examples, with the emphasis that these are only some out of a plenitude of pictures, and that many more such possibilities constantly arise and could be mentioned. It is true, we have made an effort to attach this sense of plenitude to New Work, a little as if it were a part of our "brand." Frankly, we do this in part with the hope that we can establish a different sense about the world. Not that it is closed and complete and that only in the rarest and most difficult cases a small new idea can be pressed out. Yet, very different from this, that there are possibilities all around us, like a circle of half-open doors, that a countless number of new developments, new inventions invite all of us to move them further, and that this justifies a different mood different from the hopelessness and the depression that in our culture is so widespread. Our preferred word for that different mental posture is the word "cheerfulness." An overtone that resonates with this is our hope that we are presenting possibilities that represent a staircase, the stepping stones to a more intelligent, more humane, and more sensuous culture, and also that what we offer is closely modeled on the Open Source system in computers. We toss out whatever useful suggestions and proposals we manage to garner, without any claim whatever to our owning them, and we encourage the people who come to us to make their contributions in the same abundant spirit to these accumulating possibilities. There is of course a further reason that for us is more stringent and has greater weight. The profusion, the ring of plenitude we try to create is also a necessity. It is a requirement if our effort is not to be as fatuous as the long line of efforts at liberation have so far been. The presentation of these possibilities is in our conception a foundation, a beginning, a first start. We know that we of course fall short, but also know the difference between a vegetarian choice, and the possibility to pursue an option that one after scrutiny desires, and the first step must be a breaking down of walls. If those with whom we work remain in their sense of confinement they will only slouch in the direction of least resistance; they will yield to the barest breeze of their tepid whim and drift toward the mooring which seems most convenient. They must experience an open space, a plenitude at the beginning, otherwise they will not even try; they will not even try to discover what they really, really want.

Facilitating explorations

If great portions of one's organism have grown cold and rigid, and are only barely still in motion, then it is most unlikely that there will be even one small spot of genuine passion, not to speak of a capacity for ecstasy. In almost every case the entire person must become more vigorous, must rise onto their toes, to seriously want. Therefore, our undertaking is anything but a diving down as far as one's breath will permit, and finding there amid the seaweed the golden goblet of what one ultimately wants. It is a comprehensive, step by step, arduous, painstaking ascent. The second stage, after the presenting of possibilities, is hence often a little like rubbing with snow someone who fell asleep out in the cold, so as to re-start the circulation in his frostbitten limbs.

Different people find extraordinarily various activities helpful in this phase. Some of my own favorites are sport, preferably sport that involves some risk and an element of having to fall back on unused resources inside oneself: rock-climbing, skateboarding, boxing, for example. Also dancing, theater, music, most any art can have a strengthening effect. So can of course public speaking and debate, and needless to say, there are no end of games. One quick anecdote might illustrate the diversity of what can and has been used. At one point, I worked with a group of young Wall Street bankers in New York. Upper management found them wanting in initiative, flamboyance, grit and chutzpah, and therefore a happening had to be invented. What we eventually devised borrowed heavily from "Outward Bound." The young bankers had to disguise themselves, so they could pass as homeless people. Then they were dropped off in one of the more difficult parts of New York City, without money or other resources. The assignment was to survive for 3 days until they would be picked up at the same corner.

These are preliminaries, calisthenics, aerobics for the spirit, literally, warm-up exercises. Included among these explorations are of course also individual and group counseling, but also experiential exercises, a large variety of games, but also meditation, yoga, dance, both "therapeutic dance" and "therapeutic music," as well as theater. Also practices that teach one to focus one's attention on one's body, or on the present moment, and with special emphasis exercises that develop one's capacity to seriously listen to another person. To turn one's full attention on a friend or a stranger who sits across the table from them is essential for facilitating exploration of the self. Again, we introduce people to some of the "instruments" or questionnaires that fit one's character into a set of "norms," and on that basis give one insight into their overall personality "type."

In our culture there exists at the present time an almost limitless variety of such devices, practices and approaches. For our purposes it is of no great consequence which out of this multitude are selected by this or that center. Far more important from our point of view is that the Associates who come to us realize that there literally is no part, or aspect, or dimension of them – but, emphatically also of any human being – that cannot be trained or developed in a myriad of different ways. In my own experience I find comparisons to the awesome skill involved in being a true virtuoso on the violin, or a truly great ice-skater useful, as a way of pointing out just how enormous the gap can be between a normal, average performance and the abilities and skills that persistent, concentrated exercise is able to achieve.

Clearly, many additional practices could be enumerated. However, the one most crucial point in regard to New Work can be enunciated in plain words: indeed, we do explore all of these exercises and naturally many more. So this is part of what we do. Nonetheless, what is most characteristic of New Work is that we treat all of these as mere preliminaries. They are stepping stones toward finding and performing the work that someone really wants. As such they serve a function, but we are deeply impressed with the awesome difficulty of changing or improving or helping people and on that score our view is firm. Years of experience has convinced us that the singular work that one feels to be one's calling is far more trans-formative and far more vitalizing than ever so many other paths and cures offered in our culture. A mild reserve, a gentle assigning of all these practices to their propaedeutic place is thus the other side of the special status that we assign to work which someone really wants to do.

That conviction we already held even when we established the first center in Flint, Mich. We made a great many different efforts to establish within that center a "Room of Possibilities." To make that sort of room one of the key resources in every center was from then on always one of our aims, though the realization much of the time fell far short of what we strove for. The intention, all along, however, was very clear: we wanted to make available to the people who came to us the wherewithal for a quite inordinate number of experiments, and tests, models and examples from which they could learn through observation, but on which they could also work with their own hands. Our goal was from the beginning to provide a large and airy and wide open space with books and tapes and slides, and also placards and reports and blueprints and also photographs. New technologies, like Small Shop Manufacturing or early versions of the Personal Fabricator, would be demonstrated at least on models, but there would also be exemplifications of the technologies and products that New Work was trying to perfect and to introduce in countries like India or South Africa. In addition, there would also be videos and graphs on problem areas, on situations that were in crisis, together with pamphlets or fliers on who was addressing these, and what sort of help was urgently required.

Beyond this there would be a display of "hopeful starts," of technologies in which New Work took a special interest since there were indications that one or another of them had surprising and sometimes astonishing potential to surmount problems that hitherto had seemed unconquerable. The Stirling Engine, thin solar technology, our fabled water filter were among these. Joined to these would be graphs and videos and models of possible scenarios, detailed and scrutinized step by step progressions that would show how the ascent toward a solution could be achieved. One corner of this large room, or a separate smaller space would be dedicated to "Comprehensive Scenarios." These had all some distant or closer relationship to New Work and would delineate what series of steps would lead not just to a cleaner environment, or to better health, or to less injustice, or to a more intelligent Work System; they would be attempts to picture possible paths toward an encompassing better form of life, to an entire new and greatly improved culture.

One crucial function of these Rooms of Possibilities was to exhibit and to explain the evolving technologies of self-providing. Here one would be able to inspect the cutting edge of the amazing recent discoveries and developments which have strengthened the idea of moving in the direction of HTSP. One would be able to see just how far the Personal Fabricator at this point in time has managed to advance. How close to being able to make one's own shoes, or one's own microwave-oven that technology had come.

The entire history of New Work, and in particular the idea of HTSP, is wholly misconstrued if the very great extent to which we have been fortunate is not underscored three times. The history of HTSP is quite like Anderson's tale of the ugly duckling: this duckling might have remained quite gray, and it might even have died from neglect if a spate of developments had not occurred. These technological advances range all the way from the invention of the computer itself, via Small Shop Manufacturing, to the Personal Fabricator, together with all the smaller steps that happened in between. Part of the purpose of a Room of Possibilities is to give instruction in these technologies. How their diffusion fits together into the possibility of genuine economic independence should be underscored, and there also should be constant encouragement to develop one or another piece a few steps further. HTSP is above all a project! It is emphatically not yet finished or complete and not at a stage where it can be sold across a counter like a hand-full of screws. New participants, new ideas, new contributions should be constantly invited!

A Room of Possibilities is also specifically intended to be a response to skepticism and indifference and all other shadings of detachment and ennui. The difference between actually seeing and experiencing how something is made, compared to merely hearing a description of it, is like night and day. Hence it is preferable that there are life-sized models of products, or technologies, or social strategies on which New Work is working. In my experience only a very concrete and sustained experience is here of genuine use. Once folks have seen that this particular kind of furniture can be made in a center in this highly automated way, or that this kind of clothing, or this kind of electronic device, right up to the self-assembled car, can be in large part made with their own hands, they are often far more convinced of the reality of that possibility than before.

This emphasis on a Room of Possibilities in which there are particular "models" goes hand in hand with a pronounced skepticism in regard to introspection. The attempt to determine what one really wants to do through a mere look into one's internal space, peers much of the time through an extremely dark and miserably distorting glass. This applies quite especially to work. Looking with furrowed brow into one's inmost soul is mostly useless. One week, one day of doing the work makes here all the difference. One could suggest that the fact that the Job System makes no provisions for this "trying out" should be added to the list of the pathologies of the Job System. Despite much of the excited hubbub about the rampant flexibility of work, the Job System in reality fails miserably on this score.

The majority of people still divide their life into a long preliminary period in which they learn and do not work, followed by the main and middle part in which many merely work, with all learning put on hold. Even if the Job System were acceptable in other ways, that one defect should be enough to make us close the doors on it. Clearly, there should be a mixture of work and learning from start to finish. Children, who in the earliest years are far more intelligent than grownups later are (observe how rapidly children acquire language), need to experiment with things they make and do and fashion and pursue. Whether we name this work or play is immaterial. What is crucial is that they should not be forced to have recourse only to the half-blind eyes of introspection, but should see and learn with their other, external and superior eyes.

Many people seem to assume that the discovery of what one RRW is abrupt and final. In one inspired moment one hits upon it, and that settles the matter more or less for the rest of one's whole life. Nothing could be more violently contrary to the entire general picture of our practice. We invariably stress the very gradual development of the self in any number of contexts, and go out of our way to lampoon all quick-fix expectations. I, personally, often say that finding what one wants is nothing like finding a lost green tennis ball concealed underneath a bush. It is a process of many fits and starts and setbacks and revisions. Above all it requires the chance to experiment. To reiterate: the absence of this opportunity to try out and to reject is another major disease of the Job System. That one cannot experiment with a spectrum of different kinds of work is irrational and fearfully destructive, and more particularly that one cannot try out what one is learning in the process of one's education seems like an utterly debilitating handicap. It is not uncommon that someone spends 4 years in law-school, and at the long laborious end of it discovers in the first 5 weeks of practice that he thoroughly dislikes the work, and that the costly preparation was largely wasted.

What happens is, therefore, like much else in New Work, deliberately interactive. Not one, but 50 different suggestions are put forth. If one finds favor, instantly all the searchlights are turned on. Every conceivable skeptical question is encouraged, and a painstaking assessment is performed. During this, all manner of practical questions are naturally pursued, but periodically the group returns to the central issue: is this something we want to do or not? Frequently one endeavor is begun, and after a stretch rejected after all. Which again underscores the essential point, namely, that throughout the process one confronts the fact of the poverty of one's desire. It is crucial that this should be understood as a common difficulty, which we all share; that it is like regaining consciousness after falling down into a well. The assignment is to manage somehow with whatever is at hand to work one's way out of that black hole.

In line with this whole general spirit the "exact fit" does not matter very much. The idea is not that whatever has now been dug up from under seven layers of gravel and garbage must dovetail smoothly with this or that possibility before you. The decision is in any case not final. Everything changes and evolves. Spending weeks rummaging inside oneself in the expectation of a perfect Cinderella glass-slipper fit mostly turns out to have been a waste of time. Meanwhile the foot has changed. What is far more practical and productive is an enormously expanded knowledge, but also all manner of experiments with the kinds of shoes (besides glass-slippers) that are out there, that is, knowledge and experience with the myriad work possibilities that could be conceived and created and organized, particularly if we broke out of the constraints, out of the bewitched stable of the Job System.

We stress that there will be time and opportunity to change one's mind, that mistakes can be corrected. That one begins is all-important. That one gets into the habit of asking oneself not just relative to work but relative to virtually anything: is this a jacket that I really want, or do I wear it out of laziness, or fear? What about this TV show that I am watching? Am I allowing someone to pour cow's urine into my head through my own eyes or ears, or does it give me pleasure? What of this person? Is this relationship a slumming that I permit myself? What of this goal that I have been pursuing for some time? Am I a wind-up toy? Has someone tightened a metal spring inside my belly, so that I now walk like a little soldier made of tin, or is this a goal of which I could say: "Here I stand. I cannot do otherwise. God help me. Amen." In the earlier section on the Polarity of Work we described two key examples. Both the example of the woman rescuing her son and that of the villagers struggling against the Mississippi involve a nexus. Between two things, between a person and a set of external circumstances, a high tension came into being, in fact a whole field of forces. No internal machination was performed, no knot was untied, no kink straightened. No, an unexpected fact reached out from the outside and exerted a powerful pull upon the person.

To the extent to which the mild offering of guidance does occur, the suggestion is often made that one should go out and wander, like apprentices did for centuries. Individuals and groups are gently but continuously encouraged to explore and experiment, especially to expose themselves to different configurations of external circumstances and then to observe. We do say: observe carefully, because you do not know. Try to determine which of many possibilities has the greatest power over you, which confrontation evokes in you the most powerful surge of strength? That was the cardinal point of these two examples. Observe yourself with these examples in your mind, and ask: which of these possibilities exerts on me the greatest pull? What, on the analogy of a magnet, or an electric field, will draw more energy out of me than other alternatives in view? This results in a process quite different from that associated with introspection, and ultimately it results in different actions. That also matches the logic embodied in the Rooms of Possibilities. Naturally, conversations, counseling, the discussion of emotions do occur. What we try for at the outset is an exploration, an assessment of the reality, of the objective situation in which someone is. That someone is not motivated by any of the things that she hitherto had a chance to try may be entirely appropriate and sane. Most of the fare the Job System has to offer, even people with good stomachs would not want to eat. However, the Job System draws too small a circle. If we look at the larger whole, we can see much rot and mildew, much that is foul and smells to high heaven. Why should it be surprising that very many people, and particularly young people who are not yet trapped, want distance and no part of it?

Goals worth pursuing are in our world extremely hard to find. This is a perspective which reminds me of several hospitals I visited in the Third World. The beds are filled with people who suffer from ghastly, dangerous afflictions, and the physicians have not a single injection, no sutures with which to close a wound, not even food. Helpless, they walk from bed to bed. It may be harsh to say, but there seems to me to be some resemblance between these physicians and ever so many counselors and coaches who suggest careers and jobs and try to motivate. They have no medicine, no tools, no food. They walk from bed to bed, or chair to chair and smile.

That is one way of seeing what a Room of Possibilities is for: it is not just one chest of resources and tools, it is five full rooms of them. It should create the situation where one can say: let me take a look at this right over here. Aha. I see. Here we have something that has worked well in similar cases. Why don't you give it a try?

Being of use in the discovery of what someone really wants is for us partly a matter of persistence, of relentlessness, of not giving up. We try, we match, we put together; this person with that configuration, with that object, with that external set of facts. Until, even if it is exhausting, and it has taken weeks or months, we find that now at last there is a tension, a force, a crackling electricity between this person or this group and the object or the goal that is now in front of them.

Quite often we gently hint that probing around in one's insides, trying to smooth out this or that tissue, or repairing here or there the flow of an internal artery makes matters worse. The reason for one's indifference or laxity may not lie in one's own constitution, but in the facts of one's situation. Perhaps we mean the word "possibilities" more literally than some suppose. Of course, the intention is to inspire and to excite, but the alternative possibilities must be quite real, and practical, and the more of them we can arrange, the better. To put it as succinctly as I can: the bottom line is often, change what you are doing. The problem is not in your head, is not in your lack of motivation, not in the weakness of your appetites. The problem is in your work. Survey the array that we are spreading out before you and then try to choose. And try to do something different from what you are doing now, do something else!

Self-ignorance

The fact that we have a surprisingly weak relationship to our desires is one main foundation on which a great deal of both the praxis and the thinking of New Work rests. But the Poverty of our Desires is a confined and bordered syndrome. One could make the comparison between a blind-spot and a much larger, more widespread visual deficiency. That wider incapacity, more of an affliction than that specific poverty, is our "self-ignorance," the strange bedeviled difficulty we have when it comes to knowing *ourselves*! This is not a reference to Freud. Freud's idea was actually rather mild. That the mechanism of repression protects the ego against knowledge that would be upsetting to the ego's equilibrium, seems like a reasonable, beneficent arrangement; very what one would expect in a psychology that walks in the footprints made by evolutionary theory a large span of time ago. The conception of self-ignorance that is important for New Work is far crasser, a great deal darker and distinctly more offensive.

To give a first example: we are ignorant not only of our subterranean desires, we often do not even know the very shape, the contour of the body we call our own. Great numbers force themselves to go on a diet, but are uncertain, in suspense. They wait. Finally they do meet someone from whom they have been separated for a time, and the moment that person says "you look thinner" they experience a rush of intense relief. Similarly, it is shocking for many people when they are for the first time told that they indeed have something of a belly. It is perhaps still more scandalous, with our own emotions. A close friend scrutinizes our face and tells us that we look depressed. It is not uncommon for someone to respond: "Really? Do I look that way to you? I think I am fine." And then to walk over to a mirror, and to return with the verdict: "You may be right. And now that I have seen my face, I worry. I certainly look tired and not well."

An instance of our self-ignorance that to my mind is even more extreme manifests itself sometimes in clothing stores. Frequently we do not even know in what outfits we look ridiculous, and which colors suit us. Somebody who is looking at us for the very first time can judge this far better than we ourselves. The sales lady helps me into a thin, black, loose-hanging coat and says, "That is you!" What an astounding feat of knowing. I have lived with myself all these years and cannot tell, and she has spent 5 minutes and she can! Because of our self-ignorance we stumble, like Oedipus, lost in our inner landscape. We are like a botched biological mutation. There are stories about the astounding noses of dogs, and about the incredible vision of owls at night, and there are utterly stunning facts as, for instance, that salmons can return to their spawning grounds, and that monarch butterflies even in the course of several generations find their way to one and the same Mexican mountain valley. Our capacity to know the distant worlds of the galaxy or the molecule, also the world around us and especially other people is of course even more stunning, and more amazing, and still more awesome. (From which it follows that skepticism, despite the eminence of its historical tradition, was an unbelievably long barking up the wrong tree. Cf. my lectures: "Thinking One's Way out of the Disease of Postmodernism." Delivered 1998, unpublished.)

However, it is as if our eyes were encased in antlers that reach 3 yards straight ahead out of our forehead. No matter how we turn our neck, with our eyes so set in bone, we can see what is in front of us marvelously well, but it is physiologically impossible for us to catch a glimpse of ourselves. That weird handicap, that grotesque affliction: the fact that, as if out of spite, we cannot know the one point in the whole world most important for us though we were given permission to know all else.

Thus, our self-ignorance is only one-half of the picture, and this is of cardinal importance for New Work. The other half is that we have a phenomenal and marvelously perspicacious knowledge of other people and of ever so much else in the outside world. Which means that our engagements, or encounters with other people are fundamentally, in their deep structure, awesome and wildly asymmetrical. We face each other. Both you and I are in the dark about ourselves. I know that you with your eyes can see much more clearly what I am, than I can myself, and that is equally true for you. You sit, and you feel known by me. That creates with one single flash the most astonishingly bonded mutuality between us. When it comes to yourself, you are lost, but I have the pair of eyes with which you could come to know yourself, and the other way round. You have the pair of eyes with which I could begin to see myself. Thus, we need each other in the most categorical of ways. We are so connected, one could also imagine that we are like one single complex organism that has four eyes.

The unheard of intensity of that mutuality is the subject of the ten most celebrated pages Hegel wrote in his life (the chapter on "Master and Slave" in *The Phenomenology of the Spirit*. The ideas it expressed play a central role in Sartre's *Being and Nothingness*, and also in Simone de Beaver's *Second Sex)* and in a vast literature beyond this. See, perhaps also, my paper on "Sudden Encounters" Inquiry, June 1978, and my lectures "Thinking One's Way Out of the Disease of Postmodernism," delivered 1998, unpublished. (A philosophical aside: the contentions that I have just summarized amount to a wholesale inversion of Descartes. Descartes' central idea is turned inside out: the ego is anything but "clearly and distinctly known," and it has no claim whatever on being the foundation and the base. Far from it. We are born without a self, and must build and acquire our selves as we go through life.)

As a rule, and in an ultimate and deep way, other people thus know us more quickly and more accurately than we know ourselves. That is not an esoteric fact, and in no way mysterious. It is common, ordinary and virtually universal. To the degree to which it is the case, each one of us can tell the other things about herself which she does not know. We can do this without any unusual methods or procedures. You can see that I am angry, I can see that you are sad. One could say that in this regard the basic human situation is downright weird. Perhaps, it is also wonderful. What I am describing is anything but new. It is part of a long-standing, deep-rooted and widespread tradition. In fact, the idea that we are horribly ignorant of ourselves goes back to the Greeks. *Oedipus Rex* is a play about a king who does not even know the most momentous things about himself, not even that he killed his own father and then married his own mother. How much more lost inside one's own life could one be? That is the reason for the dictum: know thyself! If we had sun-clear utter knowledge of ourselves from the moment of our birth, then this would be the most ludicrously superfluous advice!

If one accepts our self-ignorance as an obtrusive and stark fact, and comes gradually to see how that affliction holds us at a ghastly distance even from the most vital information about ourselves then an avid curiosity is of course the inescapable result. It is unbearable to be so deeply in the dark. Especially about something so important. It is far worse than being lost in fog at sea, for we feel pushed and driven by forces inside ourselves that come at us from utterly unfathomable places. This means that the tension during some exercises that mean to show an aspect of the self is very much higher in New Work groups than in most normal average workshops. It also means that there are sometimes escalations that lead from one startling surprise about oneself to others that are still more dumbfounding and baffling than the first. Our self-ignorance, however, also means that a skepticism about whatever is revealed to us through introspection or through mental exercises is justified, and this, too, is characteristic of how people associated with New Work respond to a range of practices. The natural other side of that mistrust is a turn toward, or a greater reliance on, the external senses and the external world. This posture of New Work could be connected to the famous dictum of Goethe's that you must leave yourself behind and go into the world if you want to come to know yourself. Not surprisingly that turn is still further emphasized by the other member of our concept pair: if our perspicacity in regard to others really is amazing, and if this means that others seeing us from the outside are sometimes uncannily perceptive about who and what we are, then we have every reason to fix our full attention upon them. That, too, is much encouraged in the New Work groups. Against the background of the juxtaposition of our ignorance in one and our perspicacity in the other direction the turning of our full and absolute attention on what others say and do, and the discipline of acquiring a honed and trained capacity for listening, for grasping every nuance of what they say, becomes one key endeavor.

The effect this has on the level of any number of individual customary efforts can be easily imagined. Deeply probing introspective questions do not play a major role. In my experience attempts to recall the subtleties of childhood fears, or anxieties, or attachments are of very little use in the discovery of what now in the present could be one's calling. In vivid contrast to this, there are some "games" that are emphatically external in their focus and in their attention and I believe that this occupation with the outside explains their popularity in the contexts of New Work.

One much discussed and perhaps especially illuminating instance of this is a practice that we call "Brilliances and Stupidities." The thought is that everything in everyday life can be categorized in one of these two ways. A favorite example of a brilliance is a fitted sheet: a sheet in which the corners are sewn in. If you have to change the sheet under a patient who is lying in a coma, and who must be turned, you quickly learn to appreciate the full brilliance of this invention. Conversely, garlic presses for the most part are stupidities. Why? Because one spends as much time and effort cleaning them as one saves in pressing garlic through them.

Could one invent a garlic press that would not be a stupidity? A press to which the first reaction would be: "Ah! At last how intelligent, spare and minimal, and stunningly superb!" Only one more, out of a hundred possible examples: having five lines of people waiting in front of five ticket windows is a stupidity. One is always in the one line that does not move, and as soon as one changes into the next neighboring line, that one mysteriously freezes in place. The brilliant response to this stupidity, we all know: it is one long line, where the front-person is always called to the one window that a moment before became vacant. Occasionally we do ask people to examine a kitchen or a bathroom and to locate their brilliances and stupidities. The instruction is to please come back with two of each. Spotting stupidities gives an enormous boost to one's self-confidence, but it does much else. The other side of a stupidity can easily be a first venture into the realm of the imagination, a first attempt to fly with wings that one so far has not tried.

Naturally, there are no end of questions that in the context of these conversations get often asked. Some of these are questions about preferences, talents and the like. Others are questions about experiences one has had, tasks one has performed, jobs one hated or enjoyed. One general impression in New Work groups is that many of the people who come to us have been asked these same questions numerous times before. Inevitably there are some who clearly enjoy addressing them, but on the whole we are somewhat dubious about what such questions help to reveal. To produce surprises, to confront questions that one has never come across before, to explore fresh territory seems to us more productive than the standard fare of normal seminars.

The return to the simple question

An oddity occurs both in our work and also in our lives. Despite our determined hostility to all forms of bureaucracy something of an apparatus has inescapably evolved around New Work in its 20-year-long history. To that machinery belongs the centers, but of course also the store of games and practices that I have just described. The oddity is that we fairly often shed all of this machinery and return, so to say tc our origin. That is, we ask without all embroidery, straightforwardly and directly our pivotal question: what is it that you really, really want to do? The extraordinary power of that question was a great surprise to us, right from the start when we first began to pose it to the automobile workers in Flint. Through all the years that force seems not to have in any way diminished, but from the first beginnings the sheer impact of it was for us more than a surprise. It was a puzzle, and something that for us was hard to believe. Many times over, muscular men, whose bodies were covered with hair and with tattoos, whose feet seemed to be planted sturdily on the ground burst into tears when we asked them this. More times than I can count, they explained that this was the exact reversal of what their experience had been so far. Their parents, their teachers, even morality and religion always had insisted that what they wanted needed to be held in check and controlled; it represented a danger and much was done to guard against it, to weaken and tame it. Inevitably, whatever they really, really wanted became ever more distant, ever more remote and inaccessible to them. Like ever so many others, they developed a double bottom. On one level was what they more of less in a half-hearted way sort of wanted, and far underneath was something radically different, far more stark and basic. It was utterly obscure and hidden, and yet they knew that they wanted it in truth, and seriously, and with their blood. And for that very reason their reaction could not have been more energetic and direct: Yes! Of course they wanted to know what they really wanted. And today would be far better than tomorrow.

So periodically we put all else aside, and ask without all circumstance and in a calm and plain and at the same confrontational mode that simple question, in those very words. It has stayed with us during the whole duration of our lengthy journey because it does have an astonishing capacity to give direction, and to focus people. Quite alone, without technique, without the philosophical framework of the Poverty of Desire or of self-ignorance, simply, and so to say with its bare hands that question instantly calms and centers a person, settles her or him back, and returns them to their own being. Our whole history is a tale of testimonials to that effect. It does not seem to matter what at any given moment is addressed. It can be the most everyday decision. Do I really want these shoes, this coat or this umbrella? It can also be the question: what is the one, the single aim or goal, the one accomplishment that you in utter seriousness, more than all else, want to achieve? The reactions seem remarkably alike. Always a near explosion of euphoria and relief. At last, at long last, it is my turn to be asked. And in the same instantaneous breath: I want to know! Yes, yes, what is it that I really want? It may strike you, the reader, as outrageous, or harsh, or arrogant, but what follows now is not euphoria and celebration and congratulations all around. Sadly and unfortunately not. Our experience is that even after this, and even after this has happened many times a great deal of stony territory still has to be crossed. If I were asked to make a list of the five or six qualities that seem to me most characteristic of New Work then a pronounced reserve, a skepticism, above all the knowledge that things take time, that nothing marvelous ever was accomplished in a quick revolution of a mere 7 days, would be on that list. It is hugely, dauntingly difficult to change any part of one's person or one's life, and when we work with people then we aim excruciatingly high: we truly want the person to reach the point where he or she indeed does follow her own desires. In the vast majority of cases great labors still must be performed before we are even inside the ball-park of that goal.

Facing the fact that we are only half alive

The individually attuned, spontaneously evolving process of a particular set of New Work conversations is punctuated by the oft repeated return to the asking of our most basic question. Despite the variations there also is a roughly followed structure. What is frequently surprising for many who come to us is that I put a great deal of weight onto the introduction of yet another philosophic concept. What is more, much of the time I go out of my way to put this forward quite impersonally, with no intimacy whatsoever, in a deliberately philosophical and distant tone. Also, this idea does not go away, it stays there. Reference is made to it repeatedly in irregular intervals, and gradually it evolves into one of the main categories of the framework of our thinking: it is the concept of the not-lived-life!

I explain in every case that it follows upon the Poverty of Desire and self-ignorance as a third idea in what amounts to a cumulative progression: it is more inclusively, more dramatic, a natural further step that follows through on these earlier ideas. All three contribute to a foundational conception of human nature that is sharply and dramatically different from the axioms upon which the old constraining culture was erected. I should emphasize one more time that through the entire length of the attempts to translate the New Work ideas into practice, I have been surprised by the eagerness, the avid appetite with which the precisely "plain" and "normal" people involved in the New Work projects insisted on discussions and explanations of these philosophical ideas. Often times I made genuine efforts to avoid this. Sometimes I even would purposefully participate in a particularly practical and hands-on activity. Since I had experience in these matters, I would lay bricks, or do carpentry, or help in the repairing of a machine and so on. Invariably someone would point out to me in a friendly fashion that for an amateur this was pretty decent work, but that it sincerely was not what they wanted from me. They needed me for the ideas, for the sense of purpose they got from New Work, for the knowledge of how the many pieces fitted together into an overview.

This was especially true of the kind of people that we sometimes call condescendingly "simple," or "uneducated." I could tell anecdotes for many hours on how precious and significant even very abstract ideas are precisely for such people; with how much reverence they respond to them, and how much weight and significance they ascribe to them. The sharp and to my mind embarrassing contrast here is to intellectuals and academics, and perhaps singularly to the members of my own guild, to professional philosophers. In those circles, in which I have spent much of my life, one is far more cynical about ideas. One treats conceptions much more readily as toys, as constructions with which one plays games, which one juggles as if they were balls or plates. What has impressed me many times is the gravity that many often semi-literate people attach to the objects in that world. One has to remember what incredible sacrifices always and again the "lower classes" have made in all manner of crusades and wars. Of course not always for the noblest ends, but on the contrary, how many gave their health and life for misbegotten, shoddy and ill-conceived ideas? Still, that is the point: ideas are often far more important to those who can barely read than to many who make their living inside universities.

The time and effort given to the full and vivid comprehension of these ideas is, therefore, decidedly one distinguishing characteristic of how we ply our craft. This is naturally also a continuous deep search for the primal and most determining foundations of the two cultures between which we in this epoch live. At stake is a more coherent, a more useful understanding of the first foundations on which the now fading and weakening and indeed collapsing culture was originally built. Yet also, the laying bare and the actual establishment of the new and wholly different foot-walls on which the new culture, that is not yet quite born, that is so far still unstructured, inchoate and dispersed and as if at sea, can soon be based. This unusually intense engagement with these anchoring ideas plays a decisive role in the work I try to do with projects or seminars or groups, but it is also pivotal in the sequence of conversations I have with many individuals. (I never use the words therapy or sessions.) I have talked with individuals, sometimes in connection with one or another of the New Work projects, but often also quite independent of them. They had heard an interview on the radio, had seen a report on TV, had come to a workshop or a lecture, or worked in the business enterprise, the community or the school in which a project was taking place. Nearly all were in some quandary about their present work and wanted to make a transition to work that they would believe in, or love, or really want.

In a real-live situation I very often start with some of the many ways in which human nature has been defined in the past: some have said that human beings alone can smile, or alone have self-consciousness, or language, or reason. The characteristic that distinguishes humans in all these definitions is a distinction, is a remarkable, elevating, special quality that raises human beings above all others in the kingdom of the animals. Then I am apt to ask: perhaps this needs to be reversed? Could it be that our distinguishing characteristic is a flaw, is a weakness, is a lack? Could it be that we are problematic, dubious, questionable, forever troubled and ill-at-ease, because we are missing something, because we are suffering from a peculiar defect?

Hegel wrote a sentence suggesting something of that sort. It comes up with shocking abruptness in the middle of one of his monstrously obscure paragraphs. In a tunnel of grayness, in the *Philosophy of Right*, he suddenly writes, as if with a thick black pen, "man is the creature who can lose himself." It seems natural to relate this to the story of the expulsion from Paradise. The rest of nature is at ease with itself, is tranquil compared to us, because we committed a heinous, unforgivable transgression. We have been expelled from nature. Nothing was worse in early cultures than to be ostracized or exiled, and we have been cast out, and are lost and disoriented. Our condition is more serious: we have not just lost our way, we have lost our *selves*!

There are halls, city-squares, ocean-liners full of people who are alive, but who nonetheless do not actually *live* their lives. And the relationship is easy to see: there are many ways and modes in which one can *not* live one's life. Losing one's self is one of the great variety of them. If the connection to one's self has been severed and one has drifted away from it, then it would be natural for one's life to coast, and float, and ultimately sink toward death as if it were drowning in a morass. Yet, the losing of one's self is often a euphemism, a flattery because a self never existed in the first place. We were born without a self, (indeed one could cite much evidence for this, for example, from the writings of Piaget) and we shuffled forward without ever pausing, without ever taking time and effort to create a self that would be our own. That self-less downward ambling was precisely the *not*-living of our life.

Many of the greatest writers have written on this theme. Tolstoy's *Death of Ivan Illich* tells the story of a peasant who lies dying. As his numbered days pass, he recognizes that he did not live his life, and he raises up his voice in a relentless, incessant shout, that, so Tolstoy writes, "lasted for four whole days." Once one has read this story, it is difficult not from time to time, suddenly, to hear a brief moment of that fearful 4-day long scream. In that way Ivan's long shout becomes a symbol, a permanent embodiment of how very many do not live their lives, and of the horror with which they would react if they came to recognize that fact. Samuel Beckett in a single, celebrated, much quoted sentence pulls back the curtain and uncannily exposes this pervasive condition in one single clause. He writes: "Dead – enough to be buried!" Meaning that the vast great mass of the people, the mass that fills the halls, the squares and the streets, that most of them have been dead already for a long time. A great number of them did not even survive the years they spent in school. Slowly, in those years, through relentless unending pressure they were thoroughly extinguished. Still, not quite enough to be buried. They still moved weirdly like zombies in a deep trance. That is how they continue, and for a great stretch they still pass as alive, till one further small contraction happens.

That insignificant spasm is the threshold in their case: now, on the other side of that minor dip they are officially and certifiably dead, dead – enough to be buried, even though life had actually left them years and years ago.

It is extraordinarily important to remember clearly and sharply that in nearly all of the world's great religions the idea of "coming to life" of "receiving, and being given life," plays a central role. In the New Testament this pervasive motif is expressed with quite singular and explicit clarity. Jesus says not just once but numerous times that "He is the life." Surely, here the most natural of questions to ask would be: what possible meaning and sense could it have to speak of "coming to life" or for that matter of "being re-born" if one were born and fully alive the whole time? If we were not half-dead as both Beckett and Tolstoy propose, then what meaning or reason could there be for so many of the great traditions and countless sects to promise us a new birth, and therewith the long-postponed beginning of our actual life? What sense would this promise make if we were alive *already*? There could not be such a gift, nothing of that sort could be conceivably received, if we were not distinctly *less* than alive. The view, or for that matter the judgment, that the vast "mass of men" is not truly alive is thus not in the least peculiarly stark, extravagant, or arrogant, or modern. Far from it. It belongs to the most ancient, and firmly established and most widely accepted of traditions.

This is continuous with our earlier discussion of the ideas of human nature that underlie the now passing as well as the now arising culture: in the tradition identified with Descartes and the eighteenth century and the Enlightenment, the self is "clearly and distinctly known," so much so that this knowledge is the basis of all other knowledge. (Cogito ergo sum.) The ego is the commanding captain on the bridge of his ship, whose orders every limb of our body instantly obeys. In the other, self-strengthening and self-enhancing culture the ego is conceived as basically frail, fragile, as easily influenced and led. Certainly it is not clearly and distinctly known. Instead, it is hidden through self-ignorance. It is also not from the start finished and full-fletched, not "born free," and also not a subject, complete unto itself and isolated. Much of this we have said before, but now we are adding another further dimension that goes considerably deeper and is perhaps still more important: in addition to having those qualities, we as human beings are more than all else divided and ambivalent! Yes, we are pale, and easily discouraged. But more than that: we stand tilted, held back, with one foot out of the door. One raised eyebrow is enough for us to withdraw, to surrender, to capitulate and not to really live at all; not of course to commit suicide, that would be a prodigious action, but on the contrary, to freeze, to become inert and passive, to pull back into the position where we are half-dead and half alive.

The delusional idea of the self in which the eighteenth century basked leaves very little that still needs to be done. The totality of all the facets of the culture therefore become in the end only instruments of administration. They supervise, play umpire and regulate. That turns out to be the role of the state, and of impartial morality. The now emerging wholly contrary idea of human nature begins from a creature still appallingly unformed and fetal, not much more than a swirl of protoplasm. The daunting, many-staged process of development and growth must still be accomplished. This creature that does not know its own desires, and that is so accursed that nothing in the world is harder for it to know than it itself, suffers from an affliction still worse, still more of a challenge, more of a handicap. It teeters on the brink of wanting to altogether fold its wings and not to fly at all. All other animals need to stay alert in order to survive. Human beings in contrast to that live in a protected world in which they can allow themselves great stretches of deep sleep. That weakens many to such a great degree that much of the time they feel quite overwhelmed. Surely this creature requires far more than some training and the enforcement of a little catalog of rules. To reach ripeness and maturity, to gain in strength until it becomes self-possessed, requires a plenitude of support, of care and attention for which normal nurture would be far too mild a word.

With the now added quality the contrast to the official tradition of the Enlightenment becomes sharpest and most extreme. Not a self that is a bundle of self-interest and self-assertion, that ultimately is best imagined as a mud-ball of greed, but instead a waif that is reluctant to exist at all. Both the ideas of the Poverty of Desire and self-ignorance are preparatory, important though they are. This hermaphrodite quality, this ambiguity between life and death, represents an extreme, a culmination, a summing up.

The idea that it is very common, very easy and seductively inviting to simply miss the living of one's life the way one misses a train has to be touched with cautious fingers until the cool, crass realism of it slowly takes up quarters in one's mind. This is one place where for once something like a "technique" of counseling enters in. I am a fierce believer in the power of pictures and metaphors, and I therefore often ask the people with whom I am having conversations into what single image they would condense their entire life up to this point. Have you been waiting; if so, what kind of waiting? Have you been standing on a corner, hoping that someone will come by and pick you up? Or have you been crouching like a cat, ready to pounce, to unleash your rage, to take your revenge? What are the other 25 basic postures that occur to you? Which of these seems to fit you best?

In line with this, I often ask the group to try to think of 5, or 10 or 20 of the most common ways in which life is missed. What are the devices, the strategies, the excuses, the genuine major hindrances, the distractions that cause people to postpone the living of their life until it is too late, until they scream like Ivan Illich? More specifically, what are the beliefs, the philosophical cobwebs, the absurd remnants from the now dying cultures that still fetter people, so they do not venture into the safari of their life? Pushing still further down I sometimes inquire: can you conjure up any pictures that convey the meaning of a missed life? How can the drama, the story of this happening to someone be communicated and conveyed?

This is usually difficult, so here is an example: there is a carefully researched, rare but well-known disease that afflicts young children, often between 4 and 9 years old. The effect of this illness is that all of the signs of aging appear abruptly, in a few weeks or months. You can visit a ward full of children, who in every last detail look exactly like someone in his middle or late 80s: 6-year-olds with deeply furrowed wrinkled skin, with only a few remaining tufts of wispy, white hair, with voices that for all the world sound like voices of old women and old men. The horror of these small and frail children readily lends itself as a symbol. You can sit in a subway train and to your sadness see such children in numerous seats up and down the aisle. It is true that in their case the signs of aging appear in the usual scheduled years, but it makes no difference, the signs could have arrived much sooner. They only did the sparsest amount of living between their childhood years and their old age, so they are fearfully like the children in the ward.

To make up five or a dozen of one's own pictures of this common fact might be part of the practice of a workshop; it could even be something like a request or an assignment. Still, the concept of the unlived life is like the upper half of an idea that has a second counterpart. This, too, is an idea, a concept, and it, too, corresponds to a ream of different facts that require metaphors and pictures to be captured and conveyed. Abstractly, one could express this counterpart, too, as a proposition about human nature.

Just as it is true that we come into the world quite startlingly unfinished (think of the dependency of babies and of the time it takes for a child to have the ability to walk, compared to a young horse which can do this in a single afternoon), and just as it is a paradoxical fact about us that we can know much that is very distant from us far better than we know our own selves, so it is also bitterly the case that we must constantly exert an effort and struggle just to stay on the same plane. As soon as we desist from the exertion of that energy we begin to contract, collapse or rot.

My impression is that all hands will agree that this is an inexhaustibly rich and fertile field for the invention of images but also for the pursuit of what this in fact implies. That search can truly go over vales and rivers and down into caves. Among the implications belongs, for example, the New Work interpretation of boredom. We are fond of saying that boredom is not like a mild stiffness that we feel in the morning. Boredom is apocalyptic! One should give it its place next to the plague of locusts in the Bible. The boredom which is inflicted on children in schools maims and disfigures them in ways which cannot be repaired. In the time I spent in New Hampshire, I had some encounters with authentic Arctic cold. If one sits down, or stands still, or does not protect one's face, fingers and toes, one's nose or ears freeze into pieces of ice.

That is similar to boredom. If you must sit in school, or behind your desk in the office, if there is no chance to move or to exert energy, then boredom will freeze off your nose, and toes, and fingertips, and leave you crippled, just like some forms of work. Among the implications of the fact that we *must* move, or else suffer the beginnings of gangrene is also the view New Work takes of compulsory retirement. There, too, images are not hard to find: along the coast-line of northern Mexico, for instance, are chains of American retirement communities, and walking on a burning hot day through some of these is very reminiscent of Dante's Inferno. There is no meaningful, no purposeful, no thrilling and inspiring way to exert effort. The effect this has is far more graphic, far more dramatic than one imagines. In the hot summer, people in these retirement communities soak themselves in alcohol; in the afternoons they lie, barely dressed, mostly unconscious, in clumps and heaps on their front lawns.

Far more can be said to underscore this brute necessity to struggle, to exert yourself, to move or to rot like an apple on a wet board! There are detailed statistics on morbidity soon after retirement. This, too, is one more argument to support this case. So is the much-studied difference between people who strain their minds till late into their old age, and those who allow themselves to enter this dark night ever so cautiously, gradually, and 1 inch at a time and who because of that deteriorate much faster than the others who strain their bodies and their minds on every day.

These concepts and images pulled together represent a determined attempt to communicate a different sense of what the drama of one's individual life might be about. It is very like taking someone into a theater and asking them to look for the first time at a play in which they themselves are the main character. It is an effort to depict the starting situation, the stage set upon which the curtain opens. What is the background and opening dilemma that sets into motion the play of our life? It is, for one, the double situation, the Janus-faced dybuck whom we have just described: we wake to life, at whatever point this happens, and looming above us is the dark shadow of the possibility that we will not live at all, that even though our limbs are healthy, and we have good hearing and good eyes, we will sleep through the entire journey, and only wake when the conductor cries: Final Stop! This train ends here!

The reversal

It is part of the pattern and flow of New Work conversations that we ask a manifold of crisscrossing questions. Some of these come as a surprise, some I am sure seem sometimes too direct and are seen as offensive. Many are attempts to move surface pretenses out of the way, and to lay bare deeper lying truths, but in a rhythm we do return to our simple basic question: what would you really and seriously want to do? It is true and significant that people have often intense emotional reactions to this question, that bulky rough-hewn men have broken down and cried. It is also true, and it is one of the main characteristics of New Work, that we are skeptical. That is the other side of the concept of human nature I have just described: we approach our endeavor with a towering sense of its difficulty. We know that assisting people toward a fuller sense of their own self-possession is a daunting and bedeviled task, full of tricks and feints and opportunities for self-deception. Therefore, we encourage people to second-guess and to look again. Often it turns out that the question of what work one seriously wants to do has not been even asked. One is still trapped inside the framework of jobs, and one's hope is to identify a job that is slightly more attractive, a bit more fun. One is still merely looking for a job – only now a job that wears a mini-skirt.

Not universally, but in a very large proportion of the great range of very different people who have searched for their New Work an abrupt and major break does happen in this phase. Once they have first resisted and then struggled with and then embraced the idea that they are only half alive it is very as if they have managed to break their way through a floor. The whole lot of alternatives so far considered begin to seem trivial and without weight. Not that they feel suddenly illuminated and in secure possession of their answer to the question of what they want to do. They are far from that. More nearly they are one great step closer: they now have come face to face with a desire that has an authenticity, a clarity and force that seems very new and utterly refreshing in contrast to their experience so far. This desire is sweeping and general but all the same strong and clear: they seem certain that whatever they in the long run finally will want specifically to do, surely they want to be more alive, more of a person, more fully, more vibrantly the very creature that they are.

The single expression most associated with New Work is the doubling, the reiteration, the repeat in the *really, really* of the work we want. This reiteration is much quoted, much referred to, many jokes are made about it (an element of humor was part of the intention) but many also find it puzzling. Naturally it was from the start designed to convey a multitude of meanings. Among these was also a commitment that we would seriously listen and find out what you really, really want rather than impose our ideas upon you. Central to the meaning of the repetition is also this reversal. There are the myriad things one wants prior to the recognition that above all one wants to live more fully and intensely. That desire is recognizably deeper and more authentic and is therefore what one RRW. This is strongly reminiscent of the anecdote which illustrated how afflicted we are with the Poverty of Desire. That little story narrated the progress of a therapy, where after years of weekly sessions the client for the first time ever feels that now she in her own person acted, while everything before had been capitulations, to the influence of her parents, her teachers and whoever else. In the same way these New Workers now sense a great difference between the desires which they coaxed and pursued before, and this very different incontrovertible and authentic voice. The very next thought that strikes many who for the first time admit to themselves the primacy of this desire is not surprisingly how ubiquitous the expressions of this desire actually are. Indeed, once one has focused on that wish and has named it one encounters it everywhere. There are hints of it in the advertisements for vitamins, and of course for health food, and for exercise equipment but it is blatantly also present in the descriptions of cosmetic products and the commercials for cruises and vacations. All of these lie close to hand and on the surface, but one could naturally enlarge the perspective and connect it to the perennial wistful wishing for a fountain of youth, or also naturally to the dread of old age and death, and beyond this to the most stereotypical accounts of depression: that one feels lifeless and without energy, that nothing interests one any longer, that life itself seems to have lost its flavor, that one feels so weary that enormous efforts are required to make it out of bed.

A second, immediately connected thought which is much discussed and often embroidered with great numbers of high-spirited tales is the fact that we all experience moments of fulfillment, hours in which our doltish clumsiness drops away, and we rise up suddenly to a far higher, far improved, seemingly almost perfect level of performance. Some people experience this in tennis games, when for one afternoon they play "way above their heads," others when they play the saxophone. Sometimes it happens in a conversation, when each of the two partners raises the other by a notch at every exchange until both express themselves more fluently than at any time before, and both giggle in little fits of hysterical euphoria. Many of course associate this feeling of being "more alive" with being in love, and many others also with adventure and risk and excitement.

The question which almost invariably emerges from these ebullient conversations is whether it might not be possible to stay on that higher level permanently? To not only have sporadic hours at great intervals in which one feels alive, but whether there is not a method of climbing up to that higher plane, so that one would stay on it without slipping back. Or still better: is it not conceivable that one could reach the level of experience that one has when one for once plays the violin really well and rather than descending back down to one's normal tepid life, one could pause and then climb higher, by the same distance that one has just traversed. That question turns out to be protean. It takes on countless different forms. Once one has been struck by the recognition that fundamentally one wants to be more alive, one inevitably wants to know how this could be achieved. What do I undertake, how must I live my life, so that I will not look back in terror as Ivan Illich did? If I take the question seriously then in what direction do I turn so that I am not like one of the dreadfully ill children that look like they are 90 before they are 6? In New Work groups the insistence of that question rises up in a crescendo: how shall I live, so that I do not waste my life?

We consider this a key moment; one of the crucial steps in the transition from the old to the new culture, and from the mentality of the Job System to that of New Work. Whether that question is asked desultorily in passing or stays in focus makes of course all the difference. We emphasize the amphibian half-dead–half-alive nature of human beings as much as we do because we see in it perhaps the most quintessential quality of the modern, as such. To not accept society and life as tradition hands it down to us, but to strike out anew and insist that we shall re-create society as we see fit, and live life accordingly must inescapably lead to the question of how the very life that I myself am leading could be more alive? What else could be the main criterion and measure of the society and of the life we really want? And with the serious asking of that question one is assuredly in the world of Whitman, Melville, Emerson and DH Lawrence, but also in the world of Shakespeare, Goethe, Nietzche, Hoelderlin, Gide and Blake.

In the pause that is a natural punctuation for this crucial dividing moment, this hour of entrance and of passage from the old to the new I usually make an effort to communicate three matters, and if I can, I do it in the calmest and most detached of tones. First: I explain that this is the very heart and core of New Work, namely the conviction that doing work that one deeply and seriously wants to do is the one and best way to end up living one's life with fulfillment and intensity. It is the one best way to ensure that one will not shout for 4 whole days when one is close to death.

Second: I make clear that one large part of this is a matter of plain experience. Not of course strictly speaking everyone, but nonetheless a very large proportion of the people with whom we have pursued the question of what they seriously want to do with persistence and patience reach at the end of the day the conclusion that it should be some kind of work that excites them, that pulls them into life.

Third: It is also and importantly a matter of a decision we have made. We not only tease people who are so modest they merely want a job that is chocolate coated. On another level we are fiercely determined. In the back of our minds is naturally the pathology of the Job System but in the front of our minds are the three failings that are characteristic of humanity. In light of these nothing is as urgent as to enliven, to energize and to arouse people, but the Job System does the exact opposite: it subdues people, dampens them, accustoms them to boredom and to passivity, makes them dependent and subservient.

In effect we thus go together with other people through a 180 degree turn in their and our understanding of what we are looking for, of what we hope for and expect. It is not just different, it is for many people initially unthinkable, much *more* than had ever crossed their minds. There is not one single step in the sequence of activities and conversations that constitutes an encounter with New Work which is not deeply influenced, even determined by the complex of foundations that we have now laid down.

The partly humorous phrase that one should discover what one really, really, wants has, if one cares to take a close-up look, a surprisingly exact meaning. The point is not at all that one has now at last found the most concealed of all desires buried under layers deeper down than one had dug before. We could more meaningfully speak of two different layers, actually two quite different questions. The one is: what seems to give me the greatest thrill or tickle, the momentary biggest rush? And the other very different question is: what will function most effectively in the long-range project of my becoming an autonomous, active, genuine person? What will help me most to overcome the primal failings which afflict humanity?

The first question is fairly private. Even though we often have an extremely quick and perceptive grasp of other people, whether one or another option feels more or less thrilling to the person next to us, we are *not* able to determine. This leads directly to a rather deep distinction between the kinds of counseling New Work requires and the many and widely disseminated forms of coaching that usually have some relationship to the ethos of New Age. Acceptance, affirmation and encouragement constitute a very large portion of what coaches often do. Naturally, or even, necessarily! The client says, this is what I feel like, so what else is there to do? Since it feels, and truly *is,* risky to act on a barely perceived appetite, encouragement to "go for it" is much wanted. That the longer-range results are extremely dubious is by now well known. (The most familiar statistic is that approximately 80 percent of all small start-up enterprises fail before the end of the second year.)

The New Work conversations which we arrange have a quite different content and tone. Not only does the communication of information and of unfamiliar ideas and always of specific examples play a much greater role, there are long sequences of probing questions that in effect ask, how firmly do you stand? Are you sure and clear, or not? Try to be as precise as you can about the way in which this work will enhance or strengthen you *as a person*. And by this we explicitly do not mean your financial status, but your capacity to be a developed and maybe even a splendid human being.

The great divide lies in the fundamental intent with which one approaches work. If the Archimedean point of reference is the person, if the rock-foundation question is, how will this work affect the human beings who perform it, then one has left the bewitched garden of the Job System behind. That of course is not the case in the usual start-your-own business incubator, or in the New Age scene. Far from it. A host of different phenomena make it very tempting in our culture to advertise the ambience of fun and pleasure that a job will give. One term that some, who were lured and trapped by this advertising, use is "soul-sucking" jobs. As so often, there is truth in this coinage. Many times before, the spiritual, the somewhat religious, the distinctly obscure has been used to bait the cruelest and most dastardly of traps. The promise of the fulfillment of your dream can of course be used to make you an even more assiduous, willing and obedient employee. No one needs to be told that a great deal of this has happened recently, and often quite without deceptions, but in full light of day. The Job System is in serious trouble. The pressures increase still more with every day. What is more natural than the step to a somewhat higher, more demanding job requirement: we do not just want you from nine to five, and we do not want you unwilling and morose; we need your enthusiasm and your exuberance. We need your soul. So be prepared to hand it over every time you clock in.

More mildly one might also say that there is no substitute for being on your toes. You must be alert, you must look about you with sharp eyes. If work is offered to you in our present culture then you must ask yourself whether in serious truth, and without cheating, it is work that will invigorate and enliven you and make you more of a person. In the culture and the Work System we now have, you will have to be strong and quick and extraordinarily courageous. If you become inattentive for one moment the revolving wringer will grab your arm, and maybe more. Maybe your spirit! Then you are done for. You will let your work suck the last ounce of energy out of your body and your mind. You will lie and say that you are following your dream, when actually wild horses drag you through the sand around the walls of your fallen city. Some imagine that they have already reached the goal, they wave and shout with excitement, when in fact they have only made a small adjustment. They are still in the mentality and posture appropriate for jobs, they are still very like patient beasts of burden that hold still while the bags are fastened on their backs. The difference is only that the job they now have in mind is a whit more consistent with their values. They want to work with children, or with homeless people, or in a natural park. At points like this we can be obstinately difficult, and I am sure upsetting. It would be typical of us to at that point call a halt, and to announce that this is anything but the moment for a piece of cake and self-congratulations, but on the contrary the moment for a fresh new start, for a start far more serious and intense than the one with which one has merely toyed so far. At a juncture of that sort we might reiterate that we are the very opposite of an employment agency. That obstreperous as it may seem, we are not in the business of fitting people with a meat-cleaver into the shoe of yet another job. For better or worse, we are trying to assist people in the opposite, namely in the transcending, the surpassing of that way of experiencing work, in fact of that Work System!

This is the kind of moment where we bring the concept of the not-lived-life into the conversation. Our intention is quite explicitly to shake those present by the shoulders and to wake them up; to come closer to an understanding that something quite different, more momentous, more in the face of life and death is our subject, is at stake. Of course this is only one extreme. The pendulum swings back and forth. We also turn around an instant later and declare that we are self-ignorant, and also ignorant in other ways, and that we therefore could be totally mistaken. Maybe there is no need to persist, to push further? It is possible that you indeed are coming closer, that you have come to a first answer? Do test it! Put weight on it. Make very sure that you really want this in a serious way, that it will carry you and not turn out to be thin ice.

Often a group formulates a number of different ways in which the mentality of the Job System and that of New Work can be juxtaposed not only because that is for us the single most important contrast, but also because we all know that the psychology of the Job System has an incredible hypnotic power, and the effort to free oneself from it requires a large number of ever new and fresh starts.

In that spirit we explain to each other and to ourselves that what we call "The Reversal" can also be defined in perhaps still clearer terms. Within the Job System work serves the boss or the employer. A gamut of criteria must be satisfied otherwise a job cannot exist, and all of these criteria reside in the person who hires me. He decides, he gives the orders, he must be satisfied, he makes a profit. In New Work the direction of all of these arrows is reversed. They do not point toward another, but instead point toward me. I decide what work I do, and far more important: the work must serve me; the ultimate purpose and question asked is whether the work advances my development, whether it increases my strength and vitality instead of exhausting and debilitating me as Job Work does. So far I have been a tool, a means toward someone else's ends. From here on in, I will not be serving work, but the other way around: my work will be serving me. I recognize that I am frail and flawed, and I decide that I will strengthen and build and develop and create myself through the work I choose to do.

The basic relationship to my work, the posture I adopt toward it are therefore diametrically opposed. People slide into the fundamental attitude appropriate for the doing of a job for many superficial reasons: because they lack courage and are not venturesome, because they have failed, because they are weary and want to be protected and go home. Yet there also is a layer of deeper reasons that have their roots down in the understructure of the Job System. One dark point of origin and beginning is the so-called "Labor Theory of Value." It was one of the standard tropes during the zenith of the Enlightenment for David Hume, Adam Smith, Locke, Ricardo and Kant, and it is now integral to the very fibers of our flesh. The central idea could not be simpler: it is the assertion that we acquire the right to own through work that we perform. That sounds so innocuous to most of us that calling it a "theory" seems strange or overblown. That impression, however, is mistaken. Two quick thoughts can give one a first inkling of the fact that some surprising consequences are hidden under the sheep's-clothing of this sentence. First, there is simply its inversion: if you do not work, you also do not have the right to own, and from there it is only a small step to the harsher dictum: if you do not work, you have no right to eat, or to find shelter, which comes close to saying (during the winter in a city like Detroit) that you deserve to die.

The other thought amounts to the question: what on that theory is the significance, the meaning of work? One strand of the answer is that work becomes a currency. It is transformed (you could say, degraded) into a payment that one makes; indeed it is the ultimate and final and universal currency. Everything, property, but also my own life, has to be worked for, must be earned. Turn this over and look at the not so apparent underside. If work is to function as a payment, as something that I sacrifice, that I give in return for something else, where that other thing has value and is something that I want – then work of course must be unpleasant and to be endured and something that I (at least mildly) suffer. If work is marvelous and delicious and erotic then it cannot be a payment, a "must," a condition that I am forced to meet! That would be bizarre, a mad crossed purpose of terms! Is not the basic posture that is here imposed: humility, worthlessness, a sense of doing penance for a sin? And once I have you in that posture, are you then not prepared to be patient, and to endure? And is it a wide-reaching step from there to an attitude of resignation, of capitulation, of accepting that maybe 45 years of one's whole life are a mere test of one's Stoicism and one's patience? Is it far-fetched to think that many experience their jobs as a servitude in measured time-slices? Could it be that astonishingly, marvelously (in a feat of philosophical magic that should put one's mouth agape) the so innocent seeming Labor Theory of Value prolonged subservience right through the supposed "liberation" of the Enlightenment? It would seem that within that system deep down and with only few exceptions the root experience in which work is embedded is resignation, is capitulation and a giving up. This manifests itself also in hundreds of everyday dramas and their descriptions. As typical as any of these is "growing up and coming to accept the real world." Surely this is how ever so many parents and young people comprehend it: One dreams. One is self-indulgent. One chases all manner of whims and butterflies and notions, but that is "not the way to *earn* a living." Sooner or later that phase must be outgrown and then the "seriousness of practical, real life begins." One has to shoulder work, just as a camel kneels down for its bags, or as an ox accepts the traces of a cart.

The enormity lies in the duration. Work will swallow the best part of your waking hours, and in most cases a full 45 years of your life-span, from the end of your childhood to the onset of your senility (if you have bad luck). And that gargantuan piece of your life is, despite some compensating trinkets, shining beads and mirrors, in the last analysis surrendered! Offered up. A monstrous, giant sacrifice, to appease who knows which angry gods.

If work in the Job System is ultimately a form of payment and of sacrifice, then what does work become in the existential drama that unfolds from the premises we just described? If I do not have a self, and in any case am in the dark about it, and even more ignorant of my desires, and if the danger is extremely great that I am too timid and too cowed to venture into life at all, then quite obviously the last thing needed is to browbeat me some more with wagging fingers that remind me of the harshness of the real world. If the very existence of my self is in doubt, and my desires are in any case like seedlings covered by deep snow, then the injunction that I should forego and sacrifice and pay is malicious and mad. Worse even, since it is far from assured that I will try to really live, nothing could be more destructive and downright evil than the insinuation that I should wrap the biggest part of my entire life into a package and put it on hold in a baggage room. The question is, what might draw, what conceivably could coax, what could beckon and coax the majority of people into living life with gusto and abandon? Our answer is: only one thing has that persistent, that enduring, that comprehensive, that never tiring power, and that is work; the right kind of work, work that they deeply and seriously want to do.

This opposition can be formulated in terms of the self. Given the old Cartesian self, it made perfect sense to discipline and to control the unbridled, tyrannical, maniac, selfish captain of the ego. Work could be used for these disciplinarian ends, and they are indeed the ends for which work was used. We have now stepped out of this world (this eighteenth-century lunatic asylum) into our first small corner of sanity. The self is wholly different from all of these assumptions. Our task is to do all we can so that the difficult birth of the self is first of all accomplished. Then it needs to be cared for and fed and strengthened, which swings open the door to one of our most cardinal and pivotal propositions: What if the most strengthening and most invigorating food should turn out to be work that one seriously wants to do? What if the one best way to find one's buried and concealed desires were surprisingly enough the question: what is the work I really want to do? What if the best way to assist a person who is in danger of not living life at all, were to build for him a bridge to something that he seriously wants to do?

The contrast between the two sets of basic premises thus hardly could be still more flagrant. The picture we now have of both – of the drama that much of human life is inescapably about, *and* of the role of work and its functions – is wholly different from anything that could be imagined in the old framework of the Job System (which is also the framework of the social contract theories and of the eighteenth-century Enlightenment.) Given this, what we expect from work, and how we evaluate it, and ultimately what we most want from work is naturally bound to be wholly other than was formerly the case.

In a nutshell: the primary functions inside the Job System were those we know only too well: first, and governing all the rest, was the production of wealth – getting the soil to yield harvests and fruits, and transforming raw materials into products of every conceivable use. The fun or pleasure element existed within those constraints. It was an extra, a bonus, an impressively sweet and large piece of often dangerous candy. In the emerging new framework, the primary function of work revolves not around goods, but around you and me as persons; not the production of goods but the ascent of humanity is now on center stage. The central questions now become the following: what will *enliven* those who do this work the most? What will draw them with the greatest power toward the fuller realization of their nascent and fragile humanity? What work will do the most to draw and coax this abstemious, life-denying person closer to the banquet table of what life has to offer? What work would do the most to raise up the overwhelming, enormous mass of human beings, who live in numbed discouragement at an awful distance even from their own desires, to the condition in which they will shape and fashion and above all simply live their lives?

These questions were unthinkable and unimaginable in the framework that is now sinking under the horizon in the West. In the old framework man came into life essentially complete and finished. He was *born* free! On the philosophical, metaphysical level (if I may use that word) nothing more remained to be done. We, humanity, had arrived. The rest was just administration:

getting the contract into the right form and assuring that everyone will obey and abide by it. Neither work, nor the state, nor society, nor whatever else you want to name had a genuine function on that level. The framework preempted those questions or those possibilities. You cannot intelligibly *ask* what will make a person free if he is free already. You cannot devise strategies that will assist him to become a free person if he steps out of the clouds and has his feet on the mountain top already.

All of that awakens now to a new day. There is momentous, mountainous work to be done. Given the enormous distance between what humanity is at present and what a free humanity would be, there is need and a place for everyone. The task is the protracted, difficult ascent. The very basic questions need to be re-asked. If the state is not just an administrator, not just some kind of hired guard who makes sure that the children play peacefully and nicely in the yard, if the state has a serious role in the raising of humanity up toward freedom, then how can the state begin to exercise that function? Equally with the economy: if the task of the economy is not merely to produce an ever more oppressive excess, then how could an economy be structured so it, too, would assist in the arduous ascent?

Most to the point and obviously closest to the heart of New Work: how could one re-think, and re-structure, and redesign *work* so that work would not cripple and exhaust people, but would make a totally different contribution? How could work become one, or even the main tool, the main staircase on which human individuals could climb upwards step by step in the ascent of *their own* development, their own evolution? How could work be the goad, the midwife in this process? How could work become the strongest rope that pulls us into life?

Again, the asking of this question was *unthinkable* in the cage of the old framework. That we stepped out of the womb already finished was only one of the main reasons for this "unthinkability." The other reason was how we thought about work. If work is fundamentally what we were condemned to do when we were driven out of paradise (to eat our bread in the sweat of our brow), then *with* chocolate covering *or* without, there is no way in which work can play a great or decisive role in the climb up toward *freedom*! The most that work could do for our freedom in that world is to stop. If ultimately all of work is a punishment and an oppression, then freedom from work, freedom from itself, is all that work could give.

The polarity of work is therefore all-important. Work *can* cripple and also kill us, but that is only one possibility. Work can also give us energies we never dreamed we had. Remember the images of the mother saving her young son, and of the villagers fighting the Mississippi. Since work can do this, not just in one moment or one night, but for the entire stretch of a whole life time, work may well be the best and only rope-ladder that hangs down into the well in which we hitherto still are.

It is not possible to understand New Work unless the perpetual possibility of the not-lived life has been grasped and appropriated. The fact is that the answer from nearly all the people with which we have worked comes in the end to the declaration that they want work that will make them more alive, that will lift them to a higher level, work that will pull and coax them deeper into life, and ultimately work that will make them more fully and more completely the person they now are. The sum of these statements is one piecemeal written Declaration of Independence. In their totality they are a single, multi-voiced ode to emancipation. Each of these separate affirmations is like one more fist raised in the great assembly of humanity. They declare their emancipation from and their rebellion against the first axiom of the Job System. For this is the confrontation brought down to its most antipodal terms: Within the borders of the Job System work in the final and last analysis, after the garlands of window-dressing have come down is a price paid; it is a burden, it is a means toward an external end. In its last quintessence it is a "must," a piece of coercion. Work that one RRW is in pitched juxtaposition to this the very emblem, the very symbol of work that is free. The goal of New Work is therefore the re-appropriation, the re-possession of work. In feminism one speaks of "taking back the night." In the same way we are "taking back" the huge and all-decisive realm of work. In the great stony fields of the Job System the vast majority of people were crippled by their work. In the vast asylum of the Job System people therefore experience their work as a "mild disease." On the other side of that high border, in the territory of New Work the central experience of work is as life-giving. The work I really, really want helps me "to become who I am." (Nietzsche). It gives me more of the energy which is "eternal delight." (Blake)

Chapter Seven

Life and the Work We Really, Really Want

It is downright curious: very many people take two steps with assurance and ease. They come to realize that they want to be more alive, and they of course express this in many different ways. They also, secondly, want some kind of work, whatever it's more exact description will turn out to be, that will help them toward the fulfillment of this deep desire. Now a further step presents itself. On the face of it this next realization seems to lie only inches beyond the point now reached, yet curiously, to make that last advance is frequently extremely difficult. To put it plainly: to accept that one's work should play some role in making one a stronger and more self-possessed person very many people eventually come to accept, and it seems to them a natural and plausible conclusion. It is quite different with the only slightly more demanding, slightly harsher claim that work plays an absolutely central role in this; that in fact ever so many other avenues that seem to lead in this direction are feeble if one compares them to work that one seriously wants. When this idea is proposed one gets the impression that the mentality of the Job System marshals all of the forces of resistance that still remain to it. And, naturally, it is also true that this seemingly small step represents a turn in a new direction. We move on from work to life. If the last question was, what sort of work would you seriously want, then we next raise that same question about life itself: given that we so far have been half-dead, could it conceivably be the serious pursuit of WRRW want, which could do more to lead us toward life, than anything else that we might imagine or attempt.

It is odd, but there is great resistance not just to this specific answer to this question, but even to the asking of it. Many put up barricades and strenuously look the other way. We have made it our custom to proceed at this juncture as concretely as we can, to not philosophize, but on the contrary to move forward hand over hand, from one example to the next.

The endless beach vacation

Frequently, the very first line of resistance is familiar to the point of being a cliché. "Really living," "living it up," who does not know how to wallow for a while in that? Playing golf and fishing, or lying on a beach with a bottle of wine and a good-looking woman, is it not self-evident that this is what "really living" is? In short, anything but work! The dismissive cynicism with which this is often said is, paradoxically, due to the conviction that this beach fantasy cannot be obtained; that it is of course unreal and out of reach. In that way the fantasy is both: it is as much an avoidance of the question, as it is an answer to it. So often, this has a damaging effect; for the space is occupied. The question has not been answered, not in good faith, but it nonetheless cannot be asked. The room in which it would have to be posed is taken. That is part of the strategy of the resistance, and many, for that very reason, remain in the belief that lulling about would indeed be life at its most satisfying best.

We very often point out first that it seems self-destructive not to ask oneself this question with serious tenacity; after all it is possibly the most important question one ever faces throughout one's entire life, and it is hence perverse to take time and trouble for a million other questions, but to treat this one as hopeless, as too demanding, as a question that only children ask. For many it is a sharp surprise that in the context of a Center for New Work we talk about how one can manage to live life fully and intensely, in the most matter-of-fact but also the most determined and relentless fashion. In slow degrees the people who come to us begin to realize that this is for us indeed a most practical and "daily" question; that is, a question that it is useful to ask anew perhaps not literally every day, but certainly in intervals every few months. Quite commonly we lay hold of some off-handed, smirking remark and launch into a serious, full-scale, probing discussion of it. One convenient topic is naturally the kind of description of the actual experience of retirement that we touched on earlier when we gave an impression of the retirement communities along the coast of Mexico. Another issue which among New Work people is a kind of stand-by favorite is the also already mentioned varieties of boredom. The quick confrontation with a more realistic picture of what retirement for many is actually like, far from how this is endlessly offered up on TV, is often quite enough to jar someone into a first and unaccustomed thinking. Once we have wedged a toe into the door in this fashion, we quickly follow through with larger and heftier considerations. We might ask whether this entire way of thinking is not another grandchild of the Old Testament division into 6 days of sweat and labor and 1 day of deliciously complete and thorough rest; rest without mitigation, rest that is a completely empty time.

That leads of course instantly to the question: who almost inevitably would conceptualize and fantasize bliss and happiness in this odd and peculiar white-washed way? Who, but someone who hates and loathes his work? Who, but a person who for 6 days of the week may have been driven with sticks and whips to heave monstrous stones up the side of a pyramid? Of course, understandably enough, if one spends 6 such days in the blazing sun, then utter proneness, then lying completely still would be one's fever fantasy of the ultimate of bliss.

As the delirious wish of a sun-struck slave this lust for leisure is of course wholly understandable. The fulfillment and the living out of that wish is a wholly different affair. Emptiness is just plain (here comes once more, our reiterated phrase) – "not enough!" Certainly, every now and then a piece of it, some stretch of lying in the grass, or of fishing, or of beer on a beach. Yes, thank

God! But, really? That for 15 uninterrupted years? That would be a devil's gift. Delicious as a pause, as an interruption, but for heaven's sake not as the fulfillment, as the apex, as the meaning of one's life, which is what TV ads for Florida condominiums have tried to make of it. The reality is crass and drastic; most people discover that this as a goal, this as the content of one's life, is plainly too small. One is reminded of the humorous Zen-Buddhist idea that one should put an entire coat into its own pocket. If one took this seriously and actually tried, one would of course discover that there is far too much coat, far too much material to fit into the pocket. There is a similarity. If the fantasy of the fishing, golfing life suddenly in real life descends upon one, then the main reaction is simply that it is too small. It turns out to be something like using a handkerchief for a blanket on a cold night. One can twist and turn, and pull one's legs up to one's chest, one will still feel naked and cold. We mean this almost literally. There is not enough content in that sort of life, it does not possess the required magnitude. For anything to give meaning and substance to a human life it must be larger, it must possess more volume; that for a start and of course a great deal else.

Such an exchange is for us only a minimal first step. There always is some surprise that we address this issue quite as brusquely as we do. Yet we hope that this is useful as a way of putting a wedge into a small crack. Many people experience a kind of shock since we seem to be determined to think about these topics in such a hard-headed, practical and pragmatic a fashion. That shock is important, in fact salutary for it opens a door, to the taking of a course that was not possible before.

It is all too easy to prattle endlessly about how one would want to live, what living seriously would mean, while one's mind in no way moves. It remains at rest, glued to an idea in which one in no way believes. Yet this means that no new, no better image or idea can enter and take up residence. Remaining in this posture is downright dangerous, for if one continues lamely along a path that one secretly loathes and condemns, then over time great quantities of rage and fury will accumulate. What seems important to us is to initiate thought, is to create the space in which the question (how do I in earnest want to live?) can at long last at least be raised. If we see any opening we follow through, and as often as not with a warning that one's perception is bound to change – like it or not. Once one has tasted work that one seriously wants to do, one has been spoiled. That taste is so flavorful that lying in the sand on a beach is flat and stale by comparison. What is more, this difference is so pungent and so unmistakable that it pulls a long chain of consequences in its wake. Having the experience of that kind of work will in all likelihood end the segmented and punctuated rhythm where we alternate full-time, total work, with vacuous emptiness. Since much of work will be a delicious experience one will not wait for it to end. Spending most of a year or most of a life time in the expectation of either the annual or the final endlessly long vacation will no longer be a tempting option. Very probably one will be working far less than we do now, but in a much more intelligent and intermixed arrangement. Doing the work that suits one's tastes and talents will be a delicious experience, and more likely than not one will surround these with pauses of lassitude and relaxation, where these, too, will have some genuine content and not be stretches of sheer nothingness. This quite obviously is what people who intensely enjoy their work do already now. Surely, the idea of enduring for 40 years some tedious and patience-trying work so that one in conclusion can then be driven in a large windowed refrigerator along "sights" which one's eyes are by then too dim to see, will disappear as soon as the spell of the Job System has been broken.

All of these are in our experience useful considerations, but they are preliminary compared to the confrontation of this beach life fantasy with our description of what human nature is actually like. If we indeed are so detached from ourselves that we are ignorant of our own desires, and beyond that even of who we are, and we still further are indeed half-dead for these and other reasons, then a life like an endless beach vacation is clearly the last thing we need. We will sink into an ever deeper slumber and all three of the primal failings will gradually become ever worse. The contrast here is clean and sharp and for New Work most important. If my own ignorance about my own desires indeed is a serious condition then nothing may be as needful, as directly curative for the overcoming of this affliction than an intense and sustained effort to determine what work I seriously want to do. Finding out what kind of shoes, or lampshades, or deserts I like may also be of some small help, but bearing down full force on the question of what would be the WRRW would obviously have far greater weight. This in fact has been confirmed almost universally in over 20 years of our experience: the question about work does seem to be the natural beginning. Once one has gone through some energetic and fierce bouts with that issue, all manner of other determinations seem to follow with much greater and almost natural ease. Somewhat oddly, this extends from the sort of practical matters I just mentioned, to the seemingly least practical and most intimate affairs. Very many people I have known had their very first utterly intense experience of full delight in relationship to some New Work that they were doing. Strangely, they seemed to learn from this what the experience of taking full delight in another person feels like. They needed the encounter with work in which they took delight as a measure, as an object of comparison, as a breakthrough into a new realm. In a similar way this is also true for the two other primal handicaps. That we do not know who we are is one of the great remonstrations that has echoed down to us through the ages. Very parallel to the thought just delineated: lying in the sand will not assuage that defect. The very opposite is true for the WRRW. Knowing that I am in the midst of doing work that is deeply what I want to do is often one first major step to my answering the question of who I actually am. And the same is again true for my being far less than thoroughly alive: lulling between dunes wafted by mild breezes certainly will not pull me deeper into life, but WRRW can of course do that.

The gourmet fantasy

The second, almost equally reflexive response to the question about what sort of life one would most want dumps a cornucopia of delicious tidbits on the floor. Often these tend to lie tellingly in the opposite direction from lassitude. What one wants is not leisure, but adventure, climbing mountains, going on safaris, practicing karate or Tai Chi, taking risks and having any number of close calls, hunting lions and flying through the air on kites, naturally also yoga and meditation, and exercises that in 6 weeks will give one "the body one deserves," also success, fame and power just so that nothing has been omitted. Something that fits the general stereotype of this description is raised so regularly that we have developed a standard reply to it as well.

Very many of the people who tell us that this is what they mean by "really living" merely gesture in a desultory fashion toward these appetizing possibilities. They are basically dilettantes; they want to nibble here and there, take an excursion, have a try of what a sport, or an act of daring, or an adventure would be like. Though superficially different, they often end up malcontent in a fashion similar to the one we have just described. Small pieces, again, are "not enough." Just like the premature retirees they feel that their life has no content, and no substance. Yes, once a week they practice Tai Chi, or they go out now and then and spend a weekend camping and sitting naked next to a drum, but the effect is negligible, weightless, without consequence.

One of our first responses amounts mainly to a warning. On first blush what we are saying may seem marginal, or minor, but this is actually one of the junctures where a crass misunderstanding can easily happen in an instant, and it turns out to be intractable and most difficult to repair. Many have of course often heard, long before they attended a workshop or a seminar, that New Work tries to help people discover something that they seriously want. By their own lights, these titillation hunters are entirely on the right track. These episodes are things they want, and even the ethos of multiplicity, of many-coloredness seems to fit New Work. They imagine that they understand us completely, though they actually are miles away from it. Our first warning to them is surprisingly similar to the one we give to the pursuers of leisure. It is again a matter of magnitude, of size, of the sheer volume, the quantity needed by a human life. There is a resemblance to a home-spun piece of advice that it makes sense to give to young people who accept a job they basically loath, with the excuse that they will do what interests them during the weekends and the vacations. The same adage applies also to teachers and young academics who fantasize that they can write plays and novels "on the side." The problem is that it is easy to underestimate the power of the Job System. Legions of people start out with such a resolve, but nearly all of them capitulate, often after many years of frustrating struggle. The job takes more time and energy than one imagined, and what one seriously wanted wilts. The misunderstanding of New Work is therefore flat. The intention of New Work is of course not that one should have an exciting hobby on the side. The demand of New Work is that everyone should have the chance to do something that they consider meaningful and grand in a significant and major portion of their time. Our endeavor, moreover, is a tenacious and sustained attempt to reconstruct the Work System of our culture, to put structures and institutions and financial arrangements in place that will make this possible for nearly everyone and not just for a select elite.

Therefore our question to these people is: "Do you want to take a risk, or climb a mountain once in a while, and take a lesson in Tai Chi once every 2 weeks? You can do that, of course, but it has nothing to do with New Work. We ask you, do you want to do this in earnest, as your pursuit, as the work that you really, seriously want, or only marginally, on the side, as a hobby?" If that is your plan then you are almost bound to lose. For many of the bargains people try to make with the Job System are reminiscent of legends told about the devil in the Middle Ages. On the face of it the Job System seems ever so obliging and flexible, and prepared to make all manner of concessions, very like the devil in these stories. Yet behind your back that system is very powerful and shrewd and when the final reckoning comes it will have taken vast portions of your life. It will leave you drained and eviscerated, half suffocated in good intentions which you were too weak to keep. The efforts in the margins will have been too futile and too small, and in your own eyes you will have failed on both counts. These are again the initial, probing parts of these conversations. As before, it is the confrontation of this fantasy of an imagined life with the three weaknesses of human nature which bring on the much more difficult and hard, but also the more productive exchanges. How will this kind of life advance you in the crucial task of determining and bringing to the surface the concealed and ineffable character of your own desires? The great mass of your life which will remain inside the Job System you will be bracketing and writing off. It cannot tell you much because it is in any case only a burden and a test of your patience. And the furtive explorations for which there will be enough room will be too sporadic and short-lived for you to learn from them the momentous lessons you need to absorb. This is even truer in relation to the establishment of who altogether you really are, and most important of all with coaxing you out of the condition in which you are only half alive. The bits of adventure or athletic prowess, or traveling, or practicing yoga will be too meager for you to make serious progress in either of these. Most particularly when it comes to expanding the energy with which you live: experimenting with a few appetizing samples is of no avail. The quantity of energy that flows into you from a task is proportionate to the size of the task. The vitality at your disposal increases in steps, as the undertaking into which you have burrowed expands. That, naturally, casts doubt on spending one's life on a tidbit chase. It reiterates once again the single childlike conclusion which we have reached: namely, that finding the work that you with the deepest conviction, and the most determined commitment, want to perform – that work, not hors D'oeuvre of this or that – will lead you to the life that was intended for you.

Quite often we gently hint that probing around in one's insides, trying to smooth out this or that tissue, or repairing here, or there the flow of an internal artery makes matters worse. The reason for one's indifference or laxity may not lie in one's own constitution, but in the facts of one's situation. Perhaps we mean the word "possibilities" more literally than some suppose. Of course, the intention is to inspire and to excite, but the alternative possibilities must be quite real, and practical, and the more of them we can arrange, the better. To put it as succinctly as I can: the bottom line is often, change what you are doing. The problem is not in your head, is not in your lack of motivation, not in the weakness of your appetites. The problem is in your work. Survey the array that we are spreading out before you and then try to choose. At least do something different from what you are doing now, do something else!

The entrepreneurial hype

The first responses to the question "what sort of life would you really, really want?" are frequently half-humorous avoidances of the question. To address this like any other query, straightforwardly and in cold blood, is at first too strange. One is unaccustomed to it, and has to go through an adjustment that requires time. After a short, perhaps severe, discussion of the beach-bumming dream and the gourmet fantasy the mood and tone of our conversations often settles down. The people with whom we are talking recognize that for us this is a challenging and puzzling question like any other and they make an effort to give a serious reply. A first foray in that different spirit is often a way of saying that they want to start their own business and eventually run a company of their own. To an extent that answer, too, is still a reflex action, but another element also plays a role. Some of the phrases associated with New Work echo in their ears – that we believe in self-reliance, in independence, in standing on one's own two feet – and somehow they have the impression that starting one's own business is close to what we have in mind. Their surprise is naturally sharp when we explain that this can easily be the exact opposite of New Work. Quite often we make a connection to our idea of the reversal and then clarify that "working for oneself" has for us a meaning wholly different from the one they apparently assume. In our terms the normal experience of the small entrepreneur is miles from what we mean by any of these expressions.

Always we of course allow that maybe this really is what they seriously want to do. However, small entrepreneurs are anything but "independent," and they in no way stand on their own two feet. More nearly exactly the reverse. In fact, they depend not only on the one boss who is giving them commands, but they also depend on every last customer. And since every customer has to be pleased, and the more intense the competition the more servile and obsequious that pleasing needs to become, they end by becoming the cow-towing servant of nearly everyone. No matter who knocks on their door, they fuss and bustle about him like an officious, nervous maid. Nothing is therefore as silly and inappropriate as the image of the autonomous, self-reliant, Marlboro man entrepreneur who rides through the mountains on his gorgeous horse. The follow-your-dream-idea of the small business enterprise totally misses the U-turn reversal which we have underscored. The intensely pressured work they end up doing for their small enterprise is patently not subordinated to their own personal development. Exactly the reverse. If one observes their daily grind at all closely then nothing is more apparent than the fact that everything is sacrificed to the survival of the start-up venture. Their work is if anything under even greater pressure of a coercive must, the only difference is that they have been hoaxed with ambivalent and seductive rhetoric.

Despite the fact that we normally insist on cheerfulness and humor, when it comes to the entrepreneurial hype our tone often becomes harsh. We take whatever hammers we can find to break this pottery to bits, and to beat the dust as best we can right down into the ground. There are two connected reasons for this; one is personal and the other is systemic.

Since the now dominant social system suffers from 20 different diseases, one has appealed countless times to the optimism and enthusiasm of young entrepreneurs, invariably with the declamation that if they are only creative and tenacious enough then all problems would dissolve into pink cotton candy clouds. In connection with the work I have been doing for the last 35 years I have come to know legions of the young women and young men who had been propagandized into believing this with a fanatical and blind religious faith. In the light of the pernicious pathology of the Job System, and of what we have been saying about both the Business-Job-Nexus and the Blitzkrieg automation which the global corporations have been spreading we know very well that this hype all along has only been a bright scarf with which one tried to hide atrocious ills so that the party of the ninetieth could continue in its blissfully euphoric mood.

The bursting of the dot-com bubble, that was soon followed by the beginning of the period of fear (on 11 September 2001), has effectively put that approach to rest. In fact one could make a separate study of how drastically the mood of the entire spate of journals that address specifically young entrepreneurs has changed, almost exactly from the date of that attack. The regiments of young entrepreneurs that in the last few years have been sent into the battle to bolster the tottering Job System could remind one of the Japanese kamikaze pilots. Sadly, the resemblance extends right down to the appalling survival statistics. Truly, one used these young people ruthlessly as cannon fodder. Part of their function was to cover the social landscape with an optimism as thick as the frosting on a cake, even while the number of those who failed was often 80 and 90 percent, which suggests that one could compare them also to the Polish cavalry which in the first few days of the Second World War was thrown into the battle against the German tanks. In a few hours the youth of Poland was decimated since they rode against the tanks with drawn sabers above their heads. The thoroughly indoctrinated young businessmen are similarly ill-equipped and similarly wasted in their fight against the utterly overwhelming powers that create poverty, unemployment and misery.

To see the grimness, the waste and the horror of what in fact really is a last-ditch rear-guard action still more vividly, one should make the comparison to any of the Third World countries. In all of them, whether it is Mexico, or India, or Haiti, or South Africa, or the former Soviet Union one sees literally millions of healthy, vigorous, young looking men and women in countless intersections and along many miles of the main streets. On a cloth or a piece of plastic in front of them they have tiny pyramids of fruits, or a few belts, or chains, or candy, or chewing gum, or T-shirts, or sunglasses. Every one of these desperate people has his own "small business enterprise." One should blend these images and superimpose them on each other; here are the scrubbed looking 25-year-olds, with their freshly printed business cards, which proclaims them to be the "president" of a single person company – every one his own single enterprise –

and right next to them, and very similar to them, are the herds of black boys who shine shoes, and the flocks of young girls who sell mangoes on wooden sticks.

The systemic reason behind the fierce anger of our attack on this hype should now be very plain. We on purpose detailed the pathology of the Job System, and then described the bulldoze power of the Business-Job-Nexus to convey the sheer magnitude of the forces that have been unleashed. The enormous migration from the farms into the cities in virtually all countries, and the spread of automation across the entire spectrum of all jobs (emphatically, including those in the service sector) are measures of the vastness of these developments. To pit against forces of this size the hyped excitement of young entrepreneurs is by now a ghastly black humor joke.

Nonetheless, it is powerful and only a fool would take it lightly. We need to go back and recall the image of the locked train. We live in an age in which there seem to be no solutions for the problems that swoop down upon us and hack at us like Hitchcock's birds. So, no matter how feeble and ludicrous and grotesque, the one sheath of straw that is held out to us we naturally grasp with our hands and teeth. Our jaws are clenched on that last straw of hope and we will not release it easily. And precisely that is a most crucial point: as long as people do hold on to that last straw, the process of thinking seriously about our problems, the process of at least facing them does not even start. The self-deception, the blindness, the Punch and Judy show of politics continue. That in a nutshell is why our attacks on this one delusion are as cold and harsh and devastating as we can make them: simply because it seems all-important for that process to begin.

In many cases the response to this comes as overtly as one could have wished. After a lot of workshops, or seminars, or lectures someone has approached me and explained that she or he had had some involvement with New Work possibly for years, but that the point where they actually "got it" happened only after they had heard one of my all out lampoonages of the venture hype. Up to that point they had slumbered in the notion that New Work was merely a broader and more human variation on that same theme. Certainly, they had heard our reiterated insistence that we were actually trying to evolve a fundamentally different economic system from the now prevailing one. However, they had to hear the sequence of head-on clashes with their own ears to recognize that this was not hyperbolic talk, but rightly or wrongly our actual aim.

This has been similarly the case also in numerous follow-up discussions around the endless beach vacation, the gourmet fantasy and for that matter, all manner of still other happy-life fantasies. These, too, moved many people gradually, one notch at a time, away from the deeply ingrained elements of the job mentality. These, for many initially strange comparisons, pulled them away from the conviction that work inevitably has to be a burden, or a penance, or a mild disease, and brought them closer to the idea that the very special WRRW can tutor us out of our self-ignorance and fill us with the energy to actually live.

Work WRRW and therapy

How WRRW compares to the varieties of different therapies is for many reasons an inevitable subject for discussion. Among these reasons is of course that therapy now often deals with a sense of lifelessness, a lack of affect, a general feeling of depression. For very many the connection to finding something which they intensely and passionately want is hence simply self-evident.

To set the stage I frequently tell the story of an encounter I had in a forlorn and economically bereft town in the west of Michigan, that is, in Kalamazoo. I worked in that town with a group of women who had been unemployed for a long time. One, it turned out, was a prostitute, and the story I am telling is really very simple. In a conversation she asked:

What good is the counseling I get for one hour in the week? I feel sorry for the social worker who sits and talks with me. As a matter of fact you may laugh, but I do feel genuine sorrow, real compassion. If I compare my work to hers, hers is so useless, so utterly in vain, so totally without effect. What chance does one hour of counseling have against the work that I do for the rest of the entire week?

Obviously, this is a reference to one of our favorite themes, that of the power of work. The effect that work has on people is frequently described in somewhat lyrical or romantic terms – work sculpts us like an artist shapes a human figure out of rock – or it is described in terms that lie close to the world of medicine – every work has its own professional disease: the coal-miner his black lung, the salesman his inveterate jolliness and the preacher his hypocrisy. The work of a prostitute makes a compelling example, for it would be difficult to think of work that shapes the most intimate core of a person in a more ruthless, cruel and disfiguring way. Most of us have an inkling of the contempt that prostitutes develop for men, and of the high barricades which they over time construct to separate themselves from their own sexuality. Unsurprisingly, an almost countless number of examples that demonstrate the enormous shaping power of work have run across our path during the 30-year-long history of the many-faceted New Work project. For that matter, most anyone at some time or other has probably observed a 15-year-old who is for the first time in the grip of a task that utterly electrifies him or her changes in every dimension of his being: the walk, the posture, the way the head is carried, the glance, the smile – all of that can be transformed in 3 days by work that challenges and excites, so that one is literally in the presence of another person. Similarly, many of us no doubt also witnessed how an 80-year-old seeming geezer suddenly was catapulted into a whole new vigorous period of his life, just because a turn in his composing, or his painting whirled him forward into territory that took his breath and drove him wild. It would of course be ludicrous to make out of the enormous transforming power of work a contest between therapy and WRRW. It is unabashedly our aim not to administer a therapy, but to change people's work – that in fact was what I tried for in the case of the prostitute. Still, as in so many other cases, we see our relationship to therapy as a partnership, as a possibility for supporting and strengthening each other.

In our picture of the situation, the great range of therapies now practiced should be in an alliance, in an explicit and perhaps even formalized cooperation with New Work. Surely, it is evident that a therapy can prepare the road for a dramatic change in the work one does, and the other way around, that committing oneself to WRRW can be the first phase of a therapy. Indeed, in our panoramic mural of the two cultures, we see this as yet another cause for hope. We started from the image of the locked train, but we insisted all along that the vast majority of people and of forces actually want to travel in a very different direction. This is one further measure of just how encompassing these groups or these forces are: the fact that the variegated panoply of the now prevailing therapies have the strengthening of people's selves and vitality as their aim means that they too can be counted among the harbingers of the life-enhancing culture which is now close to gaining incarnation.

One could call this the external relationship between New Work and therapy; but there is also, and importantly, an internal relationship. From our first beginnings we tried to evolve a set of extraordinarily comprehensive political ideas – in truth, they were nothing less than the blueprint for a culture that was liberating in a serious sense – but from day one we also worked with individuals. Behind this stood ultimately a very large conviction, to which we have been alluding from time to time. We have linked it closely with Paolo Freire's skepticism; with his belief that it is childishly easy to succeed in having people follow yet another freshly painted shimmering ideal. They will be speaking a new language, maybe it will be the language of dialectical materialism or of liberation theology, and their coats and caps may have buttons of a different color, but they nonetheless will still be followers. That all-decisive fact will have remained the same. They will be acting in a new play, with new costumes, but they will still be as enserfed as they were before: as far from liberated as they ever were. No ideology, no set of general ideas or general structures can circumnavigate this cliff. They all shatter on this rock. Those who follow them, will still not be individuals, they still will not be following themselves. There is no shortcut, no one-size-fits-all; people become self-possessed, they find what they RRW only one at a time, only through patient and attentive individual work. We accepted this as an ineluctable given, and therefore developed all along both a set of general ideas and an individual practice. There should be no doubt that this is one of the principal distinguishing characteristics of New Work: it exists in the intersection between the social and the individual. It rides that fence and has one foot on each of these two sides. It advances parallel and at one and the same time a configuration of political and social structures and a process in which distinct and separate people are engaged. This is so because under the last of many bottom line stands, it must be so: that freedom or emancipation or a culture in which humans will not be crippled but will grow up to be self-possessed cannot be achieved with less! There must be the conjunction and the harmonious interplay of structure and content, of political design and personal development.

When all is said and done, this may be one great advantage of New Work: where except in the domain of work can the structural and the personal be combined? Where except in the domain of work can one at one and the same time create the bones for a new system, but also many individual gardens in which separate individuals can grow?

Work WRRW and the secular

The capacity of WRRW to increase our vitality, sometimes right up to ecstasy and jubilation, is the starting point for conversations in still another topic area, and here, too, the social and the individual are paired, and are seen as necessarily in combination and in interplay. These are the conversations about the difficulty of living in our bleak and emptied modern world. Many of these talks start from a familiar list. Among the deprivations we have suffered are the loss of community or more graphically the disappearance of the traditional village, and with it also the shrinking of the extended family. We no longer feel at home, the sense of being sheltered has been taken from us. The important role played by religion has also faded, and this means that our sense of purpose, of having a meaning, of living by values that represent an ordained order has receded, but it also means that a wealth of embroideries and decorations that in times past made our life far richer and more colorful than it is now have disappeared. Along with much else, nearly all of ritual has vanished from our daily life, our holidays have been reduced to shopping sprees.

For me this last complaint is particularly vivid, for in the Austrian mountain village in which I grew up, a funeral lasted for 3 days and the whole village participated in the procession to the cemetery and also in the feasting and drinking that started right afterwards. The celebration of Christmas extended over the better part of 2 months, with pageants, trumpet trios performing in the winter snow, young girls dressed up as angels, and here, too, great numbers of festive meals stretching all the way from the first of Advent to the day of the Three Kings.

New Work does not make light of this nostalgia. On the contrary, to us it represents the reaction to a panoply of genuine facts; so much so that it is high time for a decisive improvement to correct the balance: modernity should no longer be identified merely with this coterie of losses. We deserve a compensation for the deprivations which we have incurred. If there has been such a great deal of deterioration, then there should also be an ascent, a gain in at least one large domain, and that domain could well be that of work. That is one main reason why we have made so much of the difference between assisting people in the finding of a job that wears the mini-skirt of a little fun, and helping them in the discovery of WRRW. A job, even if it brings some pleasure, clearly does nothing to offset the just listed losses. On the contrary, many would insist that the agrarian work of earlier cultures was superior to the Job Work which took its place, and that our Job Work is precisely one of the deficits of modern life. Therefore, we always insist with special emphasis that WRRW really must be work of the very highest order, that we must persevere in the pursuit of this goal, for part of our hope is nothing less than to raise the valuation of modernity itself.

Naturally, not to be fully conscious of just how towering an aim this is would be preposterous foolishness. Still, in the background stands the very large and commonly accepted picture that the entire effort of constructing our life and our culture in accord with our own intelligence, which had its onset with the French Revolution and the Enlightenment, has so far been a gray and chilling disappointment. Still, there is of course no reason why this should forever remain the case. The very conception of it was from the start, as a mind-boggling undertaking, and that the first attempt would not right away succeed, but fail quite miserably, was in truth only to be expected. The idea that we are now at long last close to a second serious start in the effort to devise a more intelligent and life-strengthening culture should in this context be regarded as no more than natural and even overdue. If in addition we face calmly and fully that this is what the vast majority of human beings at this point want, then the transition to a system of work that is not just mildly better than the one we have so far had, but to one that is a grand, impressive and inspiring step upwards is now a likelihood.

In the conversations that turn around the topic of the secular, we often make much less of the fact that discovering the WRRW requires the presentation of possibilities and the chance to pursue explorations, or the overcoming of the Poverty of Desire or self-ignorance. What we highlight, with all the lamps that we can commandeer, is the increase in energy and strength that WRRW is able to provide. We remind people of the idea of the Polarity of Work and quite especially of the fact that we hold the view that we receive strength from work. We also emphasize that a configuration of circumstances can draw unsuspected energies from us, and that this moreover is frequently a process which has no clearly defined upper limit. Therefore, the energy created between myself and a task can increase in escalating phases. That thought relates to some of the remarks we made about the gourmet people: in many cases only a task that looms large and that draws us onwards from one level to the next generates quantities of vitality and force that are truly dazzling and astounding. Nibbling, once more is "not enough." Typical examples where massive energies are liberated occur when a crucial piece of research or a monumental novel has to be completed. These are situations very different from most gourmet fantasies.

Whimsically, one could say that the image of a muse, of an attractive and enticing woman, luring us onwards is too sweet and romantic. The experience is more nearly like that of climbing an impossibly demanding mountain, in many stages, with many camps on narrow ledges. What gives us the strength to continue is not so much a muse but the ghost of the task in front of us, and that ghost seems like the ghost in Hamlet, huge and dark; he does not compel us, he does not hypnotize us, he simply floats in front of us and that seems to be enough to infuse us with powers that we never dreamed of having.

It is the sheer vitality, the extraordinary sense of exuberance and life – the condition which Whitman expressed with the sentence: "I have myriads inside me" – that is often brought on by WRRW. And that experience represents the crucial response, the real answer to the losses which the advent of modernity and the secular inflicted on us. In other words, the life of older cultures, with ritual and religion, with the protecting and comforting village life, with all manner of colorful and marvelously theatrical holiday celebrations, really had a spate of attractive features. There can be a compensating other side. If one opts out of the Job System and manages to first discover and then to realize WRRW then one is likely to experience a fullness of life, an energy that is far more valuable than the sum of the traditional features which have disappeared. To put this still more pointedly: there is a condition that must be met; it is finding and doing WRRW. If that condition is fulfilled, then a secular, modern life can be more flavorful and more dramatic than the life that our forebears had.

It helps to picture this concretely as an actual choice. I do not think that it is difficult to imagine someone who perhaps obviously and stereotypically does WRRW – say an artist, or a writer, or for that matter even an enormously productive anthropologist – walking between the huts of a village in which an early culture is still untarnished and intact. That sort of person might feel quite clearly that the village life on balance is too confining, that it happens on too small a stage, that perhaps most crucially it is too subdued, too mollified, too quiet – that when all is said and done he would never decide to go back to this sort of life, and in the last analysis his reason would be energy, vitality, simply and plainly: more life! His present work gives him this in abundance. If he tried to return to the village, he would never stay, for he would miss that sense of living fully far too much.

I use an unusual person as an example only so as to make this point graphically and concretely. Nothing hinges on the fact that he has special talents or an exceptional career. At stake is that WRRW can be seen in still one more additional perspective. We just now described the fading of religion and the arrival of the secular in general, cultural terms. Ritual and the village community disappeared. There is also the intimately personal, the existential experience of this. In the more intensely religious earlier ages many people lived this earthly life in the belief that it was only a trial; that it had no value in its own right, but was merely the passage through a valley of suffering and tears. Of incomparably greater consequence was the everlasting life to which the this-worldly life only opened or closed the door.

What has happened in the last 200 years is extremely strange. An ever-growing majority of people resigned themselves to the realization that the heavens are now empty, that there will be no afterlife. Yet again, there was no outcry, and also no great shout of liberation. One continued half-heartedly and tepidly as before. Which was madness, inexcusable apathy, the same fateful passivity which we have met before as the Poverty of Desire. If the great drama has now taken an entirely different turn, if this life is indeed the only life we have, then to live it with gusto and appetite and flamboyance is the only natural and sane response. So far this change, however, has not yet occurred. In great numbers of conversations in the context of New Work we encountered instead the resistance to even raise this question, coupled with the clumsy lurching either in the direction of open-ended leisure or of the munching of as many morsels as one can.

Many people come to New Work wearied and exasperated with their own half-heartedness. They want to make the U-turn that the vanishing of the afterlife almost demands of them; they want to live this life as fully as it can be lived, but they don't know how. To these people we then explain that the first and most intelligent step toward that goal may well be the discovery of work that they RRW. This first and difficult discovery, in our experience, leads on to others. Knowing what work they RRW, will lead them to the discovery of what they RRW from material things, and also from their relationships to other people, and onwards from there to what they RRW from life itself.

There is yet one more dimension that plays a role in these conversations. Maybe that dimension emphasized or receives attention quite especially in cultures distant from us. In my experience especially in India, Japan, also among North American native tribes, and with startling clarity among the Eskimos. The groups in these cultures that we have worked with experience New Work as profoundly different from their usual impression of the West. To grasp this one has to stress that they see the West not just as materialistic, or greed-driven, or cash-obsessed. From their angle of vision, the West is far more repulsive, more appalling, more of an offense. This is so, in part, because they are deluged by the sewage that pours out of their television sets. In all the countries of the Third World that I have visited, the TV programs and especially the TV advertisements are measurably worse than even the cow-urine in which we are soaked on our couches. It is of course a basic fact of life in the slums, that even the most tawdry shacks, even those that have no roof, are topped by a TV antenna. In endless repetitions, to which many of these people are accustomed from their schools and their religion, they listen to ads about the subtlest and least detectable of female napkins, the latest and most absurd fad-diets for losing excess weight, interminable programs on how one can develop the "abs" on one's stomach into a girdle of delight, and in especially massive doses, how teenage children compete in what are billed as beauty or talent contests. It is as if the masochism of the West has gone into a rampage; we hang out our dirtiest linen for the great majority of humankind to see. Inevitably, many of the members of these cultures are often in a frenzy of disgust and hatred. That is why they experience New Work as so wholly and redemptively different from the West that they are used to. Countless conversations have turned on the overlapping relationship they see between their own sometimes half-buried spiritual traditions and New Work. That one can experience work as a calling, and that it then gives one a sense of detachment from commercial trash, and even more that having that sense about one's own work protects one against the opinion of others, even against the shock of sudden unexpected adversity, and thus gives one calm, tranquility, a sense of ease and of assurance and of being unperturbed – that is what attracts them often to New Work. Having WRRW which could be more important than the possession of material things, so much so that these become distractions and tawdry trinkets, was of quite particular importance for New Work in India. Fancy products, stuffed chairs and elaborate serving dishes and the rest of a materially protected existence that could become irrelevant established a basic sympathy for New Work. Some aspects went beyond this. The fact that this posture came at the end of a long inward journey, which was moved forward by the reiterated question whether this was now indeed in conformity with one's inmost self, established in the eyes of very many the conviction that there existed a genuine kinship between their own spiritual tradition and New Work. In the religious communities but also and quite especially in some of the remote villages of India many emphasized that they recognized in this a relationship to the revered teachings of Ghandi. Surprisingly, they insisted on this even though we were straightforward about the faith we had in advanced technologies, that contrasted so flagrantly with Ghandi's spinning wheels. To our astonishment, they on this particular point often turned the tables. They saw precisely in the combination of the spiritual core with extremely modern technologies a step forward which made Ghandi's teachings more relevant and more attractive than they had been before. Some say that above all the consciousness of individuals must be changed. Others say the opposite, that serious change can only occur if you alter the political and economic structure. We insist that it must be both, and both in equal parts. Therefore, New

Work proposes both, the project to construct a very different future that will put the technologies we have developed to an intelligent new use, but also a path to a modern spiritual existence.

Ask yourself, is there a domain, or a strategy, or a set of minimal enumerable steps that can do both, change the structure of society and also the spirit of individual people. Our answer is that work alone can do this. Work can be changed so it will accomplish both. Both, an economy incomparably more productive, incomparably more humane and also a climb up a mountain to an honest spirituality. Work where honesty means a spirituality without cheating, without the aid of remnant superstitions. To pursue the work one RRW, therefore, makes people vastly more productive and creative, but it also helps them to achieve a spirituality that is pure, that is not mixed with fake additives.

This has deep and far-reaching consequences if you think of it as the basis for yet another partnership. Possibly the majority of those who find themselves ever more estranged from religion experience this separation, this divorce, as something of a fall, or a descent into nihilism. As their God dies they find themselves disoriented, lost and orphaned. To this multitude of people New Work offers a very different perspective.

The chaotic gloom of nihilism is not the only route, nor the only possible next stage. One can also experience it as the shift from the other-worldly to the this-worldly, from the self-deprecating to the self-affirming, in short, not as a fall into the black abyss of nihilism, but instead as an upwards transition, the beginning of the long-postponed ascent. Which would be another way of saying that the natural stage following the separation from religion is the living of a consciously and purposefully and joyously secular life, a life that is Shakespearean, flamboyant and ripe.

Put still more clearly: if you have stopped believing in a life after death, you had better turn around and make a holy deep decision to live this life as fully and as avidly as it can be lived! Why? Because the essence of a great deal of religion was the encouragement not to live your life, but instead to postpone it. Religion formed an alliance with our instinctive reluctance to expose ourselves to life, with the poverty of our desires. It pampered and reinforced this abstemiousness. As long as one believed in earnest that his life was a negligible trial period compared to what came afterwards, this was an understandable posture. However, if you do not believe in this magnificently long and far more splendid afterlife, then you must now struggle with all your might to break the habits of that earlier period of history and of your life. This will be like a difficult convalescence. It is as if you had spent your entire life up to this point in an inviting bed, and now you are asked to get up and walk. Walking in this case means much more than we normally suppose, it means that you will "raise as many moments of this life as are in your power up to ecstasy." (Emerson).

If you sincerely ask the question: what can I do so that I will have lived my life intensely, in what direction lies the answer? Then in one sentence: we have been saying, as a first, yet decisive step, consider your work. Do not allow yourself to suffer your work as a mild disease. If that is what you decide to do, only edges and crumbs and leftovers will remain. Work is far too large and too shaping to be relegated in this way. If you want to live life fully, then make a beginning with your work. Do everything you can to turn your work into an intense, a burning, a rapturous experience.

Feminism

Quite often the very first question that I am asked, right after the conclusion of a lecture, is direct and to the point. Someone asks: And what about women? I begin my answer usually by pointing out that there has been a sense of kinship and affinity between women and New Work through all the ups and downs of our mountain hike. This was so already during the initial struggles in Flint. Indeed, if a group of women had not organized their own program which they explained on the radio and on television, that they at any rate liked the idea of 6 months' factory work, and then 6 months of work they really cared about, the project might have died in its crib. Similar turns occurred whether I was teaching a course in a university, or giving a workshop in an international and highly touted bank, or going through the basics of New Work with women on welfare, or in an Indian tribe. Invariably women understood New Work long before men began to grasp it, invariably they also were prepared to act in support of New Work, when the men were still dubious and sought to impress each other with the sharpness of their critical intelligence. Nothing of course is easier to understand than why this happened all along. From the very first major thought that usually initiates the discussion; the idea that the Job System has existed only for the last 200 years, and that it is emphatically only one way in which work can be organized, and that there are naturally other forms and modes and kinds of work – other than Job Work – women are far ahead of the men. This is how most women have been thinking their whole lives. They know that there are other forms of work, and even the idea that Job Work is much of the time a grind and a chore and that there are kinds of work that are incomparably more satisfying – like the work of having and raising children – is for them an old familiar friend, if not a platitude. Very different from most men: their identity, their sense of self-worth, their conception of what structures life and gives it its rhythm are all intertwined with their jobs. These very plain opening statements to men amount to explosions that blast the foundations of their lives. So, naturally they resist and are much slower than women to grasp the concept.

The unsurprising consequence has been that in virtually all of the developments of New Work, women were in the forefront, they were leading. Their voices had weight in the various centers, they initiated new and heretofore not thought of programs, their explanations and defenses of New Work on platforms and in the media were more persuasive.

That is the first part of how I sometimes answer the question: "And, what about women?" The second part sets this practical, matter-of-fact, historical account to one side, and separates it from the philosophical, and foundational part that is to come. That part goes back all the way to the idea that we are midway in the transition from one to a wholly different culture. The old, now disintegrating culture was based on one conception of human nature, the new culture that is now being born grows out of a wholly different idea of what humans are ultimately like. The root and core of the old culture was the notion that man was very like a rapacious little animal; that he needed to be subdued, tamed and socialized so that his rampant egoism would not wreak havoc all around him. The premise of the new culture is the exact opposite: it recognizes that humans are frail, easily broken and even more easily discouraged, and that they above all, therefore, need to be invigorated and strengthened. For a host of reasons the axioms of the old culture managed to rush into the spotlight first. The effect was that most of the now traditional institutions, which though weakened still hold sway, derived their rationale from the image that humans above all needed to be tamed. The strengthening, life-enhancing culture got a much slower start – again, for a multitude of reasons. The deep and intimate philosophical relationship between feminism and New Work has a simple cause: they are both expressions of the new life-enhancing culture.

The one panoramic fact which makes this commonality and kinship obvious are the pervasive similarities especially in the counseling offered by these two. New Work does not explicitly offer seminars in self-assertion, and many feminist groups do, but such seminars would fit very naturally into the process we have been describing. The difference is that New Work would probably offer them for both men and women. Against the backdrop of this aspect of feminism, one could propose that New Work has focused on one particular, though very large, means of self-assertion training, namely that through work we can express our greater selves. Perhaps it is important to emphasize that what we have in mind is unusual and specific. Not that people are strengthened by climbing one rung higher on the ladder of jobs. Not at all. Instead that work strengthens me as a person, gives me more energy, a greater sense of competence, of autonomy and of life. I become more the kind of person that Whitman and Emerson and Blake admired and also were. This should create mutual enlightenment. It should connect some of what I have been describing with elements with which we are long familiar and at home. Conversely it should suggest that some of the philosophical ideas we have been sketching could be a foundation, a base for feminism. The explicit recognition that we are indeed born frail, and that long efforts are required to turn us into self-reliant persons, is merely a more abstractly worded repetition of what numerous feminists have said many times before.

A serious and splendid love

Some life fantasies are only comfort pillows that people keep in a corner of their couch. Not even they themselves seriously believe in them. Yet one is different. Asked for the one thing that might in earnest make them feel that they really are alive they might say: a serious, lasting and splendid love; and who would want to scoff at that? In my own mind this is something of an ultimate and last comparison. What happens if we put on one side of a scale finding and pursuing WRRW and on the other side having in one's life that sort of love? Nothing would be more pathetic and absurd than a staged contest, a list of the pros and cons on both sides. Still, there is one important and large point that needs to be made. Wonderful as love, either a single love, or a sequence of deep passionate encounters is, there is nothing political that can be done to ensure that the great majority of people will indeed meet another person with whom they will be experiencing that. Political instruments are useless when it comes to love. It would be absurd and silly to put love on a political agenda, to announce as plank seven in the platform of a party the creation of structures that will guarantee every citizen at least one great love in her or his life!

In this lies, surprisingly, a crucial contrast to work, for a one-sentence summary of New Work could well be that it aims to provide serious, meaningful and even splendid work for virtually everyone, and that it emphatically wants to achieve this through means that are political. This contrast extends to all of the world's great religions. For love in virtually all of them is the great instrument of transformation, and this naturally raises the question: are the religions when all is said and done deeply limited in their effectiveness for that very reason? If anything at all can make not just a privileged few but the mass of humanity more vigorous and more alive then quite possibly there is only one way in which this can be achieved, namely through the transformation of work! The lines along which this transformation could occur have by now been laid out in great detail, and they have been tried and proven in many contexts of actual experience. This then might be a crucial difference: love cannot be arranged through political alterations. We can change through political means the manner in which we work, and we could change that manner drastically and dramatically and from the ground up. The results would be sweeping, the results would be a new and different culture. To make the comparison to love, to insist that this cannot be done through and for and on behalf of love, makes a serious point. One begins to realize that work is maybe the only sphere of human life with which we can do this. It is alone! In this work is distinguished. It is unique.

Nothing else can equal it in this regard, or be compared with it. Work, therefore, should be made the very core and center of a political endeavor.

This is difficult because we have been so inured, so long-term conditioned to conceptualize, to view work as a punishment, as a price that we must pay. Endurance will be needed till the idea takes hold that living intensely, that living as we deeply and seriously want can be achieved perhaps only in one way, and that is solely and alone through work! As we continue to probe and move from one comparison to others, the idea begins to sink in that the quality of life that we long for can perhaps only be reached if one addresses and chooses one's work in virtually opposite ways from how most of us slouch and drift so far. It is possible that we have to set our sights much higher, that we need to demand from work what work in the form of a job cannot provide. Conceivably, nothing else, nothing other and short of work that we deeply and seriously and passionately want could ever give us the kind of life that we seem inescapably to long for.

To do work that you love will transform you. New Work is an attempt to create a structure that will give support and aid in a multitude of ways so that this change will be possible for the great mass of the people. Work that they seriously want to do should not be only a playful, a marginal possibility; not only a hobby, not only a wistful wish, but big stretches of most people's work should be that kind of work. To transform, to change the social structure so that it will support this, that is the endeavor, that is specifically and exactly what New Work is trying to do.

A summation

This does not just invite us, this forces us out on a ledge from which we have an overview. Even in the first pages of this book we spoke already of a second culture which is struggling to be born. We said then that it lacks an agenda, a sense of which strategies and steps might lead it toward substance and reality.

In one concise sentence, our answer to that question is: transcend the Job System, leave it behind and establish the foundations for a new System of Work. You cannot cure the present work situation with a few cosmetic tricks. What is needed is a gradual, cautious transition, but one to a whole New Work system. Only a dramatically new arrangement can ensure that people will indeed have the opportunity to do work that in its defining purpose will enhance and strengthen and empower the human beings who perform it. Thanks to technology, thanks to the possibility of becoming far more self-providing, thanks to the chance of from now on having machines do the work that hitherto has crippled human beings, such an arrangement is within the reach of our outstretched hands. There already exists a great array of forces and constituencies that pull in this direction. One area consists, plausibly enough, of the manifold that makes up the pathology of the Job System. The entire gamut of the pathological conditions we described are all forces and reasons for moving toward that new system. The two forms of New Work we have described, work as HTSP and work as a calling, are proposed shapes or molds. They are attempts to specify, to answer in detail questions like: what does it mean to change the Job System? How would one begin to do this? Perhaps most importantly, what would an alternative Work System, one appropriate for the new culture, actually look like? A host of additional forces, or partnerships, or alliances have come to light. Each one of these is one more reason for hope, for cheerfulness. Each is one more mosaic stone in the big pattern that is the answer to the question: why are you confident that a development in the direction of New Work could in cold and realistic practice actually occur? I proposed repeatedly and strongly that those who formerly were or still are People of the Left should make common cause with us. Also those who seriously care for art and culture and education, and the fullest possible human development. Emphatically also the four-fifths of humanity who live in the Third World, together with those who are appalled by what has happened there. Clearly also those whose principal focus now is to reduce the perceived excess of ecological requirements for human life. All of those connections are to be made, but there are more that should be added. The very close relationship to feminism should by now be utterly apparent. We also said, and only half in jest, that comparisons to the variety of psychotherapies, and even to the gaining of vitality through meditation or through food regimes and dietary supplements are our appropriate partners. The serious side of this comes more to the fore if one relates this to the shift in values I have just described. That there is a magazine that calls itself bluntly and simply "Self" is a tiny symptom of this hugely pervasive change. So, of course, are a truly huge field of occurring changes that all in different ways express a turning toward this world, this life, instead of the other one, after death. Long and careful conversations with all of these groups might be wonderfully fruitful and illuminating. We should compare notes and initiate exchanges: you believe in Buddhist exercises, or in yoga, or eating certain kind of foods. We believe in work. We have chosen work as our path to a more intensely experienced life. Maybe our hitherto separate ways should converge, should be combined. Surely, this is not a matter of one and only one being right! If we attend to a chair, a lamp, a couch, a table with concentration, it is apparent how most of them could be improved in 100 different ways. Of life itself this is naturally true 10,000-fold. We can therefore work on this together.

One further connection must be drawn. There still exists, in addition to all of these constituencies and groups, the great mass of humans who are adrift, who are not nihilists in the desperate and frenzied way Dostoevsky described in his novels. They are nihilists like boats that are becalmed. They have not made an about-turn, or a commitment, or a decision. They observe the Horror Show of our politics with the same thin and bitter smile with which they respond to virtually anything. We must acknowledge that the last century has made it very easy to become such a person. Too many hopes were disappointed, too many sacrifices were made in vain, too many promises turned out to be pied piper songs. Nevertheless, we should surely, with the palest and most modest of all hopes, have conversations with them too. The hope would be that they have patience, and in addition good ears, so they could tell what song it is that they now are hearing!

Because the crassest and most elementary difference between New Work and these pied piper songs is that the latter all invited sacrifice, whether it was for a nation, or for the three words of the French Revolution, or for some glorious future social circumstance that lay on top of a mountain of corpses. New Work is the opposite of that! It pledges you not to sacrifice, not to "let this present moment fall into the well of time, for the sake of a distant future meaning" (Camus). Different as the melodies of all these pied piper songs sounded, in their effect they were the same. They were all wedding music and wanted you to marry death. Not so New Work. There have been ever so many voices that have tried to make you fall in love with life. Incredibly enough, Trotsky in his best moments was one of these, most certainly when he wrote the sentence: "If the food does not taste better after the revolution, then the revolution will have been a mistake!" That expresses the spirit we try to convey: taste it, taste it for yourself, taste it at every moment! Do not go to sleep. Do not allow the wool to be pulled over your eyes. If the next step deeper into life does not "taste better" on your tongue, then turn around and try a different direction. Not your self-sacrifice, but your self-possession is at stake.

We mean this very plainly. We have no secret, no idea, no formula to peddle. That it is better to live than not to live is not a mystery, and not a revelation. The sparrows on the rooftops can tell you that. We are only suggesting that doing work that you, not someone else, but *you* yourself can love and fondle and play with like you play with a small child will lead you to the love of life.

Conclusion

In *The Phenomenology of Spirit* Hegel describes the French Revolution as a disaster, as a calamity, as a spiral of events that ran berserk as it dug itself ever deeper into a pit of self-destruction. The reasons for this were anything but circumstantial let alone minor. This catastrophe did not occur because something gratuitously went awry, and derailed the process so that it, like a train, fell from a bridge into an abyss. The very opposite of that. As one would expect from Hegel, the reason was singular and deep, also hidden from the sight of the participants, and most Hegelian of all, it was an idea. Indeed, one could argue that this account is one of the most persuasive illustrations that exemplifies the much misunderstood and much lampooned general contention that not material or economic but on the contrary mental or spiritual configuration govern the epochal evolutions of history. The cause of this disaster was an inversion, a gargoyle caricature of the idea of freedom. Here it is important not to mince words, but to make sure that the tone, the emphasis, of Hegel's text is not toned down, but is conveyed in the starkness of its full extremity. That life-changing idea was indeed so horrific a distortion that inescapably, and driven by the inner logic of this idea, the Revolution had to revert itself into the Absolute Terror, a period of mayhem during which in Hegel's own famous phrase, "one cut off heads as if they were cabbages," (where Hegel surely wants us to see the great basket at the foot of the guillotine in which the cut-off heads piled high) and from terror on to Napoleon and to the Restoration, that is in effect back to the status quo in which one was ruled again by a retarded aristocracy and half-whit monarchs.

What gave to this disaster the full traumatic impact with which it hit home had everything to do with what had gone before. There had been 1,000 years in which humanity was for the most part led by superstitions and unreason. Not just for Hegel, but for his whole generation of German Enlighteners (Herder, Lessing, Hoelderlin, Schiller, Goethe), one quintessential embodiment of this ghoulish time was the great war of Thirty Years (1518–48), in which armies decimated each other in battles that were provoked by theological disputes. Disputes such as whether the body of Christ was only symbolically or literally present in the host that was eaten during mass. With that as a paradigm representation of the unreason that had benighted humanity for nearly a millennium, now at long last the Rule of Reason was proclaimed. And what happened? The first grand effort to have the shining light of reason lead the way turned into this! It perverted itself into its own self-annihilation.

This is the idea of freedom, which we have come across before. It defines freedom as the absence of obstacles. As such it is one of a cluster of ideas that have their taproot source in Descartes' conception of the self, though added to that Ego had been the idea that it was governed only by self-interest, by egoism or, less politely, by greed. That made of it a kind of atom governed by only one single constant and insistent force. It is the core of a human being and is fixed and basic and clearly and distinctly known. The metaphor that we most naturally use for it is that it is like the captain of a ship, that controls and commands the body.

One branch of the Enlightenment stayed with that traditional, encrusted notion and this conjunction of ego with egomania formed the philosophical foundation for the calamitously unreasonable thinking that led to the catastrophe of the French Revolution but also to the long line of historical monstrosities that followed in its wake.

It was further this conception of the self, or of human nature, which postulated in essence that human beings were very like voracious rodents, that demanded naturally that the taming of this small dangerous beast was the item of prime priority. This taming, this subjugation, had to be accomplished by whatever means were needed. One weird instrument employed was the Social Contract. We, in retrospect, looking back upon the past 200 years have certainly learned that the Social Contract did not prevent mass-murders on an unprecedented scale. The question is: why would anyone have ever thought that a greed-ridden rodent could be bound by a mysterious legal instrument. This conception of the self also required that education be above all a process in which this egoism is gradually disciplined and controlled. Yet that same self also justified a state that had a monopoly over the use of the means of violence, and therefore a police-force and prisons. Last, but certainly in no way least, was the need for a strict morality, that took its meaning, its bite from the fact that humanity from the very first had sinned, and therefore needed subjugation and punishment. Even before the Revolution had begun, the thinkers that were developing this inverted branch of the Enlightenment thus were already busy abolishing and undermining that re-birth to come. Essentially, the culture whose ultimate foundation was this idea of human nature was, even though post-revolutionary, nonetheless in its core still an instrument of repression.

The other branch of the Enlightenment developed a wholly opposite idea of human nature, aspects of which we know already very well. In Hegel's formulation this self was in stark opposition to Descartes Ego which was fixed, immobile and a given; a self that develops with a vengeance. For in the very earliest chapters of *The Phenomenology of Spirit* Hegel in effect describes an awareness that has so far no self at all. Here he anticipates Merleau-Ponty's "pre-personal consciousness" but also a spate of later child-psychologists. Piaget is the most widely known of those psychologists and he argued from assembled evidence that the somewhat difficult conception of a human being that has consciousness but yet no ego, and no self was an empirically demonstrable fact. Piaget postulates that this "self" to begin with is not even there, that it with great difficulty develops. With great difficulty the forming "self" slowly moves through stages where it is more firmly defined until it eventually gathers some measure of self-possession and self-control. The most natural associations which grow out of these most basic notions are that the self to begin with is of course adrift; that it is highly subject to every kind of outside influence. One could say that its own desires are faint and frail and that it hence suffers not from egoism, but the exact reverse, from a Poverty of Desire, which in turn means that the journey that it must traverse is a journey through which it comes closer to itself, closer to its own identity, closer to having indeed become a self. Such a journey is also very needed since humanity on this account is not only frail, shy and easily intimidated, but also afflicted with an almost insurmountable self-ignorance. Such self-ignorance is one of the ways in which this conception of the self harks back to the Greeks – for whom coming to know oneself was close to a supreme command, because by nature humans are afflicted with self-ignorance. Such a philosophy or realization once more sets into stark relief the contrast to Descartes, for whom the self is most certainly and ultimately known. The flamboyance with which Hegel re-thinks human nature and the startling gesture with which he sets his antipode into the sharpest possible juxtaposition to Descartes made him a really great philosopher. Yet also, and this is incomparably more important, he thereby performs the historic act that places the enduring enterprise of human liberation on a proper and workable main track. After the terrifying descent during the Middle Ages, this is no small feat.

What then, in contrast to the no obstacle, reduced hindrance view is Hegel's view of the genuine, authentic, bona-fide idea of freedom? As one might suspect Hegel goes back to the Greek, the classical, the original idea most famously and succinctly formulated by Aristotle: a person is free to the degree to which his actions are determined by himself and not by something external, outside or other than the person himself. Freedom, in this conception of it is certainly not a given; we are not born with it. It is fragile, difficult to attain, easily lost and comes into existence only under favorable social circumstances. All of this clearly parallels Hegel's ideas about the development of the self. Beyond this there occurs a shift on an even deeper level. We are accustomed to think of actions as either free or unfree – and that again derives naturally from the idea that freedom is the absence of obstacles, and that the essence of freedom is the having of a choice. It is an act that is in this case rendered free. This is deeply different from thinking that freedom is a predicate of whole persons and also of states. The Greeks thought primarily of persons as being free – one was free as a man, or not. In Hegel's early writings the comparison between what human beings seem to be like in his own age – fragmented, weakened, disoriented and adrift – to the human beings that lived in Athens – who were of one piece, integrated, vigorous and alive – plays the most central role. This role was so central that it defined for Hegel the basic nature of his philosophic enterprise. His conception changed in his later years, but early on he thought that the historic task of his time was to bring back to a new birth what the Greeks had been. That was part of his idea of freedom: a society in which people would again be as fully developed, strong and vigorous as the Greeks had been. Freedom meant very much more than that one could cut off the head of a king, it meant the creation of a culture and of a state that would foster the development of impressive, splendid, admirable human beings. To achieve an overview we can now say on the deepest level we have a confrontation of two radically opposed conceptions of human nature. Out of these two juxtaposed ideas of the self grew two ideas of freedom just as dramatically opposed. For the perspective of New Work it is even more important that correspondingly there also developed two distinct and separate cultures. In the very beginning of this book we briefly indicated that one of these gained public prominence and power long before the other, which in its early phases existed more in the imagination of poets, artists and philosophers. From the start we characterized one of these cultures as disciplining, ordering and finally repressive and the other as life-enhancing and truly emancipating. The large panoramic, background picture is that the older, more repressive culture is now descending, while the younger, more liberating culture is now rising, and coming to the fore.

In this large picture New Work is one effort to assist, to be a midwife in the birth of this New Culture, to give that liberating culture more force, more visibility, most especially to assist it to come out of the realm of ideas into the domain of social structures and political realities. New Work is thus an effort to advance, to move forward by some steps the grand and enduring project of the emancipation of humanity; to lend whatever help it can in the creation of a culture that does not only flaunt one dubious, and deeply deceptive idea of freedom, but that instead is a culture that in a genuine and serious sense deserves the title that it creates people who are free.

This is one possible formulation of a summation. Though true enough, it is couched in broad, massive and for the most part abstract terms. We can add a picture that will locate New Work more concretely in a framework that is harder and more practical: focus on a crucially important three-step logic, or on the conjunction of three equations. It runs like this:

1. Choice = Freedom
2. Democracy = Choice
3. Therefore: Democracy = Freedom

We already know from earlier passages where these seemingly smooth three-steps stumble. Right at the start: it is of course an ingrained habit to assume that having a choice and being free are one and the same thing, but this may nonetheless be a crude and ultimately heavy-weight mistake.

Recall once more the simplest of examples: you are talking with someone who is a vegetarian, and you offer him the choice between pork and beef. How much freedom have you given him? How appreciative, how grateful, how liberated should he feel? To bring it closer to home: many of us felt that the choice between Bush and Gore was like choosing between pork or beef for a vegetarian. Philosophically formulated: both are cases of choosing where one does not want either of the two alternatives.

Since not only rational considerations but a firmly implanted reflex is in question, one or two more examples might be helpful. Let us go to an extreme case, one that is famous, that is known from the novel as "Sophie's choice." A troop of SS officers have captured two children and demand that their mother makes a choice. Which of the two children would she have them kill? Yes, she has a choice, but is she free? Is that freedom?

This does raise a question. What exactly becomes of the so-oft-repeated mantra, that "we" in the United States have freedom, and hence are to be envied, and are moreover in a position to liberate other countries simply because we have choices. We are only one step from the next realization, that choices are ubiquitous, that we have choices even if we are in a concentration camp or even if we are a slave. Does the fact that we have choices even in the condition that is quintessentially defined as the absence of freedom not refute choice as the defining characteristic of freedom? If having a choice is not the same thing as being free, if it is much less, then democracy which does offer us choices (like that between Gore and Bush) also offers us much less than freedom. Which makes it natural to raise the question: if not freedom, then what? If the conditioned reflex that makes us say, either to a child, or to a country: "You had a choice, and therefore you were free," is indeed not true, but just a reflex that was drilled into us, then how shall we describe, or measure, or assess what democracy does offer us?

This is far less baffling than it might at first sound. Most, even after a brief reflection have quite a clear idea. Very far from the grand euphoric associations which the word freedom mostly evokes, democracy is plain and humble, and wears solid home-spun clothes. Its essential meaning is a bundle of extremely limited, narrow, but of course nonetheless significant guarantees, or protections, or assurances, or preventions, or also rights. None of them are as sweeping as the word free suggests. One typical example is that your rights as an accused must be read out loud to you when you are arrested. That is not a world-transforming comfort, but it is something all the same. Similarly, the hard, practical value that is hidden behind the magnificent phrase: "freedom of speech." That certainly does not signify that I can say anything whatsoever with blanket immunity. Nothing of the kind. People will still judge me by, and react to, what I say. If I say something dull-witted that will have an effect. Some people will think less of me, and no government in the world can protect me against that. On the other hand, I am protected: I cannot be arrested, and even less shot for calling the president of the United States a fool. And again, parallel with the one right, that is often seen as the core of the bundle of democratic protections. To echo a saying that one often hears in the United States: I am free to vote, but I am also free to freeze to death in the streets of Detroit.

Only the very blindest of people would dismiss democracy as flim-flam, as window-dressing, as of no account. It does count, and it does make a difference, though the rhetoric that surrounds it is often wildly overblown. Virtually everyone agrees on this much, but this only brings us to the doorstep of the question which many have asked, and which is difficult in the extreme. Yes, democracy is not enough – but what has to be added? In that last half, lies the great perplexity. What is the measure of the gap? What is the plus that must be added? What more has to be put into place so that a society and culture is humane and impressive and maybe more than that, a society that is free in a serious sense, that fosters human beings that are free and emancipated and self-possessed, human beings that are not crippled but that are instead full-grown, and fully alive human beings?

Such a question leads directly to two rounded and compressed understandings of New Work. That large missing component, that bridge, the practices, structures and policies that must be added to democracy to transform it into such a society and culture are those of New Work. One of the strengths of New Work is that our conception of what needs to be done is finally simple: it comes to three things:

1. Centers of some sort would have to be established, even though they must not be exactly like we envision and describe them (the architecture could be very like that of the shopping-malls we have at present, with the difference that there would not be a variety of boutiques and shops in which one buys things, but workshops with computers and tools of all kinds and also Personal Fabricators in which one makes a pair of sneakers or a microwave-oven. Incidentally, many malls are going out of business. Using them might therefore have an economical advantage.)
2. Programs would have to be created that assist people in discovering what they seriously want, that also help them to hone and strengthen their desires and then to translate them into work with which they either earn a salary, or for which they receive a fellowship.
3. There would have to be programs that introduce and train people in the skills of HTSP.

The insufficiency of democracy, and that which it lacks has more weight, edge and cut than many might imagine. To drive that home let me remind you that the ANC won in South Africa an inspiring revolution, a revolution that the whole world watched with bated breath. Nonetheless numerous black taxi drivers who over the years have become my friends confess – often with real rage – that poverty, unemployment, crime and violence have become much worse in the 10 years of black rule. Mandela is probably the last person who wanted to surrender to the Business-Blackmail-System. Sadly though, his perception was the same as everybody else's: If there was to be any development and economic growth then it could only happen through Big Business and the creation of jobs. There was no alternative. Very many decisions of his government were therefore in line with what we call "Free Enterprise." And those policies have steadily made matters worse. This is once more an indication of the power of the Business-Job-Nexus that we by now know all too well.

The same worsening has of course been the fate of a host of other countries; one could really say in the last 20 years the same worsening has been the case everywhere. Not just in the Third World, but also in Europe and the United States. It is most especially important to apply this to Iraq, and also to Afghanistan, that is, to the countries which we have been covering with war, but also to those who probably will be next, which include Pakistan, Syria and Iran. What we supposedly seek and hope for, namely to establish democracy (at least that is the version which was most recently announced) is of course in doubt. It is far from certain that we will succeed. Still, that is not the point. The point is rather that we should not assume that "establishing democracy," if indeed that happened, would be a great turning point. Assuming that then the worst would be over, that now the ascent will start, that now we have laid the foundations, and given time and patience all of these people will live like Americans do in the Middle West is a very dangerous assumption.

Such horrible naivete is a crass miscalculation, a pathetic, foolish error. Much more likely the further development of our present style of democracy will be like it has been in 100 other places: it will get worse! It might be very like the last 10 years in South Africa, only still fiercer, still bloodier and grimmer. Even with democracy they will still be trapped in the same system, as we ourselves of course are. The situation will be less stable, less established than it is now, and these countries might be careening down into the butcher's nightmare in which Zimbabwe has recently been. It might be useful to still give an overview of what New Work is most actively pursuing at this moment. I believe four areas deserve to be singled out. The most telling indication of where we are in the Third World, but also the most exciting prospect for the near future, is developing in South Africa. The Johannesburg branch of the Friedrich Ebert Stiftung has agreed to sponsor the establishment of a "National Policy Forum." That is the culmination of several years of slow preparatory work. This is not to be a conference, but instead a permanently existing body that will convene in sessions from time to time. The principle item on the agenda will be to compare and confront the two alternatives that have now emerged as contenders, the Business dominated strategy vs. the policies suggested by New Work. Invited will be high-level government officials, people that are important in the struggle against poverty and violence, as well as widely known business leaders, intellectuals, artists, and "opinion makers." The discussion will focus on the reaching and the implementation of decisions, and the intention is to persist in having these meetings until decisions have been reached. How it all turns out is still a mystery. We are all part of this process.

In our own perception these forums represent our moving upwards from the level of individual projects to that of national policy, which has been one main hope of ours for many years. If these forums happen and succeed on at least some level, we will be on our way out of the locked train. Our hopes on this score do run high, but we also remember and emphasize that changing ideals is not easy and takes time. Maybe more time than we have estimated, or more time than some may wish to tolerate.

In second place I would list the establishment and the rapid growths of the New Work enterprises. My long-time friend and close associate John Glaser has been the moving spirit in this endeavor. For a long time he has been the savvy CEO of a company, and a few years ago we both agreed that living from the deadline of one grant application to the next was no longer fitting for New Work. We needed much larger sums of money and the only way to obtain these was to earn them through business ventures. In the meantime we have created a corporation (an LLC) and are now midstream in a good number of negotiations with a rapidly growing number of business firms.

What we are developing is best explained with an example. A small but extraordinarily well-run firm in Germany evolved a remarkable small water filter that in its quality is decidedly world-class. In essence one can pour dirty and foul water that may be poisonous into the top and drinkable water comes out at the bottom. In Germany the firm barely managed to survive, simply because drinkable water in Germany is still far from rare. The exact reverse is of course true in large parts of Africa. Since we have a great diversity of various connections in Africa, we offered to advance the idea that this filter will be manufactured in small, possibly mobile plants, for example, in South Africa. To reduce a complex business arrangement to a few words: the German firm will be making money from license and consulting fees, many African villages might have safer water and in addition some small factories, and New Work will be paid for initiating and facilitating the arrangements. The money will be used to support further projects, and in particular to fund New Work Fellowships, that is, stipends that allow someone to do work that she or he "really, really" wants to do. In the chapter on the New Work Economy we listed a number of HTSP technologies on which we are presently working. Since HTSP is in the last analysis a lifestyle that is dramatically different from the one most people have been living, the number of these products might very well become much larger. In some sense what is really needed would be a parallel HTSP twin product for every product we are using now. If a development in that direction were indeed to occur then we might be in a position to fund a very great number of New Work fellowships. As a third promising development I would describe the Network of Associates. It is a fact that the number of "laptop people" is extremely large, that they represent a worldwide community of the most talented and gifted people, and that above all they always wanted to experience their work as a pursuit or a calling, as we have said before. Many of them are also furiously opposed to the direction in which the culture has been moving, and on top of that they feel that their ideas were stolen from them. There is no question that a large portion of them are chafing at the bit. If a chance to make common cause with New Work appears on the horizon they will pounce on it. Since the frontier of further development in the case of New Work is enormously extended (it stretches from writing new software to making films and TV shows, to teaching college courses on New Work, to designing New Work programs for numbers of individual professions, to the development of further products and still more advanced manufacturing techniques) the growth of the Network of Associates might eventually have some resemblance to the famous parable about putting one grain of rice on the first square of a chessboard, and doubling this for every square, till all the rice in India would not be sufficient for the last square on the board.

The last field I would like to mention is that of education. The movement to create alternative schools is powerful both in Germany and the United States. Another close friend and associate of mine, Lienhard Valentin, is a prominent figure in the German branch of that movement. We have teamed up for the holding of many workshops and conferences, and a strong bond between this movement and New Work has begun to form. One major strand of this web is the fact that work used to be boring, and that the traditional and still dominant existing schools were the appropriate preparation for this Job Work. The schools gave one extensive training in the enduring of large amounts of boredom. Work has changed, not just New Work, but also the work that most people are still doing. A majority of people must now think in their work, they must assess a situation and have the wit and the self-confidence to make a decision. In short the schools of the old culture no longer prepare students for the work that they will have to do. These schools will be transcended. The schools for the next generation will no longer be "schools." They will not look like barracks, but very much more like Centers for New Work. You remember: Centers for New Work look like train stations from which trains into a more cheerful future leave every hour. The first impression that one will have upon entering one of these centers will be that one would have to be utterly determined to experience boredom in them since the atmosphere in them is so alive, and so diverse, and so exciting. The chances seem excellent that one will soon see such schools in many villages and towns. It is a fact that a massive majority of people hate and loath the direction in which our culture has been moving. They capitulate, they remain passive, they go along because there is no alternative – not to be seen, and not to be imagined. For a long time, many associated with New Work have used the term: the Problem of Visibility. What they have meant is that we live in a peculiar moment. A very small event, an event in people's minds, not a huge exertion like Mao's march across the bigger half of China, could make a surprising upheaval of a difference. It is possible that we are close to that event in people's minds. If so, the birth of a culture more humane, more intelligent, more cheerful, more sensuous and more flamboyant than the one which we have suffered is under way.

Capitalist Realism
Is there no alternative?
Mark Fisher
An analysis of the ways in which capitalism has presented itself as the only realistic political-economic system.
Paperback: 978-1-84694-317-1 ebook: 978-1-78099-734-6

Rebel Rebel
Chris O'Leary
David Bowie: every single song. Everything you want to know, everything you didn't know.
Paperback: 978-1-78099-244-0 ebook: 978-1-78099-713-1

Cartographies of the Absolute
Alberto Toscano, Jeff Kinkle
An aesthetics of the economy for the twenty-first century.
Paperback: 978-1-78099-275-4 ebook: 978-1-78279-973-3

Malign Velocities
Accelerationism and Capitalism
Benjamin Noys
Long listed for the Bread and Roses Prize 2015, *Malign Velocities* argues against the need for speed, tracking acceleration as the symptom of the ongoing crises of capitalism.
Paperback: 978-1-78279-300-7 ebook: 978-1-78279-299-4

Meat Market
Female Flesh under Capitalism
Laurie Penny
A feminist dissection of women's bodies as the fleshy fulcrum of capitalist cannibalism, whereby women are both consumers and consumed.
Paperback: 978-1-84694-521-2 ebook: 978-1-84694-782-7

Poor but Sexy

Culture Clashes in Europe East and West

Agata Pyzik

How the East stayed East and the West stayed West.

Paperback: 978-1-78099-394-2 ebook: 978-1-78099-395-9

Romeo and Juliet in Palestine

Teaching Under Occupation

Tom Sperlinger

Life in the West Bank, the nature of pedagogy and the role of a university under occupation.

Paperback: 978-1-78279-637-4 ebook: 978-1-78279-636-7

Why Are We The Good Guys?

Reclaiming your Mind from the Delusions of Propaganda

David Cromwell

A provocative challenge to the standard ideology that Western power is a benevolent force in the world.

Paperback: 978-1-78099-365-2 ebook: 978-1-78099-366-9